BERKELEY'S PHILOSOPHY OF SPIRIT

Continuum Studies in British Philosophy:
Series Editor: James Fieser, University of Tennessee at Martin

Berkeley and Irish Philosophy – David Berman
Bertrand Russell's Ethics – Michael K. Potter
Boyle on Fire – William Eaton
Doing Austin Justice – Wilfrid Rumble
The Early Wittgenstein on Religion – J. Mark Lazenby
Coherence of Hobbes's Leviathan – Eric Brandon
Francis Bacon and the Limits of Scientific Knowledge – Dennis Desroches
Hume's Theory of Causation – Angela Coventry
Idealist Political Philosophy – Colin Tyler
John Stuart Mill's Political Philosophy – John Fitzpatrick
Popper, Objectivity and the Growth of Knowledge – John H. Sceski
Rethinking Mill's Ethics – Colin Heydt
Russell's Theory of Perception – Sajahan Miah
Thomas Hobbes and the Politics of Natural Philosophy – Stephen J. Finn
Thomas Reid's Ethics – William C. Davis
Wittgenstein and the Theory of Perception – Justin Good
Wittgenstein at His Word – Duncan Richter
Wittgenstein's Religious Point of View – Tim Labron

BERKELEY'S PHILOSOPHY OF SPIRIT

Consciousness, Ontology and the Elusive Subject

TALIA MAE BETTCHER

continuum

Continuum International Publishing Group
The Tower Building, 11 York Road, London SE1 7NX
80 Maiden Lane, Suite 704, New York, NY 10038

British Library Cataloguing-in-Publication Data
A catalogue record for this book is available from the British Library.

ISBN-10: HB: 0-8264-8643-6
ISBN-13: HB: 978-0-8264-8643-1

Library of Congress Cataloging-in-Publication Data

Bettcher, Talia Mae.
Berkeley's philosophy of spirit : consciousness, ontology, and the elusive subject / by Talia Mae Bettcher.
p. cm.
Includes bibliographical references.
ISBN-13: 978-0-8264-8643-1
ISBN-10: 0-8264-8643-6
1. Berkeley, George, 1685–1753. 2. Spirit. 3. Self (Philosophy)
4. Consciousness. 5. Ontology. I. Title.

B1348.B48 2007
192–dc22
2006033156

Typeset by Aarontype Limited, Easton, Bristol
Printed and bound in Great Britain by Biddles Ltd, King's Lynn, Norfolk

Contents

To Helen Leary

that your spirit shall not be forgotten

Acknowledgments

Several earlier versions of chapters were presented at conferences. A version of chapter two was presented at the Midwest Seminar in the History of Early Modern Philosophy, The University of Chicago, April, 2001 as 'Berkeley's New Substance.' Portions of chapters two and three were presented at the New England Seminar in the History of Early Modern Philosophy, Dartmouth College, May 2002 as 'Berkeley, Ontology, and Self-Consciousness.' A major portion of chapter three was presented at the International Berkeley Conference, Texas A & M, April 2003 as 'Berkeley on Self-Consciousness.' Portions of chapter three were presented at the Southeast Seminar in Early Modern Philosophy, University of Florida, April 2004. Portions of chapter five and six were presented at the International Berkeley Conference, University of Tartu, Estonia, September 2005 as 'Berkeley on the Privacy of Ideas.' In responding to Charles McCracken's talk 'Was Berkeley a Common-Sense Realist?' at the fifth annual Southern California Philosophy Conference, California State University, Long Beach, October 2001, I developed some of my views in chapter five.

I am grateful to all who offered comments and criticisms at these presentations. I am especially grateful to Margaret Atherton, Michael Ayers, Geneviève Brykman, Stephen Daniel, Charles McCracken, Tom Stoneham, and Ian Tipton. I am also grateful to three anonymous referees for comments on an earlier manuscript that became chapter three.

I express my deep appreciation to Roberta Morris and Henry Mendell for their helpful comments on earlier versions of the monograph. Susan Forrest, Randall Parker, and Kayley Vernallis have been tirelessly invaluable in their assistance, commenting on the monograph as well as earlier, rudimentary versions of chapters. Thank you. This monograph is based on my dissertation work. I give special thanks to my adviser, John Carriero. Aside from helping my views to flourish, his guidance deepened my understanding of what it means to be a philosopher.

Introduction

That we have first raised a dust, and then complain, we cannot see.[1]

The views of Descartes, Hume, and Kant on self and self-consciousness have secured an almost mythological status in philosophy. According to the famous philosophical story, Descartes claimed to perceive an 'I' which accompanied his mental states. But when Hume 'entered most intimately into what he called himself' he perceived only perceptions and concluded the self was nothing but a bundle of perceptions. Failing to find anything to hold the bundle together, Hume ultimately abandoned this account. Kant would show that Hume had left out the 'transcendental unity of consciousness' which secured this unity without any metaphysical soul.[2]

By contrast, Berkeley's views about self and self-consciousness have been relegated to virtual ignominy. Alas, Berkeley's commitment to spiritual substance has been the subject of controversy and, not so infrequently, an object of derision. In another traditional story, Berkeley is the middle figure of the 'empiricist triumvirate.'[3] He rejects material substratum on the basis of a Humean argument (it cannot be perceived; there is no idea of it) but attempts to retain spiritual substratum despite the fact that it, too, cannot be perceived.[4] Inevitably, Berkeley's notorious and seemingly *ad hoc* claim that while we lack an idea of spirit, we nonetheless have a notion of it has been met with considerable scepticism. It is easy to see Berkeley as a double-sided or torn figure: He has the philosophical sharpness of a Hume; he is blinded by religion.[5]

The fact that Berkeley intended to publish a second part of the *Principles* to treat of spirits more fully, yet failed to produce it, has only underscored the concern. Berkeley writes to Johnson:

> As to the Second Part of my treatise concerning the *Principles of Human Knowledge*, the fact is that I had made considerable progress in it; but the manuscript was lost about fourteen years ago, during my travels in Italy, and I never had leisure since to do so disagreeable a thing as writing twice on the same subject. (*Works* II 282)

It has been easy to speculate that the *real* reason Berkeley never re-wrote his lost manuscript was the fundamental incoherence of the account itself.

Adding to the dramatic appeal of this story, in his early notebooks, Berkeley appears to have endorsed a proto-Humean conception of the mind – something of the type that Hylas defended (3D III 233). Beginning with entry 577, 'The very existence of Ideas constitutes the soul,' there is a set of entries: 578–81, 637–38, 672 in which Berkeley makes claims such as the following: 'Mind is a congeries of Perceptions. Take away Perceptions & you take away the Mind put the Perceptions & you put the mind' (PC 580). This, and the incoherence which allegedly blights Berkeley's published account of spirit, has yielded speculation of a more duplicitous Berkeley who kept secret his *true* account of the mind, while officially offering up an indefensible theory.[6] Whether Berkeley is viewed as simply blundering or duplicitous, this over-arching story places a philosophical Berkeley at odds with the more theological one.[7]

Berkeley's Philosophy of Spirit

The purpose of this monograph is to vindicate Berkeley's conception of spirit from this long-standing concern as well as other difficulties which plague it. Far from incoherent, Berkeley's philosophy of spirit reflects an important transition from the older notion of a subject as supporter of accidents to the more modern notion of subject (as opposed to object). Indeed, Berkeley's views can be used to illuminate the modern notion of subjecthood and its connection to the theme that the self is mysteriously elusive. In my estimation, Berkeley ought to be placed alongside Descartes, Locke, Hume, and Kant as a great early modern figure in issues concerning self and self-consciousness.

According to the view that I shall defend, Berkeley's rejection of material substratum is embedded within a general rejection of substance–mode ontology. While retaining a notion of substance, Berkeley dispenses with the notion of mode thereby escaping parity of reasoning concerns. Because Berkeley rejects the older ontology, he is led to a transformed model of self-consciousness which grounds his dualism between perceiver and perceived, provides content to the view that spirits support ideas by perceiving them, and enables Berkeley to address the concern that we lack an idea of the soul.

By taking Berkeley's view seriously, we find that Berkeley (not Hume) is better viewed as an originator of the theme that the subject cannot be an object. The sneaking fear that Hume has 'left something out' can be given content by his refusal to address Berkeley in the *Treatise*. Far from viewing

Berkeley's position as incoherent, Hume views it as 'unanswerable.' Hume proceeds from a very different starting point and simply explains away the considerations which motivated Berkeley without ever addressing him in a non-question-begging way.

In addition to this vindication of Berkeley's philosophy of spirit, I have two goals. First, in addressing the problems which have been supposed to afflict Berkeley's account of spirit, I illuminate his metaphysical views more generally. For example, Berkeley is alleged to hold 'the identity principle' according to which ideas are nothing but mental states of perceiving. Yet Berkeley also endorses 'the distinction principle' (the view that spirit and idea are 'entirely distinct').[8] How can spirits and ideas be entirely distinct, if ideas are merely *states* of spirit?[9]

Even if one denies that Berkeley held the identity principle (and I do deny it), Berkeley still appears to hold that spirits are substances which support ideas. The distinction principle, if read like a Cartesian 'real distinction,' undermines what we can call the substantiality principle. Yet reading the distinction principle to allow ideas to depend upon spirits for their existence seems to deflate it. Both principles are important to Berkeley. The substantiality principle seems fundamental in securing Berkeley's thesis that sensible things are mind-dependent. The distinction principle appears to capture a kind of dualism which, as we shall see, is central to his argument for the natural immortality of the soul. Resolving this tension is crucial to understanding Berkeley's ontology.

My second goal is to situate Berkeley's philosophy of spirit within some of the philosophical and theological questions of the day. While I will develop several of these issues in the opening chapter, let me mention some related themes now.

I follow David Berman in emphasizing the importance of the Irish philosophical and theological context of Berkeley's thought.[10] John Toland's (1670–1722) infamous deistic attack on the Christian mysteries, *Christianity not mysterious* (1696), must be recognized as a focal point of dispute concerning the status of the mysteries and human knowledge of the Divine.[11] Indeed, Berkeley's Provost, Peter Browne (1666–1735), had made his name through his response to Toland, *A Letter in Answer to Christianity not mysterious* (1697).

In opposition to Toland's claim that God only speaks to us through our common notions, Browne thought that he used our common notions 'analogically' to represent the supernatural.[12] While we lack any 'proper and direct' ideas of God (and his properties or anything else supernatural), the ideas we do have can be used to partially understand the supernatural, as a blind man might come to understand sight by having it described to him through appeal to his other senses. This position, endorsed by Archbishop of Dublin, William King (1650–1729), Peter Browne, and Edward Synge, formed the basis of what Berman has called 'theological representationalism.'[13]

Among other things, I shall argue that through his rejection of the older ontology and the model of consciousness informed by it, Berkeley comes to view the distance between spirits and corporeal things (ideas) as far greater than the distance between finite spirits and God. This distance is central in his own account of our knowledge of God and the Christian mysteries.

Methodological Considerations

Because it is hardly obvious that Berkeley's philosophical views remained the same over the course of his career, let me clarify that in elaborating Berkeley's philosophy of spirit, I have mostly in mind his views as expressed in the 1710 *Principles* and the 1713 *Dialogues*. Undeniably, Berkeley's views underwent considerable development in his 1707–8 notebooks.[14] There are also important changes between his 1708 Manuscript Introduction to the *Principles* and his 1710 Introduction.[15] While I wish to be sensitive to these changes, my goal is not to provide a reconstruction of the development of Berkeley's thought.

I will also draw on Berkeley's work up to his 1734 revisions of the *Principles* and the *Dialogues*. His later work *Alciphron* (1732), as well as his private letter to Browne (1733), contain invaluable information about Berkeley's views on the relationship between metaphor, analogy, and spirit.[16] This is important in situating Berkeley in the controversy over Christian mysteries as well as in understanding his reaction to the 'theological representationalism' that prevailed. I will also sometimes draw on Browne's 1728 *Procedure, Extent, and Limits of Human Understanding* in order to situate and understand young Berkeley's views about spirits as well. Both moves are controversial.

Let me clarify that my overall argument for Berkeley's philosophy of spirit depends upon neither. I do think, however, that reading Berkeley in this way will illuminate his philosophy of spirit more powerfully, while shedding light on his views about analogy and his conflict with Browne.

I will later provide reasons why *Alciphron* is relevant to Berkeley's philosophy of spirit. Let me point out now that Berkeley's response to Percival about Archbishop King's *Sermon on Predestination* (1709) indicates Berkeley's unhappiness with the account, as well as his early familiarity with Irish analogy: ''Tis true he holds there is something in the divine nature analogous or equivalent to those attributes,' writes Berkeley, 'But upon such principles I must confess I do not see how it is possible to demonstrate the being of God. . . .'[17]

Let me also observe that Browne claims in the *Letter* that he has an argument for the immateriality of the soul and an argument against the possibility of superadding thought to matter which are beyond his present purpose to share. These are subsequently presented in the *Procedure*.[18] This suggests that some of Browne's views expressed in the *Procedure* are already well-developed when Berkeley is a student at Trinity. And if Jonathan Swift is at all correct in his assessment of Browne ('. . . you must flatter him monstrously upon his Learning and his Writings; that you have read his Book against *Toland* a hundred Times . . .'), it would not be surprising that Berkeley should have been made familiar with them, whether he wanted to hear them or not.[19]

Additionally, Browne and King were in attendance when Berkeley presented 'Of Infinites' to the Dublin Philosophical Society (November 19, 1707).[20] At this point, Berkeley accepted a Lockean account of meaning (all categorematic terms require ideas). Yet by Berkeley's first extant sermon, 'Of Immortality' (January 11, 1708) he had rejected this view.[21] The presentation at the Dublin Philosophical Society may very well have led to a clash between Berkeley and Browne/King and a subsequent alteration in Berkeley's views.[22]

There is further evidence of Browne's influence on Berkeley very early in his notebooks. At PC 176 Berkeley abruptly raises a worry about the metaphorical use of language. He claims that insensible things are described in terms borrowed from sensible things. At PC 176a, Berkeley claims that we lack ideas of reflection ('this is metaphorical dress we have not'). Both are views articulated by Browne in his rejection of Lockean ideas of reflection (*Procedure* 97). At PC 177, Berkeley wonders how our idea of God can be complex when his essence is simple. Again, this can be found in Browne (*Procedure* 82). Up to this stage in the notebooks, however, Berkeley had supposed that there is a complex idea of the soul which includes willing and perceiving (see PC 44, PC 154). This suggests Berkeley's abrupt change is possibly inspired by Browne.

Moreover, these men share similar views about abstraction. In the *Procedure* Browne devotes an entire chapter to the topic, echoing some of the arguments of Berkeley. To be sure, there are important differences in terms of the sort of abstraction they are attacking, as well as their arguments against it. My point is that there is sufficient overlap to raise the question of influence. And it seems plausible that Browne influenced Berkeley rather than the other way around.

While there is little change in Berkeley's published philosophy up to 1733, an apparently substantial change comes in Berkeley's second edition of the *Principles* and third edition of the *Dialogues* in 1734. Among other things, Berkeley adds two important exchanges between Hylas and Philonous about the concern that spiritual substance ought to be rejected, and he draws a distinction between *notions* and *ideas* claiming that while we lack ideas of spirits, their mental operations, and relations, we nonetheless possess *notions* of them (PHK I 27, 89, 140, 142).

I resist the view that Berkeley's defense of his philosophy of spirit requires this appeal to notions. In the first edition of the *Principles,* Berkeley purports to answer important puzzles about the nature of self-knowledge (PHK I 135, 136). He claims to answer the worry that there is a deficiency of knowledge with respect to spirit. He begins, 'The great reason that is assigned for our being thought ignorant of the nature of spirits, is, our not having an idea of it' (PHK I 135). The peculiar answer to this problem, according to Berkeley, is precisely that there *cannot* be an idea of spirit: 'But surely it ought not to be looked on as a defect in a human understanding, that it does not perceive the idea of *spirit,* if it is manifestly impossible that there should be any such *idea*' (PHK I 135).

It is curious that Berkeley felt he had something interesting to say about our knowledge of spirits without appealing to notions. This fact sits uncomfortably with the view that Berkeley introduces notions as a way to salvage his account of spirit. Berkeley's solution to the worry that our knowledge of the soul is deficient turns on the very denial that there can be an idea of spirit, unapologetically announced in the first edition of the *Principles.* Let me forewarn, then, that my defense of Berkeley's philosophy of spirit shall have the possibly dubious distinction of failing to centralize Berkeley's alleged 'doctrine of notions.' Instead, I focus on Berkeley's philosophy of spirit *prior* to his appeal to 'notions' in 1734. It is the 'pre-notion' view which I defend from the charge of incoherence.

To be sure, the Berkeley of the first editions has views about meaning that seem relevant to his account of notions. In the first edition of the *Principles,* Berkeley writes, 'In a large sense indeed, we may be said to have an idea of *spirit* that is, we understand the meaning of the word, otherwise we could not affirm or deny any thing of it' (PHK I 140); in the second edition this is changed to include 'or rather a notion.' However, it is only by understanding Berkeley's initial account of spirit that we can begin to assess whether the subsequent deployment of 'notion' flags a substantive philosophical position that can itself be viewed as a development in Berkeley's position or whether it was already there present in his 1710 work.[23]

Let me conclude by remarking that this monograph is a systematic argument. Each chapter builds upon the preceding one. Some claims that I defend in one chapter will be subsequently defended through additional arguments in later chapters or illuminated in new ways. As my view is confirmed in different ways in different chapters, as it renders other aspects of Berkeley's philosophy understandable, and as it illuminates Berkeley's response to the salient issues of his day, the interpretation derives what I take to be the best argument in favour of it: Simplicity and explanatory power. The interpretation is at its strongest when taken as a whole and my hope is that it will be assessed accordingly.

Chapter One

Berkeley's Project

My present goal is to place Berkeley's project within the context of prevailing philosophical and theological issues of his day. But it is impossible to do justice to the range and richness of discussion during that time within a single chapter. Indeed, the very task risks an overwhelming complexity. In order to minimize confusion, I begin with a brief account of Locke and examine some of the themes that emerged in the shadow of his great *Essay*. I then discuss Berkeley's project and its relationship to some of these themes. After, I examine Berkeley's argument for the immortality of the soul in light of specific problems raised by contemporaries.[1] I conclude by foreshadowing how these themes and problems will be addressed in subsequent chapters.

In discussing these themes, my aim is not to be exhaustive. There are obvious issues that inform Berkeley's account of spirit that I do not discuss in this chapter. For example, Berkeley explicitly indicates in his notebooks that he intends to answer Malebranche's occasionalist view that we do not cause our own bodies to move (PC 548). My aim is to draw attention to an important set of interrelated themes that have not been sufficiently explored in the literature. As we shall see, such themes do in fact connect to some of the more obvious ones – especially Berkeley's concerns about self-knowledge.

I draw on the following exchanges: The correspondence between Locke and Edward Stillingfleet, Bishop of Worcester (1635–99) during 1697–99[2,3]; Browne's *Letter* to Toland (1697) as well as his *Procedure* (1728); Henry Dodwell's (1641–1711) argument that the soul is naturally mortal in 1706[4] and the responses by Samuel Clarke (1675–1729) in 1707[5] and John Norris (1657–1711) in 1708,[6] the subsequent dispute between Clarke and Anthony Collins (1676–1729) conducted in 1707–8[7] concerning the immateriality of the soul, as well as Collins' 1707 critique of the mysteries,[8] King's 1709 *Sermon on Predestination*,[9] and Collins' response to King in 1710, *A Vindication of the Divine Attributes*.

Part I: Background Issues

Locke

According to Locke we lack an idea of the real inner constitution of body and of what he calls 'spirit.' While we know that body is extended and can transfer motion, we do not understand how this is so. While we know that spirit is capable of thought and motion, we do not understand how this is so (E. 2.23.30, 312–13).[10] In claiming that we fail to grasp both essence of body and spirit, Locke may be taking issue with Malebranche's inversion of Descartes' view that the mind is better known than the body. Malebranche claimed that we have no idea of the soul and cannot know its modifications *a priori* (we know it only by 'conscience').

While Locke provides a demonstration of God's existence, he does not see fit to establish the immortality of the soul. He argues that whether the soul is material or immaterial is beyond human understanding. He suggests that this area seems fraught with perplexity (E. 4.3.6, 542). On the one hand (perhaps with Hobbes in mind), Locke claims that when our thoughts are focused on matter, it is hard to conceive *substance* distinct from *body*. Yet on the other hand (perhaps with the Cartesians in mind), when our thoughts are focused on thought itself, it is hard to conceive how inert matter could think.

For Locke, we know that we exist and are capable of thinking. For all we know, God may superadd the power of thinking to that same essence from whence arises solidity (540–1). Despite our ignorance whether the soul is immaterial, the ends of morality and religion are not thereby undermined since God can resurrect us come Judgment Day, rewarding and punishing us according to our deeds (542). Locke's innovative theory of personal identity underwrites this view.

Given that personal identity is accounted for in terms of memory and consciousness, it is not difficult for God to assign a certain body all of one's past memories, creating a thinking thing that would in effect be oneself. It bypasses the need for the continuation of the numerically same body or even the numerical same soul, thereby eliminating the importance of the immortality of the soul with respect to the ends of morality and religion

Mystery and the Divine Attributes

John Toland argues that our ignorance with respect to the Divine Nature hardly constitutes a mystery.[11] It suffices that we have ideas of some of the

Divine Attributes. In making this claim, Toland appeals to Locke's distinction between nominal and real essence, as well as the Lockean position that soul and body are equally (un)known. He concludes that our ignorance of God's nature no more constitutes a mystery than our ignorance of the real essence of bodies or finite spirits. In response to this, Browne renders mysterious not only the Divine Nature, but the properties and attributes of any spirit whatsoever. As a consequence, one is in no position to look at one's own mental operations as a way of (however inadequately) understanding the Divine Attributes. Instead, one may understand any spirit only by way of analogy.

In particular, Browne notes that we can only comprehend God's infinity (e.g. eternity, power) through a confused process of accumulation; we lack any positive idea of it (*Letter* 44–5). He denies that our own ideas of spiritual properties can provide us with a 'direct and immediate' conception of the properties of a pure spirit (such as God, or even the pure spirit that is within us). Thinking in human beings is performed 'by help of material Organs, and more immediately by the Fibres of the Brain' (*Letter* 42); consequently human spirits are far too interblended with matter for the mental operations we are conscious of to be representative of a pure spirit.

Browne denies that our ideas of the properties of spirit are equally clear and distinct as our ideas of the properties of body. We know many properties of matter (extension, solidity, divisibility, gravity), we know only one property of a spirit (namely thought) which itself has many different modifications (*Letter* 127–8). The only reason we attribute thinking and motion to spirit is because we can demonstrate that matter cannot think and matter cannot self-move (43). We cannot even clearly distinguish between thought and motion in a spirit; they may actually be the same. We know immaterial substance only through negating the properties of matter. Consequently, Browne denies that we know spirit positively and immediately.

In the *Procedure*, Browne likewise denies that we can turn reflection upon our mental operations and form simple ideas of reflection of them (*Procedure* 412). One of his concerns is that the objects we immediate perceive come in through sensation, and the mind operates upon such ideas as are stored in the memory. In doing this, the mind is conscious of its operations, but cannot reflect upon itself. The supposition that reflection is possible involves an illicit abstraction of the operation from the object itself upon which it is operating.

It is in part because of the fact that these operations cannot be separated from the materials of sensation that they are incapable of yielding direct (non-analogical) knowledge of God's (or any pure spirit's) operations. Instead of simple ideas, Browne thinks, 'complex notions' are formed which are mixtures of our conception of the mental operation (as presented in consciousness itself) with various ideas of sensation which attend the mental operation and which perhaps purport to elucidate it in some way (*Procedure* 66–8). The only way to know God's attributes and any pure spirit, argues Browne, is through divine analogy.

In his *Essay Concerning the Use of Reason in Propositions* (1707), Collins renews the attack on the mysteries made by Toland. He takes up two related issues treated by Edward Stillingfleet in the sermon *The Mysteries of The Christian Faith Asserted and Vindicated* (1691). One issue concerns the eternity of God. Stillingfleet argues that God's eternity is mysterious. As one instance, he argues that it is hard to reconcile Boethius' view that 'Eternity ... is the complete, simultaneous and perfect possession of everlasting life'[12] with the variable activities that God appears to have engaged in over time (*Mysteries* 21–2).

In response to this, Collins argues that this Boethian view is incoherent: '... *to say God exists all at once*, &c. is to say that he actually exists in time past, present, and to come; that is, that time past is not past, and that time to come is come, and was always come' (*Essay* 54). Collins adopts the view that God exists in time, undergoing succession as there are distinct operations of God over time (55).[13]

The other issue concerns the compatibility of Divine prescience with genuine human liberty. While Stillingfleet views this as a mystery, Collins argues for an incompatibility between the two and defends a watered down view of liberty as the '... Power to do or forebear several Actions, according to the Determination of his Mind ...' (47). This is part of his larger project of undermining the doctrine of human liberty. And it is related, in some degree, to Locke's own treatment of the will.

Now the compatibility of divine foreknowledge and human liberty is the central issue taken up by King in his *Sermon on Predestination* (1709). King appeals to a notion of analogy in order to allow that while human foreknowledge of events and liberty are inconsistent, we understand God's foreknowledge only analogically and consequently any concerns about inconsistency are avoided.

King has much the same notion as Browne. However, he claims that terms such as 'loving' and 'wise' apply to God in the same non-literal way that physical terms apply to him: Saying that God is wise is like speaking of the finger of God. For Browne, this is a misunderstanding of analogy, and he complains about King's slide into metaphor in his *Procedure* (13–16).

The difference between the two views is not so great in the end. Browne had appealed to the notion of analogy in addressing the compatibility of divine foreknowledge and human liberty in his *Letter* (45–6). Browne (just as Locke and Clarke) had rejected the Scholastic notion of the *punctum stans* (permanent instant) (*Letter* 126).[14] And Collins' *Vindication of the Divine Attributes* shows how close King's (and Browne's) view comes to yielding a negative theology that surrenders the game to agnosticism: 'And therefore by understanding *Foreknowledg* [*sic*] in a different sense from what is suppos'd in the Objection, and not assigning any determinate sense to the word, all Objections whatever are prevented; for no Man can object to he knows not what . . .' (16). The problem is that understanding God's foreknowledge as similar to our own leads to an incompatibility with genuine human liberty. Yet to depart from our common understanding of knowledge is to drain the claim that God is all-knowing of any sense whatsoever.

Spirituality

According to Hobbes since 'body' and 'substance' mean the same thing, 'incorporeal substance' is a contradiction in terms. The word 'spirit' in common usage means 'subtle fluid, and invisible body, or a ghost, or other idol or phantasm of the imagination.' It can also have metaphorical significations as in 'spirit of contradiction.' If 'spirit' is ever used to signify 'God' then this usage

> . . . falleth not under humane Understanding; and our Faith therein consisteth not in our Opinion, but in our Submission . . . For the nature of God is incomprehensible; that is to say, we understand nothing of *what he is*, but only *that he is*; and therefore the Attributes we give him, are not to tell one another, *what he is* . . . but our desire to honor him with such names as we conceive most honorable amongst our selves.[15]

In his response to Stillingfleet, Locke defends his decision to use 'spirit' in such a way that doesn't exclude its being material. The Latin *spiritus* (literally – breath), as it was applied by Cicero and Virgil to the soul, Locke argues, was meant to contrast with the 'gross visible parts of a man' without a commitment to its immateriality. It might be applied to air, fire, or *quinta essentia*. Locke cites Ecclesiastes 3:19–21 to argue that the Hebrew word רוח (literally – breath) is used in a way that applies to both beast and man and does not exclude the materiality of it.[16] While Locke affirms that God is not extended, his account of spirit moves him closer to Hobbes.

By contrast, controversial Irish theologian, Henry Dodwell (1706), distinguishes between spirit and soul in a way that emphasizes the associations between 'spirit' and 'Divine.' He argues that the souls of men are naturally mortal. However, the souls of men who are baptized are 'supernaturally immortalized' to happiness by partaking in the Divine Baptismal Spirit. The souls of those who are not baptized are immortalized by the will of God to eternal damnation. While yet other souls (those who have not heard the Gospel) perish naturally.

According to Browne (in some way echoing Dodwell) there is a distinction between the soul and spirit.[17] The spirit is the immortal, divine principle within us, while the soul arises from the interblending of spirit and body. The soul contains a superior and inferior part. Pure spirit is predominantly responsible for the superior (thinking and willing), while our animal spirit is mostly responsible for the inferior (the irregular passions). While the pure spirit survives the death of our body, the animal spirit dissolves with the body at death.

Although in the *Procedure*, Browne provides an argument that thought cannot be superadded to matter,[18] Browne does not treat this demonstration as sufficient for establishing the immateriality of the soul. Instead, immateriality is established by an appeal to an interpretation of Ecclesiastes 12:7 and an interpretation (against Locke) of Ecclesiastes 3:21. In the former, 'And the Dust shall return unto the Earth as it was; and Spirit shall return to God who gave it,' he finds that dust (the body) has a natural tendency or gravity towards the earth, while spirit is by its own nature disposed to ascend upward. In the latter, Browne reads 'Who knoweth the Spirit of a Man that goeth upward, and the Spirit of a Beast that goeth downward to the earth?' in a way that puts an opposition between the two kinds of spirit. He renders 'Who knoweth' according to Hebrew idiom 'How few are there who consider' and reads the entire verse as meaning that the spirit *of itself* (of its own nature) ascends while the spirit of beasts *of itself* descends to the earth.

For Browne 'spirit' is used equivocally in this passage. In its original usage רוח means 'breath' but is subsequently used to mean 'animal life,' and then the immaterial part of us, and finally the Divine Nature. In the last two cases the word is used only because we lack a proper and literal word to express this immaterial part which we know through no idea, but only analogically. On this point, the contrast between Browne and Hobbes (for example) is illuminating. While Hobbes denies that 'spirit' has any significance when used in ways that depart from common or metaphoric applications, Browne allows for a significance that derives from the analogical use of common notions. It is a use, however, which is entirely dependent upon scriptural revelation.

Revelation and Natural Religion

Generally, the existence of God and the immortality of the soul were taken as the two basic doctrines of natural (as opposed to scripturally revealed religion). According to Stillingfleet, Locke's position strips away the rational foundation for belief in the soul's immortality (the argument to immortality from the immateriality of the soul).[19] And while Locke denies that his position has any tendency to undermine faith, he is also happy to accept the immortality of the soul on the basis of revelation alone.[20] He points out that most Christians base their belief in immortality upon revelation, rather than philosophical argument.[21]

Like Stillingfleet, Samuel Clarke, in his *Letter to Mr. Dodwell* (1707), raises the worry that Dodwell's view that the soul is naturally mortal may have a tendency to undermine faith in a future state. Those who come to believe in the soul's natural mortality, Clarke argues, will be inclined to believe that it perishes at the dissolution of the body and will be disinclined to believe that God will work 'a perpetual miracle' to keep the naturally mortal soul in existence in order to inflict eternal punishment upon it.[22]

By contrast, in the *Procedure* Browne grants that while he has provided no demonstration of the soul's immateriality, it is founded upon the highest moral certainty which is sufficient to render the refusal of assent inexcusable to God. While mathematical demonstrations (based upon clear and distinct ideas) compel assent, moral proofs (based upon analogical knowledge) ought to determine the judgment but leave latitude for the will. Even natural religion requires faith, since it is grounded in analogy. This accords with his confidence in the *Letter* that he could give a proof for the immateriality of the soul, which while not as strong as a mathematical demonstration, was at least '. . . as good proof for the *immateriality* of the Soul, as we can reasonably expect for any *natural* or *moral* truth' which is 'sufficient for the conviction of any, except those who by their Principles are oblig'd to oppose it' (*Letter* 131). Yet this proof is ultimately drawn from passages of the scripture which he views as a '. . . a plain and express Revelation of the *Immateriality* of the Human Soul; and of the *Materiality* of that in Brutes' (*Procedure* 362). The reason for this is that all religious knowledge, for Browne, depends upon analogical knowledge, and therefore requires faith in scriptural revelation. Consequently the line between natural and revealed religion is significantly blurred.

Resurrection

Some thinkers went on to challenge the very notion of an immortal soul as antithetical to Christian doctrine. Henry Layton (1622–1705) argues that there is no evidence in the scripture for an immortal soul. Instead, he argues, the entire person is supposed to be resurrected on Judgment Day.[24] And according to William Coward (1657–1725), the notion of a naturally immortal soul is a pagan invention. The truth is that we are resurrected without any soul that survives in between.[25] Particular difficulties emerged, however, concerning resurrection itself and Locke's theory of personal identity.

In his correspondence with Locke, Stillingfleet worries that Locke's account of personal identity eliminates the need for the resurrected body to be numerically the same as the one which had died. So long as the person who remembers the deed is conscious of some particular body as his own, this is sufficient for resurrection. This contradicts revelation, argues Stillingfleet.[26] In particular, it contradicts St. Paul's analogy of the seed which is buried (like the body) only to become a new and beautiful plant (I Corinthians. 15: 35–8). For Stillingfleet there is an underlying numerical identity between seed and plant which makes this a case of resurrection. For Locke, there is nothing in the scripture requiring the numerical identity of the body in the final resurrection of the dead. Since our bodily particles are always changing throughout our life, argues Locke, it makes no sense to resurrect the numerically same body on Judgment Day.[27]

In his dispute with Collins, Clarke argues that if the soul is nothing but a material system, the scriptural doctrine of the resurrection cannot be sustained. Should the same particles be reassembled on Judgment Day, it is clear that personal identity cannot consist in those particles since they are ever fleeting. But to restore the power of thinking to the resurrected body would simply be to create a new person.[28] In response, Collins appeals to Locke's theory of personal identity.[29] But Clarke points out that in Collins' account of resurrection, it would be possible for God to create several beings at Judgment Day, all of whom had memories of the same former life.[30] Obviously, this would wreak havoc in terms of the distribution of reward and punishment, not to mention lead to the conclusion that these many resurrected individuals would be the same person. But, Collins has no reply except a surprising appeal to the scriptural basis of Stillingfleet's views of resurrection and mystery itself.

Part II: Berkeley's Project

In a letter to Percival (November 1709), Berkeley recommends Plato's *Phaedo* to him. He touts the *Phaedo* as containing 'the thoughts of the wisest heathen on that subject which the most deserves our consideration, I mean the immortality of the soul.'[31] He praises Socrates as follows:

> Socrates spent his time in reasoning on the most noble and important subjects, the nature of the gods, the dignity and duration of the soul, and the duties of a rational creature. He was always exposing the vanity of Sophists, painting vice and virtue in their proper colours, deliberating on the public good, enflaming the most noble and ungenerous tempers with the love of great actions. In short his whole employment was the turning men aside from vice, impertinence, and trifling speculations to the study of solid wisdom, temperance, justice, and piety, which is the true business of a philosopher.[32]

Berkeley's explicitly professed philosophical project reflects this admiration of Socrates. He clarifies in the Preface to the *Dialogues* that his work is principally addressed to 'men of speculation' (as opposed to 'the vulgar'); his goal is to retrieve them from a useless philosophical speculation and to return them to everyday affairs. In particular, he aims to have 'speculation referred to practice' (3D Preface 168). He announces in the opening sentence of the Preface:

> Though it seems the general opinion of the world, no less than the design of Nature and Providence, that the end of speculation be practice, or the improvement and regulation of our lives and actions; yet those, who are most addicted to speculative studies, seem as generally of another mind. (3D 167)

On this point, Berkeley is even more specific about what he means in the concluding paragraph of the *Principles*.

> For after all, what deserves the first place in our studies, is the consideration of *God*, and our *duty*; which to promote, as it was the main drift and design of my labours, so shall I esteem then altogether useless and

> ineffectual, if by what I have said I cannot inspire my readers with a pious sense of the presence of God .... (PHK 156)

It seems that for Berkeley 'reference to practice' concerns everyday virtue and piety. Specifically, he wants to dispose men of speculation 'to reverence and embrace the salutary truths of the Gospel, which to know and to practise is the highest perfection of human nature' (PHK 156).

Although Berkeley does not direct his philosophical work to 'the illiterate bulk of mankind,' (PHK I Intro 1) he expects real consequences in restoring men of speculation to practice. He believes that this would have 'a gradual influence in repairing the too much defaced sense of virtue in the world' (3D Preface 168). He fingers 'the prejudices of philosophers' as hitherto prevailing 'against the common sense and natural notions of mankind' (168). Berkeley's concern is that practicing speculation in a way that is divorced from the practicalities of the everyday, while amusing is also irresponsible. The scepticism that ensues makes philosophers ridiculous in the eyes of the world (PHK I 88).

One of Berkeley's major strategies in addressing the learned is to convince them that such speculation is largely vacuous. While this negative philosophical approach can show that much standard philosophical speculation for its own sake has no genuine content, Berkeley wishes to motivate men of speculation to return to the everyday practice of Christian virtue. In order to do this, Berkeley believes he needs to establish the existence of God and the natural immortality of the soul as 'the readiest preparation, as well as the strongest motive, to the study and practice of virtue' (3D Preface 167). His positive philosophical account has a decidedly motivational role to play.

The motivational nature of his project is underwritten by belief in an innate desire for immortality which is 'deeply rooted in mankind.'[33,34] This tendency towards a better state[35] is manifested by a satiety which attends sensual pleasure and a restless yearning for unknown things of a perfect nature.[36] It is no doubt because of this desire that 'the vulgar' have a natural propensity to believe in eternal life.[37]

Eternal life is our greatest good, 'the very End of our Being.'[38] The means to obtain our chief end is salvation through Christ who revealed our end to us through his resurrection. Yet salvation does not consist in inert belief; it is action-oriented: 'The faith of a true Christian must be a lively faith that sanctifies the heart and shews it self in the fruits of the Spirit.'[39]

For Berkeley a belief in eternal life is necessary for virtuous conduct. In *Alciphron*, Berkeley argues for this extensively.[40] In the *Principles*, he claims that the view of the soul as 'perishing and corruptible' 'hath been greedily embraced and cherished by the worst part of mankind, as the most effectual antidote against all impressions of virtue and religion' (PHK I 141). Indeed, he writes that it is '... impossible that a nation should thrive and flourish without virtue, or that virtue should subsist without conscience, or conscience without religion....'[41]

Yet Berkeley denies that people necessarily possess a rational desire for eternal happiness (a desire which is in proportion to the goodness of the object and the probability of attaining it). Otherwise, Christians would act like pilgrims '... on earth walking in ye direct path to Heaven.'[42] One of the major reasons for the difficulty of forming a rational desire, is that we lack determinate ideas of the pleasures that are in store for us in the future life given our limited faculties.[43]

Berkeley uses the trope of the blind man (so central in the Irish notion of analogy) in order to help free-thinkers better understand the afterlife: A man is born blind and deaf.[44] Yet, at some point in his life, he loses his capacity to feel, taste, and smell but acquires the capacity to see and hear. In this way, we get a sense of how one may acquire new inlets of perception in the afterlife: 'Behold him amazed, ravished, transported; and you have some distant representation, some faint and glimmering idea of the exstatic state of the soul ....'[45]

Were God to give us a taste of the coming joys, there could be no virtue or vice whatsoever since the desire would so drive us, we would not be free-agents at all.[46] The future state must remain a mystery to us. It must suffice that we have faith that it shall be excellent beyond our imagination. The difficult task for Christians is to pull away from the distraction of the senses, to think about the great prospect of eternal happiness. In considering the prospect rationally, one would thereby develop the rational desire requisite for appropriate conduct.[47]

Since eternal happiness constitutes our chief end, it makes sense that Berkeley holds the human soul itself has a natural tendency toward that end. It is worth noting that in several places, Berkeley argues for the natural immortality of the soul on the basis of this appetite: 'Nay, I defy any man to produce any parallel to this in any part of the creation, or to assign one single instance wherein God hath given appetite without a possibility of satisfying it, or on purpose to teize and disappoint his creatures.'[48]

This elucidates why, for Berkeley, those who teach against the immortality of the soul undermine the very well-being of people in this life.[49] Indeed, it would appear that such free-thinkers hold unnatural desires, preferring annihilation to eternal happiness. Berkeley writes, '... I have often wondered that men could be found so dull and phlegmatick as to prefer the thought of annihilation before them ....'[50] Presumably, men who have this unnatural desire for annihilation will be predisposed to believe in the mortality of the soul. According to Berkeley, these men are unable to conceive of any eternal state devoid of sense perception.[51] Perhaps it is for this reason that they never move beyond immersion in senses to yearn for spiritual things – our natural trajectory.[52] They only experience an ultimate satiety of the senses, and prefer annihilation to life eternal.

Since Berkeley's aim is to motivate men of speculation to virtue through establishing the natural immortality of the soul, it is clear that relegation of the doctrine of the immortality of the soul to a matter of revelation (as opposed to natural religion) would be anathema to him. According to Berkeley, the immortality of the soul was a truth possibly discovered by some of the heathen philosophers.[53]

Yet, I doubt he would have followed Stillingfleet in worrying that the shift from natural religion to revelation would have served to undermine faith (at least of 'the vulgar'). Berkeley is clear that while the ancient philosophers may have used reason to attain this knowledge, this would have simply left most men in the dark.[54] Consequently, he appeals to the monumental significance of the revelation of life immortal through Christ (which people are predisposed to believe). He is in agreement with Locke that most people do not believe in the immortality of the soul on the basis of its immateriality.

However, he would have worried (along with Clarke) that the thesis that the soul is naturally mortal has pernicious consequences. As Clarke points out, men who do not reason subtly may latch on to this idea and conclude straightaway that the soul dissipates with the body at the moment of death. In this way, such a belief can have a tendency to undermine faith. No doubt, Berkeley would have likewise worried about Locke's understanding the word 'spirit' in such a way that tends toward viewing it as inflamed air.

Given his views about our chief end and happiness, it would be imperative for Berkeley to stop free-thinkers from teaching against the soul's immortality. Yet any appeal to faith or revelation would be insufficient to address such men. Consequently he would view Locke's (and Browne's) relegation of the immortality of the soul to a matter of revelation as having dangerous consequences, making it impossible to address free-thinkers by reason.

Berkeley's abiding concern with Lockean ignorance is central in the Introduction to the *Principles*. It is hard not to suppose Berkeley has Locke's explanation of philosophical perplexity and endless dispute in mind when he says: 'It is said the faculties we have are few, and those designed by nature for the support and comfort of life, and not to penetrate into the inward essence and constitution of things' (PHK I Intro 2). Indeed, if Locke's solution to philosophical perplexity is to have us 'sit down in a quiet ignorance,' it is perhaps with Locke in mind that Berkeley speaks instead of having to 'sit down in a forelorn scepticism.'[55] Consider Berkeley's reply:

> We should believe that God has dealt more bountifully with the sons of men, than to give them a strong desire for that knowledge, which He had placed quite out of their reach. This were not agreeable to the wonted, indulgent methods of Providence, which, whatever appetites it may have implanted in the creatures, doth usually furnish them with such means as, if rightly made use of, will not fail to satisfy them. (PHK Intro 3)

The parallels between this argument and Berkeley's appeal to innate desires in arguing for immortality are hard to miss. I don't think that it is surprising that our knowledge of the soul should be of such concern to Berkeley in the *Principles*. He needs to address Locke, Browne, and certainly Malebranche himself.

Part III: The Natural Immortality of the Soul

In the 1710 Preface to the *Principles*, Berkeley promises a demonstration of 'the natural immortality of the soul.' By 'natural immortality' Berkeley means that it is '. . . not liable to be broken or dissolved by the ordinary Laws of Nature or motion' (PHK I 141). This does not preclude annihilation by God, Berkeley argues. However, that would constitute Divine intervention in the natural state of affairs.

The task of establishing the natural immortality of the soul is a difficult one. And it is harder still, since in arriving at an account, Berkeley needs to contend with the question of analogy between the human and God. It is perhaps not surprising that his *Dialogues* demonstration of the incorporeality of the soul is embedded within a discussion of how we know God (3D III 231), an issue which remained of concern to Berkeley.

Indeed, in a letter to Percival (1709/10) Berkeley says the design of his *Principles* is to '. . . demonstrate the existence and attributes of God, the immortality of the soul, the reconciliation of God's foreknowledge with freedom of men. . . .'[56] This alleged reconciliation is never made explicit in that work, but it shows that Berkeley is deeply concerned with the issue. Notice Berkeley's desire to demonstrate 'the attributes of God' in the very same letter he has faulted King's method. The letter also indicates that Berkeley had written to Clarke to see what he thought were the best arguments for God's existence.

At any rate, the demonstration of the incorporeality of the soul seems a good step in establishing its natural immortality. If spirit is incorporeal, it has no parts. Since it has no parts (and is in this sense simple) it cannot be corrupted. Thus, in the *Dialogues*, Berkeley argues that since spirits are not ideas, they are not extended and therefore indivisible. There are three problems, however, which afflict this overall strategy.

1. Consciousness

Collins argues that even if Clarke succeeds in showing the natural immortality of the soul, to secure the ends of religion and morality it must be shown that we continue to exist in a state of actual thinking after death. To do this it must be demonstrated that the action of thinking is inseparably connected to the immaterial substance of the soul.[57] While Clarke may show that the soul insofar as it has the capacity to think is immortal, this is no proof that it actually continues to think.[58] Unfortunately, Clarke ultimately does not have much to say on this point except '. . . *my* argument is evidently *useful* to Religion, by proving at least the *Possibility* and *great Probability* of the future state of Rewards and Punishments. . . .'[59]

By contrast, Clarke argues it is absurd that consciousness could exist in so flux a substance as matter. Because personal identity consists in consciousness, the view would require the transferring of consciousness from one subject to another (making consciousness quite independent of any particular subject).[60] To this, Collins replies that it makes no sense to make personal identity consist in the continuation of the numerically same consciousness, since consciousness is fleeting with each passing thought. Instead, he appeals to a Lockean account of personal identity. Clarke complains this is nothing but a fiction since it would attribute to a subject that which was not in fact done by it.[61]

If Collins is correct, it is insufficient to show the soul is naturally immortal. It needs to be shown that the soul as actually thinking is naturally immortal. But, if Locke is correct in his criticism of Descartes that the soul does not always think, then this would be ruled out as an option. Neither does the Lockean self seem to be an especially good candidate, if Clarke is correct. The only other solution is to identify the soul as that which is given in consciousness at any one moment. The difficulty with this move is that the soul would seem to perish with each passing thought.

2. The Soul as Perishing

In his response to Dodwell (1708),[62] Norris identifies natural immortality as a property that flows from the essence of the being that possesses it. By contrast, positive immortality is a property that is bestowed upon a being from without (5). Norris then distinguishes between immortality as it concerns incorruptibility and as it concerns being.

According to Norris, since the human soul is immaterial, it has no parts and is therefore naturally immortal with respect to incorruptibility. Even God would be incapable of corrupting it. Yet there is nothing within the essence of soul which requires it to persist; the soul is every moment sustained by God. And should God withdraw his support, the soul would cease.

As a consequence the soul has only positive immortality with respect to its being. Here, the soul is on par with matter which is likewise not self-existent and must be sustained by God. However, the only changes we observe in nature are instances of corruption, not annihilation (54). So no creature can bring it about that matter is annihilated any more than a creature can bring it about that a soul is annihilated.

Yet, while there are no examples of annihilation in nature for Norris, this is hardly the case for Berkeley whose world is built out of sensible ideas which he describes as fleeting (PHK I 89). Why aren't our souls likewise fleeting and therefore perishing? This is a point of concern raised by Johnson. He worries, 'if . . . the *esse* of a spirit be nothing else but its actual thinking, the soul must be dead during those intervals; and if ceasing or intermitting to think be the ceasing to be, or death of the soul, it is many times and easily put to death . . . I don't see upon what we can build any natural argument for the soul's immortality.'[63] The difficulty is that in Berkeley's account, just as ideas regularly perish in nature, it seems that the soul itself should perish, too.

3. The Soul as Corruptible

In their dispute, Collins presents Clarke the following dilemma: If God can destroy a property of a thinking thing without altering any parts, short of some argument distinguishing the cases, there is no reason to believe there is any repugnancy with this occurring due to forces of nature. If, however, destroying a property of a thinking thing involves the alteration of parts, then the capacity of God to destroy a power that he has superadded to a spirit, shows the discerptibility of the soul. If God can superadd a property (as Clarke grants), why can't he take it away?[64]

Clarke's response to this last dilemma is curious. Accepting none of these possibilities, he claims that if God were to destroy a property of the soul, this would involve some alteration in the substance which is analogous to an alteration in parts but nonetheless distinct from it. Thus, the soul would continue to be indiscerptible since it still lacked parts.[65] Yet, one worries, if souls can have something analogous to parts, such that God can remove powers that are superadded to them, it isn't clear that the soul will be naturally incorruptible.

Now Norris distinguishes between two kinds of natural incorruptibility. The one is absolute (where the being lacks parts), the other allows that a thing possess parts 'which are united as not to be capable of separation' (42). In this latter sense a thing (like the resurrected, spiritualized body) might be incorruptible in that nothing can break it apart except God. This latter kind is inferior to the former. So one might worry that in allowing that God can remove 'parts' of spirit, its incorruptibility will no longer be absolute.

Indeed, while Norris doesn't allow for this sort of 'divisibility' of the soul, he does flag an interesting way in which soul may be called 'corruptible': '. . . yet still in every *Change* there is a sort of Corruption, or at least something that carries some Resemblance or Proportion to it, since what ever is changed, does as such cease to be what it was before. And therefore that may be said to be eminently and transcendentally Incorruptible which is perfectly *Immutable*' (97–8). The overall problem is that even if the soul lacks spatial parts, its possessing variable properties at all apparently undermines its incorruptibility in some important sense.

Toward a Philosophy of Spirit

Berkeley's views appear to emerge out of these issues. His notebooks begin in 1707 (A.A. Luce dates the beginning of the notebooks around June 1707).[66] And the nature of his reflections suggests that he was inspired by some of the Clarke–Collins correspondence as well as Collins' *Essay*. He starts with an investigation into time, the immortality of the soul, and the nature of God's eternity. Berkeley asks whether there is '. . . a succession of ideas in the divine intellect?' (PC 3). And he proceeds with something like a Lockean self. In one his earliest entries, Berkeley writes:

> Eternity is onely a train of innumerable ideas. hence the immortality of ye Soul easily conceiv'd. or rather the immortality of the person, y^{t} or ye soul not being necessary for ought we can see. (PC 14)

He also seems to have been concerned by the question 'about the Soul or rather person whether it be not compleatly known' (PC 25). Indeed, Berkeley seems to have been trying to work out a view about the soul as substance by using the self as a kind of starting point:

> Qu: whether being might not be the substance of ye soul or (otherwise thus) whether being added to ye faculties compleat the real essence and adequate definition of the soul? (PC 44, cf. PC 154)[67]

It is clear that Berkeley ultimately comes to reject Locke's account of personal identity over time.[68] Even early in his notebooks, Berkeley worries whether memory is supposed to be actual awareness of a past event or a potential for such awareness. If the former, then the identity will obtain only when we think on it; if the latter then 'all persons may be the same for ought we know' (PC 200). Berkeley departs from the Lockean account of personal identity fairly early on. Rather than linking identity with memory, he seems to be identifying the self with ongoing momentary consciousness. He writes: 'Men die or are in state of annihilation oft in a day' (PC 83).

Later in the notebooks Berkeley identifies the soul with the will (PC 712). He suggests that by viewing the soul in this way, any problems about personal identity can be solved (PC 194a, 681) and the immortality of the soul established (PC 814). While the relationship between this move and the earlier views about momentary consciousness is not clear, it is worth noting that this identification of soul and will is coincident with the use of the term 'spirit' to apply to the soul. The association of 'spirit' to the Divine comes out in one of the earliest uses of the term at PC 610 where he speaks of 'God & Blessed Spirit.' Indeed, the overlap is plain at PC 712: 'The Spirit the Active thing that wh^{ch} is Soul & God is the Will alone The Ideas are effects impotent things.' From this stage of the notebooks until the very end, there is an abundance of entries on spirit as Berkeley's view seems to go through some rapid developments. Given the controversy over the use of the word 'spirit,' Berkeley's decision to use it amidst this development is by no means inconsequential.

By the time we reach the *Principles*, the distinction between spirit and idea has become crucial. It is the backbone of his argument for the natural immortality of the soul: Spirits and ideas are 'more distant and heterogeneous ... than light is from darkness.' Here Berkeley opposes the view that the soul is '*perishing* and corruptible' (PHK I 141, my emphasis). He defends its incorruptibility on the basis of its indivisibility, incorporeality, and lack of extension, and he does not infer the indivisibility of the soul from its lack of extension. The 'simple, undivided' claim is made as early as PHK I 27 suggesting there may be more to it than indivisibility into spatial parts. Berkeley then argues that 'motions, changes, decays, and dissolutions which we hourly see befall natural bodies' cannot affect a spirit, suggesting that he is going beyond incorruptibility and defending its imperishability. In order to demonstrate the latter, Berkeley obviously cannot demonstrate that finite spirits are self-existent; he needs to allow that God can destroy them. But he does need to show that spirits don't come and go in the way that ideas do. As we shall see, his answer depends on his controversial views about time.

Conclusion

While it is illuminating to examine Berkeley's philosophy within the context of the afore- mentioned themes and issues regardless of whether he was familiar with the actual philosophers or not, let me conclude by considering the extent to which Berkeley was familiar with them. On the basis of his letter to Percival, we know that Berkeley was familiar with King's work. I have already presented reasons for taking seriously Browne's impact upon Berkeley. Certainly, Berkeley was familiar with the Locke-Stillingfleet dispute (see my note 3). The same letter to Percival also indicates that Berkeley had already written to Clarke about proofs of God's existence. So it seems almost certain that he was familiar with the well-known Clarke-Collins dispute. It therefore seems likely that he was aware of Dodwell's work, especially since this fellow Irishman was a friend of Browne and King. It is plausible (although somewhat less clear) that Berkeley was familiar with Norris' reply. And insofar as Clarke discusses Collins' *Essay* in the correspondence, it seems probable that Berkeley was familiar with that work, too. I should add that to the extent that I can show how Berkeley accommodates these themes and issues, I provide further evidence that Berkeley was aware of them, and took them quite seriously.

Many of the themes and problems mentioned in this chapter will be elaborated throughout the course of the monograph. In chapter three I discuss how Berkeley answers Malebranche's claim that we lack an idea of the soul. In chapter four I show how Berkeley addresses Browne's view that we cannot know spirit except by analogy, and how Berkeley defends the absolute incorruptibility of the soul. In chapter five, I expand the preceding chapter by providing an account of Berkeleian operations, enabling finite spirits to be similar to God in their capacity to create ideas. In chapter six, I explain how Berkeley addresses concerns about bodily resurrection, and link his reason for believing that spirits are imperishable with his accommodation of God's eternity and his reconciliation of divine foreknowledge with human liberty. Before we can proceed, however, that famous concern confronts us: Insofar as Berkeley addresses Lockean ignorance about real essences by effectively jettisoning them, how can Berkeley prevent the soul from being relegated to a collection of mental properties just as sensible objects have been so reduced? It is to this initial question that I now turn.

Chapter Two

The Rejection of Mode Ontology

While many commentators see Berkeley as firmly committed to the view that spirits are substances, others suppose that Berkeley abandons the traditional conception of substance altogether, possibly concealing his anti-substance views or endorsing an account so thoroughly departed from the traditional one that it scarcely looks like substance at all.[1] The position I defend lies in between these extremes. I argue that Berkeley retains a robust, satisfying account of spirit as substance, but one that departs from the prevailing tradition.

This already invites difficulty. It is hardly obvious that all philosophers of Berkeley's day held to a monolithic conception of substance. To be sure, we can sketch out some general features of substance to which all philosophers were committed (e.g. basic persistent, underlyer of change, independent, etc.).[2] However, the worry now is that either Berkeley's account will turn out to be another variation within these general parameters, or else it will depart from those parameters, and thereby fail as an account of substance in any suitable sense.

The substance, however, is only half the story. The other half concerns *the mode* or *accident.*[3] The traditional notion of substance involves the view that substances support accidents or modes. In my view, Berkeley abandons such items. By this I mean that he rejects the ontological framework which divides up reality into *substantia* and *inherentia.* To be sure, spirits provide ontological support to other items, they serve as the only causes, and they persist through change. But they are no longer viewed as subjects which support accidents since what I call 'mode ontology' has been rejected.

Interpretations which see Berkeley as genuinely committed to spiritual substance have to some degree assimilated Berkeley's notion of substance into mode ontology. The most straightforward way to do this is to identify the relation of support between spirit and idea as one of inherence. According to what has been called the 'inherence interpretation', Berkeley argues for the mind-dependence of sensible properties on the grounds that since there is no material substance in which they can inhere, they must inhere in something else; spirits are the only candidates.[4] In 'the adverbial interpretation' this assimilation involves explaining the mind-dependence of sensible ideas by identifying them as *ways* of perceiving.[5] Or else, one may simply straightforwardly identify sensible ideas with mental states (sensations, perceptions).[6] Of course, the mere acceptance of 'the identity principle' is insufficient to yield a Berkeleian conception of substance; one must hold that these states and acts are bound to a substance which has them. Once one does this, one has assimilated Berkeley's view to the older ontology.

There are other ways in which Berkeley is seen as committed to mode ontology. It is tempting to construe the mind's operations as modes, properties and the like. If operations are not viewed in this way, it is difficult to understand their ontological status and their relationship to spirits.[7] Even if one recognizes that ideas are not modes which inhere in spirit, it is tempting to think of ideas and their relationship to spirit as at least analogous to modes and inherence.[8] By stressing the analogy between Berkeleian ontology and mode ontology, it is easier to see Berkeley as belonging to the older tradition.

In what follows, I argue against the view that Berkeley retains substance–mode ontology. Furthermore, I show that by understanding Berkeley's argument correctly, we can avoid the traditional concern that Berkeleian spirit collapses into a bundle of perceptions. In the subsequent chapters, I elaborate Berkeley's account of substance and thereby demonstrate some of the serious ways in which Berkeley's ontology is disanalogous to this older tradition. In doing so, I hope to show something of importance without sliding into merely verbal issues.

Substance–Mode Ontology

The tradition of substance–mode ontology may be traced to Aristotle's division of the things which are individual and numerically one into those which are 'in a subject' and those which are not.[9] This division of 'real being' into substance and accident is of central importance in Scholastic ontology. Although altered in ways, it remains important in Cartesian metaphysics as well; to some degree, it is accepted by Locke. Of course one must recognize that the distinction between substance and accident is handled differently by different thinkers. Nonetheless, there are some key features which are fairly important (if not quite universal) to this type of ontology and which justify speaking of a tradition.

First, regardless of the specific underlying metaphysical picture at work, inherence roughly concerns subject–predicate structure. The relation involves viewing the dependent items as property-like, property-instances, or at least some way bound up with substance–property ontology. This is at its clearest when we consider the Aristotelian-Scholastic thought that accidents are predicated of a subject.[10]

In a Cartesian view, it is likewise clear that the relation in question concerns substance and properties or property-like items which 'belong' to them and to which they are 'referred.' Of course there is but a conceptual distinction (not a distinction in being) between the substance and the principal attributes thought and extension. However, a body is modally distinct from various items such as its shape, motion, and so forth where the latter concern the various properties of the body.

This means that the ontologically dependent items must be viewed as dependent in a specific way: It is impossible for a particular shape to exist without the thing itself which has the shape. This dependence is nicely captured by Stillingfleet's truth that 'it is a Repugnancy to our first Conceptions that *Modes* and *Accidents* should subsist by themselves.'[11] In a similar vein, Descartes writes:

> ... we should notice something very well known by the natural light: nothingness possesses no attributes or qualities. It follows that, wherever we find some attributes or qualities, there is necessarily some thing or substance to be found for them to belong to; and the more attributes we discover in the same thing or substance, the clearer is our knowledge of that substance. (*Principles of Philosophy* Part One, 11, AT VIIIA 8–9, CSM I 196)[12]

Modes or accidents are not merely dependent. They are dependent in a way that is to some degree connected to notions of subject and property.

A second feature, related to the preceding, is that the admission of modes or accidents into the ontology involves a serious commitment; they secure a distinctive ontological status. According to the Scholastic view, while substance and accidents/modes all count as real (as 'being'), privations and negations do not. Consider Aquinas' distinction between two senses of 'a being.' In the first sense it is 'divided by the ten categories.' In the second sense, 'anything can be called a being if an affirmative proposition can be formed about it, even though it is nothing positive in reality.' He writes, 'In this way privations and negations are called beings, for we say that affirmation *is* opposed to negation, and that blindness *is* in the eye.'[13] Consequently, while there is one sense in which blindness exists and is a being, in the more robust metaphysical sense, blindness is not so much a being as a privation of being. By contrast, substances and their inherents have real being. As such, they have an essence.[14]

To the extent that accidents can count as 'being' they are likewise ontologically downgraded. St. Thomas remarks '. . . we use the term "a being" primarily of substances, and secondarily and with qualification of accidents . . . .'[15] While a substance is a being or thing properly speaking, an accident is only a being in a derivative sense.

In Cartesian ontology, ontological gradation is likewise maintained. Descartes writes, 'There are various degrees of reality or being: a substance has more reality than an accident or a mode; and infinite substance has more reality than a finite substance' (*Second Set of Replies*, AT VII 165, CSM II 117). This, and the fact that a modal distinction between substance and mode and also between two modes of the same substances is withal metaphysical in nature requires us to recognize that for Descartes, modes constitute an ontological commitment. No doubt the fact that, on the Cartesian model, modes are represented as nothing but the principal attribute (extension or thought) existing in a determinate way might encourage one to suppose that Descartes does not make the same type of ontological commitment. Yet, the fact that Descartes assigns to modes some positive degree of reality (which is different from that of finite substances themselves) makes it clear that there is an ontological commitment at stake. Indeed, it seems clear that for Descartes, modes inhering in the same substance are modally distinct, countable items. It is precisely knowledge of the many modes of thinking – knowledge that is augmented anytime we know anything of the world at all – that helps Descartes claim that the mind is more clearly known than the body.

The point that ought to be stressed is that the admission of modes or accidents into one's ontology is a robust move. Consider the fact that accidents/modes are supposed to be individuated by the particular substances in which they inhere. Even though two substances may be the same size, they will have distinct modes inhering in them. This metaphysical doctrine which requires numerically distinct modes per substance is far more metaphysically weighty than banal observations that sugar is sweet, snow is white, my eyes have sight. So certainly, the ontological admission of modes is controversial. Yet once one has adopted these items into one's ontology, one is committed to Stillingfleet's truth that it is a repugnancy to our first conceptions that modes should subsist by themselves. Insofar as modes/accidents are defined as property-like items which cannot exist except by entering into some specific metaphysical relation (*inherence*) with a substance, once one accepts the existence of such items one is thereby required to infer the existence of a substance.

Berkeley's Rejection of Mode Ontology

Berkeley recognizes and distinguishes two ways in which a sensible thing might 'exist in' something else. Berkeley calls the first way 'existence in by way of idea or as a thing perceived in that which perceives it' (PHK I 49, 3D III 237), and the second way 'existence in by way of mode, attribute, or property' (PHK I 49, 3D III 237). The latter (I believe) is meant to capture the notion of 'inherence' and substance–mode ontology.

To some degree, Berkeley makes his rejection of this relation clear in both the *Principles* and the *Dialogues*. In the *Dialogues* Philonous says of sensible qualities that they exist in spirit '. . . not by way of mode or property, but as a thing perceived in that which perceives it' (3D III 237). And in answering the concern that extension will be predicated of spirit because it exists in it, Berkeley writes in the *Principles*: '. . . those qualities are in the mind only as they are perceived by it, that is, not by way of *mode* or *attribute*, but only by way of *idea* . . .' (PHK I 49). He then says: 'As to what philosophers say of subject and mode, that seems very groundless and unintelligible.'

However these passages are not as decisive as one might think.[16] For example, Descartes distinguishes between different ways of viewing ideas. They may be viewed (materially) as modes of mind; or they may be viewed (objectively) as objects of thought.[17] In light of this distinction, Descartes can say that the sun itself exists in the mind (in the way that objects are normally there) without committing to the view that the mind itself is extended.[18] Berkeley's contrast between existence in by way of idea and existence in by way of mode does not rule out this move. He may be saying that the contents of perception exist in the mind by way of idea (rather than by way of mode) without committing to the stronger view that ideas don't exist in the mind in that way at all.[19]

Moreover, while his claim that 'subject and mode' is unintelligible seems pretty damning, it can be taken in different ways. First, one may read it as applying only in the case of sensible things, rather than spirits.[20] After all, Berkeley goes so far as to claim that 'thing' does not apply univocally to spirits and ideas. Perhaps his claim about subject and mode should not be taken to apply in the case of spirits. Second, one may read this claim as applying only to one account of substance–mode ontology. Perhaps this attack only concerns a Scholastic position and leaves a Cartesian account of substance intact.[21]

However, there is good reason to believe that Berkeley means to reject substance–mode ontology. This can be seen by examining Berkeley's argument against Lockean material substratum. I think this argument generalizes to all substance–mode ontology, and for Berkeley this generalization is both anticipated and desired. If so, a fairly serious problem emerges.

After attacking the intelligibility of 'subject and mode' at PHK I 49, Berkeley mentions a die which is said to be extended, hard, and square. He writes, '. . . to me a die seems to be nothing distinct from those things which are termed its modes or accidents. And to say a die is hard, extended and square, is not to attribute those qualities to a subject distinct from and supporting them, but only an explication of the meaning of the word *die*.' The concern is that if Berkeley rejects substance–mode ontology, the mind should likewise collapse into a collection of properties. I am confronted by the challenge of explaining how Berkeley can reject substance-mode ontology without losing spiritual substance altogether. My contention is that a proper understanding of Berkeley's argument against Locke provides a way to answer this problem.

Berkeley's Argument Against Locke

In his most scathing critique of substance–mode ontology, Locke attempts to deflate the philosophical importance of the Scholastic terms '*substantia*' ('substance') and '*inherentia*' ('accident') by replacing them with the English terms 'under-propping' and 'sticking-on' (E. 2.13.20, 175). Locke's point in doing so is to help us see that while we possess a rather obscure and relative idea of what substance does (it supports) we have no positive idea of what it *is* (E. 2.13.19, 175; E.2.23.3, 296).

Although Locke's views about substance are hardly clear and uncontroversial,[22] it seems one of Locke's major points is that while we have some relative idea of substance *qua* supporter, we are unable to form a positive, robust conception of 'being' (*ens*), not even by some process of abstraction. According to Locke we do not have adequate ideas of the real essences of substances. Because we do not have a handle on the essences of substances, we are not in a position to produce an abstract positive idea of substance in general. Consequently, we are left with only a relative idea of substance as the subject of inherence.

This is a point of contention. Stillingfleet appeals to the importance of substance *qua* essence, 'that which makes the real being as distinguished from modes and properties.'[23] In claiming that our idea of substance in general is nothing but the idea of a mere something which supports accidents, Locke is deflating the Scholastic notion of 'being' by denying that our simple ideas of qualities are any less beings than the substances which support them.

Yet Locke remains committed in some ways to this older ontology. He endorses the principle that modes exist and that they cannot subsist alone. He writes in reply to Stillingfleet:

> So that I have the good luck here again to agree with your lordship: and consequently conclude, I have your approbation in this, that the substratum to modes or accidents, which is our idea of substance in general, is founded in this, "that we cannot conceive how modes or accidents can subsist by themselves".[24]

Berkeley's argument against Locke's notion of (material) substratum amounts to the further challenge that the (material) support relation be explicated. Berkeley writes in the *Principles*: 'Now I desire that you would explain what is meant by matter's *supporting* extension . . . you must be supposed to know what relation it bears to accidents, and what is meant by its supporting them' (PHK I 16). Again in *Three Dialogues*: 'Be pleased therefore to let me know wherein that relation consists' (3D I 197). His conclusion in both cases is that there is no way to make intelligible the relation of (material) support.[25] In both versions Berkeley considers the suggestion that the (material) support relation be understood in a 'literal' and 'common' sense which he takes to be spatial. In the *Principles* he dismisses the spatial explication of (material) support out of hand (PHK I 16); and in the *Dialogues* he argues that the proposed explication leads to an infinite regress (3D I 198).

Toward the end of the *Dialogues*, Berkeley also has Hylas mount the very same challenge against Berkeley's claim that sensible things 'exist in the mind by way of idea' in an explicit charge of parity of reasoning (3D III 249–50). He announces proudly, 'But what would you say, Philonous, if I should bring the very same reasons against the existence of sensible things in a mind, which you have offered against their existing in a material *substratum*?' Again, the starting point is that the expression under discussion cannot be understood in the literal and common (spatial) sense; the challenge, again, is how one is supposed to understand the expression at all. Philonous answers the challenge by explaining that 'exists in the mind' means 'is perceived by mind.' While the philosophical and metaphorical use of 'support' in the case of material substratum cannot be explained (translated into non-philosophical and literal words), 'existence in the mind' can be so explained (as 'perception by the mind').

Berkeley's demand that terms such as 'support' and 'existence in' be given explanation is neither gratuitous nor regressive. Berkeley's denial that Lockean 'support' (and even Berkeleian 'existence in') can be understood literally not only successfully rules out that possible explication, it also motivates his insistence that an explication be given in the first place. Berkeley's concern is that the philosophical deployment of such expressions departs from the common meanings. His point is that when philosophers use common expressions in uncommon ways, they owe an explanation of what they are talking about. Otherwise, they are deploying unexplained metaphors. For Berkeley, this means that philosophers must actually provide some 'common' translation of the philosophically appropriated and figuratively re-deployed expressions.

Berkeley's Rejection of Mode Ontology: Beyond Lockean Metaphysics

While Berkeley's argument is largely focused on Lockean (material) substratum, Berkeley is also clear that it can be generalized to (material) substance more generally. In the *Dialogues*, Hylas attempts to explain 'substratum' by appealing to 'substance.' 'The word *substratum*,' he claims, 'is used only to express in general the same thing with *substance*' (3D I 198). For Berkeley, however, the same problem of explicating the support relation applies. In the *Principles* Berkeley goes on to claim that what 'most accurate philosophers' mean by 'material substance' involves the idea of 'being in general' and the relative idea of 'its supporting accidents.' He dismisses the former on the grounds that it is an abstract idea, and then claims that the relative idea of 'support' is vulnerable to the vacuity argument that he has just deployed (PHK I 17).

Berkeley is interested to oppose not only the Lockean conception of (material) substratum but also (perhaps more specifically) an inflated conception of (material) substance which advances some positive idea of 'being or substance in general.'[26] It seems that Berkeley might have a Scholastic conception of substance in mind, taking up earlier, derisive remarks from Malebranche who complains about the Scholastic conception of substance:

> Yet, if they are asked to explain this thing in addition to extension that they pretend to see in matter, they do so in ways that indicate that they have no other idea of this thing than *being or substance in general*. . . . (SAT B3, P2, C8, 245, my italics)[27]

Berkeley's point against this idea of 'being in general' is that it is an abstract idea, hence there is no such thing. In this way, he rejects both Locke's deflated notion of 'a mere something' and the more robust notion of *ens*. The key move is the rejection of the relation of support ('existence in by way of mode') as vacuous. By undermining the relation which was supposed to obtain between substance and accident, Berkeley destroys the notion of a metaphysical subject of inherence, and with it the ontology altogether.

What is interesting about Berkeley's criticism of 'the most accurate philosophers,' is that he excludes any discussion of the Cartesian alternative. Not only does this come out plainly at PHK 17 where Berkeley speaks of the dreaded 'being in general,' it also comes out in the *Dialogues* formulation of the argument, in which Hylas remarks, 'I tell you, extension is only a mode, and matter is something that supports modes' (3D I 198). This assumption, central to the regress argument, would be rejected by a Cartesian. Such considerations have made it seem permissible to believe that Berkeley remains committed to substance–mode ontology through accepting some tenets of the Cartesian conception of mind.

It is plain that Berkeley did not take the Cartesian approach seriously; and the reason he does not mention the position is simply that he does not accept it as a viable contender. Rather, Berkeley's philosophy situates itself as a direct engagement of Locke's enlightened clearing away of 'the old Scholastic rubbish.'[28] The question is not whether Berkeley rejects Cartesian ontology, it is why he does. Some of Berkeley's most noteworthy concerns come out in a letter to Molyneux.[29] He writes:

> I am of your Opinion that Descartes flounders often in his Meditations and is not always consistent with himself. ... In Med. 3 and in the Answer to the 3: Objection of Hobbes he plainly distinguisheth betwixt himself & Cogitation, betwixt an extended Substance & Extension, and nevertheless throughout his Principles he confounds those Things as do likewise his Followers. (*Works* VIII, 26)

These remarks suggest that if one adopts a substance-mode ontology, one ought to distinguish self and cogitation, matter and extension. But in doing so, Berkeley's explication challenge would remain in full force. The Cartesians apparently 'confound these things,' while Descartes is inconsistent on this point, adopting Berkeley's preferred view (in response to Hobbes) while rejecting it in the *Principles*. Similar themes are expressed in the notebooks. He writes, 'Descartes owns we know not a substance immediately by it self but by this alone that it is the subject of several acts. Answer to 2d objection of Hobbs' (PC 795). And then, 'Descartes in answer to Object: 3 of Hobbs owns he is distinct from thought as a thing from its modus or manner' (PC 798).[30,31] And Descartes does write in reply to Hobbes' third objection, 'I do not deny that I, who am thinking, am distinct from my thought, in the way in which a thing is distinct from a mode.'[32]

Philonous works hard to have Hylas agree that '. . . extension is only a mode, and matter something that supports modes' and that '. . . the thing supported is different from the thing supporting' (3D III 198). So in confessing that 'I, who am thinking, am distinct from my thought' has Descartes not granted an important premise in Berkeley's argument? It isn't clear, I suppose. What is clear is that Berkeley takes Descartes to make this commitment in his reply to Hobbes, and possibly sees Descartes as open to his argument. By contrast, a view which does not make this distinction is guilty of a 'conflation.' Berkeley presumably rejects this latter position on the grounds that it involves an abstraction from particular extensions to extension in general (3D I 192–4) and from particular thoughts to thought in general. It cannot be maintained that Berkeley adopts a Cartesian account of mind.

Berkeley's Rejection of Mode Ontology: Against Spiritual Substratum

An odd feature of Berkeley's argument against Lockean substratum is that it is explicitly geared toward Lockean *material* substratum, despite the fact that Locke's notion of substratum concerns both body and spirit. This perhaps, raises the worry that Berkeley wishes to retain Lockean spiritual substratum. Yet while Berkeley's argument against the traditional support relation explicitly concerns only material substratum and material substance, it is easily generalized to apply to spiritual or mental support of properties and modes. If 'support' may not be understood spatially in the case of matter, it may not be so understood in the case of spirit. The only sort of support that Berkeley explicitly assigns to spirit is existence in the mind as a thing perceived in that which perceives it. However, this is not the kind of support that is supposed to obtain between a spirit and its properties, faculties, or actions.

The pressing question is whether Berkeley adopts a conception of spiritual substance that allows for 'existence in by way of mode' in addition to 'existence in by way of idea.' If he does, it appears that Berkeley is open to a parity of reasoning objection. 'Existence in by way of mode' may likewise be challenged by Berkeley's argument. Should it be understood spatially? Then how should it be understood? The charitable answer is that Berkeley accepts only 'existence in by way of idea.' The worry is that if, in rejecting 'subject–mode' as unintelligible, the die is reduced to nothing but 'what are termed its modes and properties,' why would it not be the case that spirit is likewise reduced to its modes and properties?

Berkeley's Rejection of Modes

Locke offers an account of simple ideas and our perception of them which is deeply informed by the traditional ontological framework. For according to Locke, there is a contrast between two ways of understanding ideas. He writes:

> To discover the nature of our *Ideas* the better, and to discourse of them intelligibly, it will be convenient to distinguish them, as they are *Ideas* or Perceptions in our Minds; and as they are modifications of matter in the Bodies that cause such Perceptions in us. . . . (E. 2.8.7, 134)

He continues: '. . . the Powers to produce those *Ideas* in us, as they are in the Snow-ball, I call *Qualities*; and as they are Sensations, or Perceptions, in our Understandings, I call them *Ideas* . . .' (E. 2.8.8, 134). In Locke's view, white may be viewed as a sensation or perception, and it may also be viewed as a modification or power of matter. When one receives a simple idea of white, one perceives the accident white, which 'doth really exist, and hath a Being without me' (E. 4. 11.2, 631). Insofar as 'all simple ideas, all sensible qualities carry with them a supposition of a substratum to exist in, and of a substance wherein they inhere,'[33] we may be said to have sensitive knowledge of the existence of the thing which is white (the thing which has the quality whiteness) through the perception of the simple idea of white alone.[34]

In rejecting the support relation as unintelligible, Berkeley must not only reject the notion of a (material) substratum – he must also reject this notion of mode as well. Such items are informed by the relation of inherence, and cannot be understood without it. In short, once we reject the relation, we must likewise reject both relata. That Berkeley explicitly rejects this modal way of viewing ideas emerges in his *Dialogues* version of the argument against Lockean substratum. He has Hylas draw this Lockean distinction between viewing white as an idea or sensation and viewing it as a quality or power in the object. Hylas says:

> I acknowledge, Philonous, that upon a fair observation of what passes in my mind, I can discover nothing else, but that I am a thinking being, affected with variety of sensations; neither is it possible to conceive how a sensation should exist in an unperceiving substance. But then on the other hand, when I look on sensible things in a different view, considering them as so many modes and qualities, I find it necessary to suppose a material *substratum*, without which they cannot be conceived to exist. (3D I 197)

The argument concludes with the explicit rejection of ideas viewed as 'so many modes and qualities.' Philonous claims: 'That is to say, when you conceive the real existence of qualities, you do withal conceive something which you cannot conceive' (3D I 199). Berkeley does not only reject Lockean substratum. He rejects the supported items themselves.

According to Locke, the compound idea of substance in general arises because our simple ideas carry the supposition of support. Lacking the positive idea of anything specific, we use the abstract, indeterminate idea of 'something' (which is derived from our simple ideas) and compare it with the idea of an accident in order to form the idea of the relation of support. The indeterminate idea of 'a mere something' together with the idea of support are combined to yield the relative notion of substance in general.[35]

So Locke might appear to have a good answer to Berkeley's challenge to provide 'support' with content. Yet Berkeley's argument remains effective, because he challenges Locke's unquestioned assumption that simple ideas may be viewed as accidents in the first place. In making this move, Berkeley does not deny that various properties can be affirmed of various different objects. Berkeley has Philonous remark, 'That the colours are really in the tulip which I see, is manifest' (3D I 195). Just as such claims needn't be seen as requiring a subject in addition to a collection of properties, they needn't be seen as requiring accidents in addition to the thing itself. Indeed, once one commits to the existence of modes or accidents articulated within substance–mode ontology, one may not flout the principle that modes cannot exist on their own. The only way that Berkeley can avoid this conclusion is to refuse the starting commitment altogether.

This means that it is not correct to see Berkeley as identifying sensible qualities with ideas, if we understand the former as 'modes' or 'accidents'. Consider the passage which probably most clearly suggests that for Berkeley common objects are collections of qualities. He writes, '... to me a die seems to be nothing distinct from those things which are termed its modes or accidents.' (PHK I 49). Notice Berkeley's careful wording. He avoids committing to the actual existence of modes or accidents, saying that the die is not distinct from 'those things which are *termed* its modes or accidents.' Rather, such objects are clearly collections of sensible ideas. Berkeley writes, 'Since it is not a being distinct from sensations; a *cherry*, I say, is nothing but a congeries of sensible impressions, or ideas perceived by various senses ...' (3D III 249).

The point can be pressed by recognizing that for Berkeley there is hardly a one–one correspondence between quality and idea. Locke writes that while qualities are blended and mixed together in the object, ideas of those qualities (such as cold and hard) enter the mind as simple, unmixed ideas

(E. 2.2.1, 119). Berkeley, presumably representing Locke's view in an altered (and antagonistic) way, suggests that what enters the mind is a compounded or mixed idea, which is submitted to an illicit process of 'abstraction' whereby each quality is singled out.[36] He writes:

> For example, there is perceived by sight an object extended, coloured, and moved: this mixed or compound idea the mind resolving into its simple, constituent parts, and viewing each by itself, exclusive of the rest, does frame the abstract ideas of extension, colour, and motion. (PHK I Intro 7)

Berkeley denies that one can 'abstract one from another, or conceive separately, those qualities which it is impossible should exist so separated . . .' (PHK I Intro 10). So he appears to be rejecting the view that the mixed idea of an object extended, coloured, and moved can be broken down into distinct simple ideas of its extension, color, and motion. Rather, Berkeley endorses the view the one may selectively consider certain aspects of a mixed idea without attending to others (3D I 193). So one needs to be careful in interpreting Berkeley's claim that a die is nothing but what are termed its modes and accidents. The die is a congeries of mixed ideas. The qualities are at best aspects of those ideas that may be selectively considered.

The point that I insist upon is that in rejecting 'existence in by way of mode' as a viable relation, Berkeley cannot retain modes. Yet if Berkeley does not admit such items into his ontology, how is such a collapse into such items possible? While Berkeley does not explicitly address Locke's spiritual substratum, he does address something close in another passage. He writes:

> If any man shall doubt of the truth of what is here delivered, let him but reflect and try if he can frame the idea of any power or active being; and whether he hath ideas of two principal powers, marked by the names *will* and *understanding*, distinct from each other as well as from a third idea of substance or being in general, with a relative notion of its supporting or being the subject of the aforesaid powers, which is signified by the name *soul* or *spirit*. This is what some hold; but so far as I can see, the words *will*, *soul*, *spirit*, do not stand for different ideas, or in truth, for any idea at all . . . . (PHK I 27)

Locke does not think that we have a positive idea of substance in general. But the rest of this account applies to Locke. While Berkeley does not explicitly draw on his earlier criticism of the support relation, there is also no reason to believe Berkeley wouldn't be critical of this notion for similar reasons. Indeed, it is hard not to believe that Berkeley wants us to read this passage in light of his earlier comments at PHK I 16 and 17 about the support relation and 'being in general.'

While it is true that Berkeley's argument applies to Locke's notion of a spiritual substratum, it does not follow that we are left with free-floating powers. We are no more left with a collection of mental properties or powers than we are left with a collection of sensible accidents. In rejecting the relation of support, Berkeley has rejected all of those items. Berkeley writes instead: 'A spirit is one simple, undivided, active being: as it perceives ideas, it is called the *understanding*, and as it produces or otherwise operates about them, it is called the *will*' (PHK I 27). His claim is that there is just one thing which gets called the will and the understanding. Instead of taking the Lockean properties, grouping them together, and calling them 'a mind,' these properties/powers have vanished as viable ontological elements. Instead there is one 'simple, undivided' being which itself gets considered both faculties.

One might worry about a collapse of spirit into actual perceptions and volitions, rather than some collapse into powers or faculties. Yet, Locke recognizes these general powers as the chief 'properties' of the mind. So, if we were worried that a mind was going to collapse into its properties, this is precisely the worry we ought to have. And if we are worried about a collapse into perceptions and volitions, we need to recognize that in Berkeley's view they cannot be construed as modes and accidents. So there appears to be no obvious reason why spirit should collapse into perceptions and volitions – especially since we don't know what they are.

As it turns out, the underlying ontology doesn't matter very much in terms of Berkeley's account at PHK I 49. After claiming that a die is nothing but what are termed its modes and accidents, he goes on to claim, '. . . to say a die is hard, extended and square, is not to attribute those qualities to a subject distinct from and supporting them, but only an explication of the word *die*.' He does not claim, 'To say a die is hard, extended, and square is to attribute group membership to those qualities which together comprise a die.' His explanation is so general that it works just as well in the case of spirit. He can claim 'To say a spirit wills and understands is not to attribute those faculties to a subject distinct from and supporting them, but only an explication of the word *spirit*' without it turning out that a spirit is a collection of properties. Instead, the ontology of subject and property has been rejected. There is a simple, active being which is called both will and understanding.

To be sure, it is a profound and perplexing question what this 'simple, undivided' being is supposed to be and why Berkeley believes he is entitled to it. There are other questions, too. What, if not modes or accidents, are ideas? What are mental operations? How do they relate to spirit? In brief, what sort of picture do we have once substance–mode ontology is stripped away? I answer these questions over the next several chapters. The important point now is that this situation is different from the traditional, inevitable, sad state of affairs in which Berkeleian spirit has been immediately and without further ado relegated to a collection of ideas, perceptions, and volitions.

Chapter Three

The Ruptured *Cogito*

Berkeley claims that a spirit is a simple, undivided active being that is called both will and understanding (PHK 1 27). Given Berkeley's early notebook entries as well as the considerations generated by the Clarke–Collins debate (discussed in chapter one), it seems reasonable to believe spirit is deeply bound up with consciousness. Yet this is complicated by the fact that within this very section Berkeley claims '. . . there can be no idea formed of a soul or spirit . . . ;' and '. . . *spirit* or that which acts, that it cannot be of itself perceived, but only by the effects which it produceth.'[1]

The position is shocking. In the first edition of the *Principles*, Berkeley often uses 'idea' and 'notion' interchangeably. Andrew Baxter remarks in his *Enquiry* (1733), '*Notion* extends not only to the images of corporeal objects in the fancy, but to whatever is the object of the understanding.'[2] Does Berkeley mean to deny that spirit is an object of understanding at all? Or does he simply mean to deny that it can be 'painted in the imagination' as Baxter (and Descartes) would likewise agree?[3] I propose the former. At PHK I 1, Berkeley surveys all the objects of human knowledge. And spirit is absent from this list, only mentioned after in section 2.[4]

Yet the view that Berkeley denies that spirit is an object of knowledge is paradoxical: How can Berkeley provide a demonstration of the natural immortality of the soul if it isn't an object of knowledge? Only by salvaging some room for knowledge of spirit without rendering his denial trivial can we understand his view. Showing how this can be done will constitute our entrance into Berkeley's philosophy of spirit.

The Problem of the Unperceived Perceiver

Berkeley's denial is two-fold. First, a spirit cannot be immediately perceived in the way that an idea is immediately perceived. A spirit cannot be immediately perceived *as* an idea. Second, a spirit cannot be perceived by means of an idea (where the idea functions as a representing image of spirit). Berkeley means that one may not consult an idea as a way of learning something about spirits. By contrast, it is by using our own selves as a kind of model that we can understand spirits more generally. We function as images which represent through resemblance other, even greater, spirits such as God (PHK I 140, 3D III 231–2).

Yet if we can use ourselves as a way of understanding what a spirit is, why shouldn't we say spirits are perceived? And if by 'idea' Berkeley means 'object of knowledge,' why shouldn't spirits be ideas? An initial answer is offered by Berkeley himself: 'It is therefore necessary, in order to prevent equivocation and confounding natures perfectly disagreeing and unlike, that we distinguish between *spirit* and *idea*' (PHK I 139).[5] According to Berkeley, spirits and ideas are so entirely different that they have nothing in common but the terms 'thing,' 'being,' 'object of knowledge.' He writes:

> *Thing* or *being* is the most general name of all, it comprehends under it two kinds entirely distinct and heterogeneous, and which have nothing common but the name, to wit, *spirits* and *ideas*. (PHK I 89)

In highlighting the dissimilarity between spirit and idea, Berkeley points to two main features. The one that he most emphasizes is that while spirits are active, ideas are passive and inert (PHK I 27, 89). He also cites the fact that while spirits are substances that support ideas, ideas are merely the supported items (PHK I 135). It is in part because of these differences that ideas cannot represent spirits through resemblance (PHK I 27, 3D III 231).

Although these are differences between spirit and idea, this is insufficient to elucidate Berkeley's stronger claim that spirit and idea are so different that they have nothing in common at all (save names such as 'thing'). The fact that spirits and ideas are different in important respects, does not mean that they are not also similar. Spirits and ideas are related to each other in a least two ways, namely through perception and causation. In this sense, spirits and ideas do have the relations between them in common. However, the relations themselves are asymmetrical. Spirits are perceivers, ideas are perceived. Spirits are causes, ideas are effects. So while they may be bound together by relations, it does not follow that they are similar. It is the denial of any similarity which is at work when Berkeley claims that spirits and ideas are entirely distinct. Indeed, this stronger claim does much of the work in motivating Berkeley's denial that spirits can be perceived.

If spirits and ideas are in some ways similar, Berkeley's claim that there can be no idea of spirit would be false. At least with respect to this similarity, ideas could deepen our understanding of spirits through resemblance. Yet Berkeley himself is quite emphatic on this point. He considers the objection, '... that though an *idea* cannot resemble a *spirit*, in its thinking, acting, or subsisting by it self, yet it may in some other respects: and it is not necessary that an idea or image be in all respects like the original' (PHK I 137). His response is to deny that there is anything more to spirit than these respects of difference, 'Do but leave out the power of willing, thinking, and perceiving ideas, and there remains nothing else wherein the idea can be like a spirit' (PHK I 138).

From this it may be concluded that Berkeley does not view ideas as accidents, modes, properties, or states which exist in the mind. Indeed, Berkeley's claim that spirit and idea have nothing in common entails the denial that ideas are modes or properties of the mind. There is a kind of commonality basic to the very substance–mode relationship. What substance and mode have in common is the very substance itself. By this I mean that knowledge of a substance's modes, properties, and the like constitutes knowledge of the substance as well. It is through properties that one knows a substance. For this reason, according to Descartes, thinking substance and the various modes of thought which belong to substance do have something in common and that is why he places them in the same category, under the same heading of things '. . . which pertain to mind or thinking substance.'[6]

Assume that ideas are modes which belong to spirit. Then we can look to ideas as a way of augmenting our knowledge of spirit. While ideas cannot resemble spirits in all respects, they can certainly resemble other ideas. Yet ideas, themselves, are by hypothesis modes of spirit. So they could be used to secure at least a partial knowledge of spirit by facilitating knowledge of spirit's properties. We have already seen, however, that Berkeley explicitly denies that there is any respect in which ideas can resemble spirit. Ideas cannot, therefore, be viewed as modes and properties of spirits. Indeed, it is the error of viewing ideas as modes or states of mind that leads to the confusion that they somehow constitute at least partial knowledge of mind. It is for this reason, in part, that Berkeley wants to guard against confounding natures perfectly disagreeing.

The *Cogito*[7]

According to a fairly common view of consciousness among Berkeley's predecessors, 'consciousness' (consciousness that one is thinking) is inseparable from thought itself. This consciousness contrasts with a second-order examination of one's thoughts, involving a second act of perception. The distinction is best drawn by Arnauld who says of the former, '. . . our *thought* or *perception* is essentially reflexive upon itself; as it is expressed more happily in Latin, *est conscia sui*, for I never think without knowing that I think.'

He calls this reflection 'virtual' ('réflexion virtuelle') in contrast to a more *explicit* reflection ('réflexion expresse'), '. . . in which we examine our perception by another perception. . . .'[8]

Descartes, Malebranche, and Locke hold the view that consciousness is thinking itself. Descartes writes that the perception we have of our own volition is 'really one and the same thing as the volition.'[9] Locke says that '. . . thinking consists in being conscious that one thinks.'[10] And Malebranche writes, 'For it is the same thing for the soul to receive the mode called pain as to perceive or sense pain, since it cannot receive pain in any other way than by perceiving it.'[11] I take this as the view that thinking is essentially reflexive.

Although he is not always clear on this point, Locke distinguishes between reflection as a major inlet which delivers ideas of our mental operations 'pretty late' (E. 2.1.8, 107), and consciousness which is constitutive of thinking. It is the former 'unnatural squint' which Browne rejects, denying that we can form simple ideas of mental operations, while affirming that we are immediately conscious of them.

Likewise, Descartes distinguishes between what one might call a 'prereflective' consciousness of one's thinking and a second-order reflection on one's mental operations. He denies that we require this second-order reflective knowledge in order to know what thought is and what existence is. 'It is quite sufficient that we should know it by that internal awareness which always precedes reflective knowledge' (*Replies to Sixth Set of Objections* AT VII 422, CSM II 285). This internal awareness is 'innate to all men' (285) and it is the defining feature of the expression 'thought' which is used '. . . to include everything that is within us in such a way that we are immediately aware of it' (*Replies to Second Set of Objections* AT VII 160, CSM II 113).

In a letter to Arnauld, Descartes also distinguishes between direct thought and reflective thought (AT V 221, CSMK III 357). One may engage in the latter at the same moment that one is thinking the thought (*Conversation with Burman* AT V 149, CSMK III 335). This second-order thought, although blended with the initial awareness, yields the sort of memory-specific knowledge that one would expect of second-order knowledge of one's thoughts (e.g. awareness that one has experience a *new* sensation).

This reflective thought is secondary and inessential for Descartes. He ridicules the view of an architect who must 'employ a reflexive act to ponder the fact that he has this skill before he can be an architect' (*Replies to Seventh Set of Objections* AT VII 559, CSM II 382). He thinks that reflection 'cannot in any way be regarded as essential' (382). In this way, Descartes stays in line with the Scholastic distinction between *direct* and *reflex* thought where the latter is an explicit re-direction of attention to oneself and one's mental states. Yet this direct thought, for Descartes, also exemplifies Arnauld's virtual reflexivity.[12,13]

Consciousness that one is thinking involves two elements – a variable element (one's thoughts – mental states, acts, etc.) and a constant element (one's existence). This is why Descartes writes: 'When someone says "I am thinking, therefore I am, or I exist", he does not deduce existence from thought by means of a syllogism, but recognizes it as something self-evident by a simple intuition of the mind.'[14] It is also why he writes 'This inner awareness of one's thought and existence is so innate in all men that . . . we cannot, in fact, fail to have it' and why he speaks of 'this puzzling "I" which cannot be pictured in the imagination.'[15] Malebranche writes, 'Of all our knowledge, the first is of the existence of our soul.'[16] Locke writes, 'In every Act of Sensation, Reasoning, or Thinking, we are conscious to our selves of our own Being; and, in this Matter, come not short of the highest degree of *Certainty*.'[17] Awareness of one's existence is of a piece with consciousness that one is thinking.

This awareness of one's existence includes (or rather, is tantamount to) an awareness of one's thinghood. Insofar as one is aware of one's existence, one is aware that one is something rather than nothing. Moreover, one is not merely aware that there is some thing which exists, one is aware that this thing, which one knows to exist, is oneself. Or rather, one is aware of some thing which exists, namely, one's self *qua* existing thing as revealed in consciousness that one is thinking.[18,19]

Berkeley claims that in a large sense we have an idea of spirit insofar as we understand the meaning of the word (PHK I 140). To be sure, this raises many questions including how words have meanings without ideas being annexed to them and how one understands words without possessing ideas. Yet Berkeley must hold that there is something more to knowledge of spirit than merely our knowledge of what various words mean. Human language is culturally variable and it would be strange if something so weighty as the (naturally) immortal soul should turn out to be only known to us through our own human words. Minimally, it is hard to see how the soul's existence could be gleaned from words alone.[20]

Fortunately, it seems that for Berkeley we have a kind of immediate awareness of our own existence which does not derive from or reduce to a mere understanding of the word 'I.' In the *Dialogues* (as early as the 1713 edition) Philonous explains: 'I do nevertheless know, that I who am a spirit or thinking substance, exist as certainly, as I know my ideas exist' (3D III 231). This is quite distinct from any additional point about understanding the meaning of the words, as Philonous goes on to add, 'Farther, I know what I mean by the terms *I* and *myself* . . .' (3D III 231). Likewise, in *De Motu* (§ 21), Berkeley writes, '. . . but the sentient, percipient, thinking thing we know by a certain internal consciousness' (*Works* IV 36). A similar remark appears to be added in the second edition of the *Principles*: 'We comprehend our own existence by inward feeling or reflexion, and that of other spirits by reason' (PHK I 89).

It might seem that the evidence for this view is less clear in the first edition of the *Principles*.[21] Berkeley denies that spirits can be perceived except by the effects produced. Here it seems that Berkeley is denying any direct awareness of spirit at all. One would come to know spirit only through its effects and consequently one would have (at best) a relative notion of it.

Yet Berkeley can allow for *non-perceptual awareness* that one exists. Berkeley goes on to claim that 'What I am my self, that which I denote by the term I, is the same with what is meant by *soul* or *spiritual substance*' (PHK I 139). Does Berkeley think 'What I am myself' and 'that which I denote by "I"' is unavailable to awareness? It seems hard to believe, especially when he then writes, '. . . we know other spirits by means of our own soul, which in that sense is the image or idea of them, it having a like respect to other spirits . . .' (PHK I 140). Indeed, this is a claim which is reiterated in the 1713 *Dialogues*, where Philonous says, 'My own mind and my own ideas I have an immediate knowledge of; and by the help of these, do mediately apprehend the possibility of the existence of other spirits and ideas' (3D III 232).

The point can be cinched, by recognizing that in the first edition of the *Principles*, Berkeley writes 'But if I should say, that I was nothing, or that I was an idea or notion, nothing could be more evidently absurd than either of these propositions.' Berkeley recognizes that one's own existence (and distinction from ideas and notions) is self-evident. He then continues, 'You'll perhaps insist that this . . .' (and then this is retained in the second edition):

> . . . is only quarrelling at a word, and that since the immediate significations of other names are by common consent called *ideas*, no reason can be assigned, why that which is signified by the name *spirit* or *soul* may not partake in the same appellation. (PHK I 139)

If this 'I' (that we know to exist) is in danger of being called an idea, it is hard to believe that this knowledge isn't a kind of datum or inner feeling (as Berkeley suggests in the second edition).[22] I take it that the intuitive awareness of the 'I' is something that Berkeley inherits from Descartes and

Locke. For Berkeley, we have a consciousness of our own existence in a way that does not reduce to or derive from a mere understanding of human discourse and which is not merely inferred.[23]

There is, however, a question that concerns Berkeley's use of the expressions 'reflexion' and 'reflex act.' When Berkeley says we comprehend our existence by 'inward feeling or reflexion' is he calling this inward feeling a form of reflexion? Is he taking reflexion as second order? The issue is further complicated. In the first edition of the *Dialogues* Berkeley claims that we know God '. . . by reflecting on my own soul heightening its powers, and removing its imperfections' (3D III 231–2). He goes on to say that we know our own mind 'by a reflex act' (232). Is the reflex act by which we know our own existence distinct from the reflexion we use to comprehend God? Moreover, Berkeley occasionally speaks of ideas of reflexion (PHK I 13 and 25). How do these ideas relate to Berkeley's account? At present, let me say that I take the sort of immediate awareness that accompanies all our thinking (the 'I') to count as 'inward feeling.' I think we should count this inward feeling as a 'reflex act,' if we understand the sort of reflexivity inherent in all thought.

The Ruptured *Cogito*

Prior to Berkeley, awareness of one's own existence is trivially viewed as perceptual. Locke, writes, for example, 'For if I know I *feel Pain*, it is evident, I have as certain a Perception of my own Existence, as of the Existence of the Pain I feel . . .' (E. 4.9.3, 618). Locke consistently claims that we perceive our own existence. And when he uses the term 'perception,' he uses it interchangeably with terms such as 'awareness' and 'knowledge.' This is in line with the tradition that Locke inherits. St. Thomas writes, for example, 'In this sense, no one can assent to the thought that he does not exist. For, in thinking something, he perceives that he exists' [*percipit se esse*].[24] Descartes claims to '. . . achieve an easier and more evident perception of my own mind than of anything else' [*cognoso nihil facilius aut evidentius meâ mente posse a me percipi*].[25] And Malebranche speaks of '. . . simple perception, such as that by which I know that I am, what I am thinking of, or that twice two equals four [*simple perception*].'[26] So the pressing question is this: Given that Berkeley recognizes such awareness of our own existence (following Descartes, Malebranche, and Locke), why does Berkeley deny that it is perceptual?

In the older view, while there are two elements of consciousness, the variable element and the constant element, there is also an important relation between them. That is why Malebranche goes on to write, '. . . all our thoughts are incontestable demonstrations of this [the soul's existence]. . . .'[27] And Locke says 'If I doubt of all other Things, that very doubt makes me perceive my own *Existence* . . . .'[28] Insofar as doubting, thinking, willing, and the like are mental acts, it is clear there must be a subject that has them. This is why Locke can speak of hunger and pain as capable of convincing somebody to stop doubting her own existence. Yet, Descartes, Malebranche, and Locke appear to agree, there is no proof involved in the perception of one's existence. Rather – in perceiving that one is thinking, one thereby also perceives one exists. Variable elements of consciousness are referred to the constant element such that both are constitutive of *self*-consciousness. The latter involves the knowledge that I exist and that I am an entity, whereas the former involves knowledge of *my* various thoughts, where these thoughts are viewed as modes, acts, properties – items, in effect, that are 'predicated of' or 'referred to' me. Consciousness has for its primary object oneself.

In my interpretation, Berkeleian ideas are the variable elements of consciousness, no longer viewed as properties. This might seem surprising. If consciousness involves an awareness of one's existence and one's states, and if ideas are not to be identified with states, then what could they have to do with consciousness? Berkeley talks about willing, perceiving, and various operations of the mind, so it is quite natural to apply the traditional model of consciousness of mental properties (one's states, acts) and self (one's being) to Berkeley as well. Ideas would seem to be foreign items, related to spirit in some other sort of way; and any analysis of Berkeleian consciousness would focus only on spirit and its operations and leave ideas to the side.

I claim we can understand Berkeleian ideas as the consequence of changes Berkeley is making in the older conception of consciousness. If Berkeley proceeds with the traditional model, but refuses to view the variable elements as states or properties of the mind, then he has a transformed model of consciousness. This seems an unavoidable conclusion since, for Berkeley, mode ontology has been rejected.

For Malebranche, sensations are modifications of the mind one is aware of through inner sense or consciousness.[29] If Berkeley refuses to view sensations as modifications of the mind, why would he suddenly refuse to think of them as elements of consciousness *at all*? Why would he not, instead, say they are non-modal elements of conscious awareness? Consider the thought that one might think to oneself 'What a pretty sunset.' Is that a mental state? Perhaps it is. But we can also say that it is an object of consciousness and an effect of willful production. It hardly seems unreasonable for Berkeley to view sensible ideas as objects for consciousness, but to deny that they are mental states, episodes, properties, and the like. Certainly Malebranchean sensations such as colours, sounds, odours, and tastes, may quite easily be viewed as objects but not mental states.

In the older model, consciousness can be viewed as *singular* insofar as consciousness is a single consciousness of *oneself* (and one's thoughts *qua* properties). In Berkeley's model, consciousness is viewed as fundamentally *bifurcated* between a consciousness of items distinct from oneself and consciousness of self. What had hitherto been viewed as a consciousness of one's own properties has now been transformed into consciousness of items distinct from oneself (non-'proprietary' items) and as a consequence of this, the original singular consciousness of self has been split into a consciousness of self and a consciousness of other (idea). It is no longer true that in perceiving the variable elements, one thereby perceives oneself. Consciousness is no longer a single mode of awareness that takes oneself as the object. In splitting the *cogito* awareness in two, the reflexivity inherent in all thought is limited to one's existence.

In Berkeley's model, 'the perceiving of an idea' would be nothing more than the very *consciousness* of such an idea. We can say that perceiving (taken as the consciousness that one is perceiving) involves the awareness of *two* elements, oneself and the variable object; and we can hold that the perception is nothing more than the *relation* of consciousness itself between a self-conscious being (oneself) and the object. This is a notable departure from any view according to which the perception of anything besides one's own mind (i.e. 'external objects') involves an intrinsic state or act of mind which facilitates the perception of that object. Just as mental states had been hitherto immediately available to consciousness, 'external objects' would be likewise available, if only because the variable elements of consciousness constitute the objects of external perception.

It is crucial to understand the important shift that has taken place. In the older view a 'perception' could be viewed as a mental state or act which inhered in the mind. However, in Berkeley's view a 'perception' is nothing but a relation which obtains between spirit and idea. Indeed, there is an important sense in which the relation 'perception' may be said to reduce to its relata, spirits and ideas. In terms of consciousness, one is not aware of any such state (or perception) as a kind of thing or element of consciousness. Rather, to be in such a state (to perceive) is simply to be conscious of oneself and one's objects. In the older model a change in variable elements of consciousness constitutes an intrinsic change in the mind that has the states. In Berkeley's model, because the 'state of perceiving' is nothing but a relation between the 'I' and its various objects of consciousness, a change in the variable element is merely a relational change. One may perceive as many objects as one pleases, there will be no corresponding augmentation in self-awareness.[30]

This account of Berkeleian perception may reveal another respect in which spirit and idea have 'nothing in common.' Knower and the known share nothing in common (such as vehicle of cognition, which on the one hand inheres in the mind, while on the other helps represent the object cognized). The point is impressive given that the transmission of 'likeness' appears to have been an important feature in Scholastic accounts of perception. Aquinas writes: '. . . that by which the sight sees is the likeness of the visible thing; and the likeness of the thing understood, that is, the intelligible species, is the form by which the intellect understands.'[31] In Berkeley's view there is no such transmission of likeness. There is no such mediating vehicle of cognition at all.

To be sure, whether one analyses the awareness that one hears a sound in terms of a singular model (which involves awareness of self and the mental state of hearing a sound) or a bifurcated model (which involves awareness of self and a sound), this is still a species of *self*-knowledge (namely that one hears a sound). However in the first case, the variable element is a state of mind (the state of hearing the sound), and consequently the awareness of the element is *itself* an awareness of self. By contrast, while it is true that in the second case the variable element is a component in self-awareness, the awareness of *it* does not constitute a species of self-awareness. Being aware that one hears a sound may involve, in part, awareness of the sound itself. But it is hardly obvious that this awareness of the sound is itself an awareness of the self.

Moreover, knowing the various intrinsic states or properties of a mind seems essential to knowing it. This is quite different from trying to know a mind by knowing the various things that it has perceived. While to know about the various things that a mind has perceived – to know its perceptual history – is perhaps also to know something about the mind, this knowledge does not seem to be bound up with knowledge of the mind in quite the same way. It seems that one only knows about the various relations that the mind has entered into. Any changes that the mind has undergone are merely relational and determined by the appearance and disappearance of ideas. If this counts as knowledge of the mind, it counts in only the thinnest of senses. In this way, because variable elements of consciousness are no longer viewed as mental states and one's consciousness of them is itself transformed into the perception of external objects, what had hitherto constituted self-consciousness has now been sheered off, leaving a mere consciousness of one's own existence distinct from idea.

Berkeley's Dualism

My interpretation of Berkeleian consciousness enables us to understand Berkeley's solution to the problem of our knowledge of the soul and explain (at least in part) why he is so concerned about confounding ideas and spirits. Begin by noticing the perversity that Berkeley should purport to address the alleged ignorance of the soul by denying that we can have an idea of the soul, instead of saying that we do have an idea of it. If possessing an idea of the soul would have provided us with some useful information about the soul, how does the impossibility of possessing such an idea demonstrate that this is no defect in human understanding? How does it make things better, rather than making them worse?

In denying that we know the soul by consulting a clear idea, Malebranche means to point out that we do not have the kind of understanding of thought that might enable us to determine the various properties of thought – the various modifications of which the mind is capable. By contrast, we do have the kind of understanding of extension such that we can determine the various properties of which extension is capable.[32] With respect to the soul, we merely learn about the various modifications of the soul through 'conscience' on a piecemeal basis.[33] It is even sometimes unclear whether a modification (such as colour and sound) belongs to the soul at all. In order to determine whether sensations such as colours and sound belong to the soul, one needs to first recognize that such modifications do not belong to extension.[34]

In my interpretation we can see right away what Berkeley would say to this complaint. He would say that all of the difficulties which concern Malebranche are non-starters. If our concern is to determine all of the modifications of the soul, then the concern is answered once we recognize that spirit has no such modifications. The changes in question are merely relational. Certainly, there are various objects which spirit perceives – colours, sounds, and the like. But these are not modifications that can themselves be counted off as distinct intrinsic properties of spirit. We know that spirit perceives ideas and once we know that we know all that we need to know. The problem how we determine that modifications such as a colour or sound belong to the soul is obviated by Berkeley's position that they aren't modifications. Indeed, Malebranche's minimal criterion for possessing a clear idea of the nature of some being (namely, that we be able to compare its modifications)[35] simply vanishes in Berkeley's model. Understood in this way, Berkeley's claim that it is impossible to have an idea of spirit does solve the problem since we are attempting to find knowledge of something that is ultimately founded on confusion.[36]

We can now understand Berkeley's concern that we distinguish ideas and spirits to avoid confusion. By taking awareness of Berkeleian ideas (variable elements of consciousness) as similar to the mind insofar as they count as modifications of mind, one is led into the false view that one has a partial understanding of mind (an awareness of its various mental states or properties), inviting the hope that one possess a knowledge of its nature that would enable one to determine all of the modifications of which the mind is capable. This is simply to mistake awareness of idea as awareness of spirit; this is simply to lump the two together as elements in a singular self-consciousness. As I have argued, it is because Berkeleian ideas are not to be viewed as properties of spirit that Berkeley can deny that there is a Berkeleian idea which resembles spirit even partially. This confusion is what leads to all of the difficulties.

In an important sense, spirits are not objects of understanding in a way that they are in the older model of consciousness. In the older model, consciousness is a mode of self-awareness that takes oneself as the object. Yet in Berkeley's view, one is not conscious of one's mental states. One is conscious only of objects that are distinct from oneself. Little wonder that Berkeley's response to the desire that '... we want a sense ... proper to know substances withal, which if we had, we might know our own soul, as we do a triangle' is that '... in case we had a new sense bestowed upon us, we could only receive thereby some new sensations of ideas of sense' (PHK I 136).

Given this distinction it is also little wonder that in order to avoid confusion, Berkeley warns that one ought not say that spirits are perceived or construe consciousness of one's own being as a kind of perception; one ought not view oneself *qua* spirit as some sort of idea (object of understanding), so that this confusion is avoided. The distinction is important, minimally, because failing to heed it leads to errors about whether the soul can be known and to what degree. In denying that we have an idea of spirit and that spirits can be perceived, Berkeley is not merely making the trivial Cartesian point that the 'I' cannot be pictured in the imagination. Rather, he has rejected substance–mode ontology, and the *cogito* has been split into two distinct modes of awareness. Berkeley's point is that spirit can never know itself (not even partially) as a variable element of consciousness.[37]

This is by no means inconsequential in terms of Berkeley's ontology. The sheer relational distinction between perceiver and perceived simply cannot yield a dualism at all, any more than can the relational distinction between scratcher and scratched. A robust dualism requires two distinct classes of things; so if perceivers can perceive themselves, we will have no dualism whatsoever. In short: The very success of Berkeley's dualism depends on the thesis that spirits cannot be perceived. As we have seen, by splitting the *cogito* in two he has secured such a dualism.

Perception and Support

This reading also provides an explanation why Berkeley appeals to 'perception' as a genuine relation of support. The *prima facie* difficulty is there is nothing in the notion of perception itself which yields any interesting notion of dependence. Descartes wrote of the sun 'existing in the mind' in the way that such objects are normally there, yet he hardly concluded from this that the sun was somehow dependent upon the mind in which it so existed. Berkeley's answer to this problem emerges by recognizing the following.

For both Descartes and Locke, the perception of objects outside the mind involves vehicles of cognition through which the perception is mediated (mental states, acts). By contrast, unmediated awareness of thought is constitutive of thinking itself; no thought or mental act can exist at all except insofar as it is present to consciousness. Descartes writes, '. . . we cannot have any thought of which we are not aware at the very moment when it is in us' (*Fourth Set of Replies* AT VII 246, CSM II 171). Locke writes, 'Our being sensible of it is not necessary to any thing, but to our thoughts; and to them it is; and to them it will always be necessary, till we can think without being conscious of it' (E. 2.1.10, 109). And: 'For to be happy or miserable without being conscious of it, seems to me utterly inconsistent and impossible' (E. 2.1.11, 110). This is to say, the very existence of a thought *consists in its being present to consciousness.* In addition to being dependent items (as modes, states), thoughts are likewise dependent as elements of conscious awareness.

Berkeley rejects the first relation while retaining the second. Because he rejects the first, the variable elements of consciousness are no longer viewed as modes. They are sheered off from self-consciousness; one is conscious of items *other than oneself.* These items are 'ideas' insofar as they are objects of immediate perception (consciousness). Consequently consciousness of mental acts has been transformed into the outright perception of 'external' objects. It is a relation of dependence insofar as no such item can exist *except as a variable element of consciousness.* Just as thought cannot exist except absent from consciousness, so intense heat (pain) cannot exist so absent.[38]

Berkeley is not merely insisting upon a mandatory 'luminescence' of thought. Rather, insofar as thoughts must be elements of consciousness, they are therefore bound to an 'I.' This is because consciousness involves two elements, the variable and the constant one.

One might question Berkeley's dependence relation by denying that there is any such 'I' that need exist as a constant element of consciousness. Deprived of this anchor, we would be left with only the many elements of consciousness. In fairness to Berkeley, however, the following case can be made.

Consciousness is a relation that obtains between a subject and an object. The notion of conscious and unconscious thoughts only makes sense within the context of a subject that is aware of them or not. Thoughts cannot be 'conscious' on their own. One needs to provide *some* sort of an account of a subject which has some sort of relation to its objects (even a meagre 'subject' constructed out of the elements). The question, then, is whether ideas can exist independently of this 'subject' or mind.

Now in translating the expression 'I' (a barbarism) into what is suggested by it, Berkeley's position hardly seems bad. His point is that whenever one thinks, one is aware that *one* thinks. One is, in this way, aware that *one exists*. The question, then, is how this self-awareness, possessed by the 'subject' or mind, is to be analysed. Clearly, this self-awareness hardly seems reducible to one's awareness of one's various ideas. Instead, it is a distinct awareness of oneself which appears to accompany all of one's ideas. Consequently, this awareness grounds Berkeley's talk of a distinct spirit; and the generally accepted view that thoughts cannot exist except as elements of consciousness requires that they be accompanied by this 'I'.[39]

One might further worry that it isn't true that one is always aware of oneself whenever one is thinking. When one is absorbed in one's thoughts, one is altogether lost to oneself, thinking, for example, about the film one watched the other day. This seems to be a more general objection to the early modern view that thought itself is inherently reflexive. If so, it is not a special problem for Berkeley's notion of mind-dependence. More importantly, this objection ignores the distinction between second-order reflection and the sort of reflexivity inherent in all thought. It is true that when one is thinking about the film, one is not thinking about oneself or the fact that one is thinking about film. So, too, when the architect works she may not be thinking about the various activities in which she is engaged. There is nonetheless a sense in which she is aware of what she is doing and that she is doing it. Similarly, there is a sense in which we are aware that we are thinking (whether we expressly reflect upon that or not). Again, we are aware that we ourselves exist, whether we expressly reflect upon that fact or not. And insofar as this awareness is ineliminable from all perception, Berkeley can claim that our immediate objects of perception cannot exist without a spirit to perceive them.

Chapter Four

Purity of Spirit

Several consequences of my interpretation converge to shape my account of mental operations. First, since Berkeley has rejected 'inherence' as vacuous, mental operations cannot be viewed as modes which inhere in spirit. Second, they cannot be variable elements of consciousness since they are not ideas. Third, if Berkeley were to allow different sorts of operations (doubting, loving, etc.), constituting discrete intrinsic states of spirit, the Malebranchean concern about how we determine the various states of the mind in advance would re-emerge. It follows that Berkeley must reject the view that mental operations are discrete intrinsic states which are variable elements of consciousness.

Some confirmation of this rejection is found toward the end of Berkeley's notebooks: 'Will, Understanding, desire, Hatred etc so far forth as they are acts or active differ not, all their difference consists in their objects, circumstances etc.' (PC 854). One gets a sense of how this might work by considering sensation: The difference between seeing and hearing is determined by a difference in object. In both cases there is simply the 'I' that perceives a particular object (a colour or sound). There is no difference in spirit itself, but only its various relations with sensible ideas.

However, such an account of operations also invites deep questions that arise from Berkeley's view that spirits are both active and passive (PHK I 29, 3D III 240–1). Of such difficulties, I defer treatment until the following chapter. Instead, I provide further evidence in favour of this interpretation. In doing so, I examine Berkeley's view that we can form something like an image of God to understand some of his attributes. By exploring Berkeley's views on analogy and mystery as well as his response to Browne, we will be better enabled to understand his views about mental operations.

Part I: Berkeleian Dualism

Analogy and Metaphor[1]

Berkeley's claim that spirits and ideas are so different that they have nothing in common seems radical. It suggests that terms such as 'thing' and 'knowledge' apply to spirits and ideas equivocally. Indeed, Berkeley warns of equivocation. Does Berkeley mean that spirits and ideas are to 'thing' as financial institutions and river-sides are to 'bank'? Scholastic examples of pure equivocation do not go that far. For Aquinas dog (the animal), dog-star, and dog-fish (*canis marinus*) are equivocals.[2] In such cases it seems that the only connection is the fact that the star and the fish are named after the animal.

Yet, if Berkeley means that spirit and idea are equivocates in this sense, the position remains extreme. One wonders whether Berkeley doesn't mean something else. Aquinas recognizes analogy as a mean between the extremes of pure equivocation and simple univocation.[3] Analogical predication would allow a kind of equivocation without going too far. Medicine, urine, and the animal itself are all called 'healthy' where 'health' is predicated of them analogously.[4] Given that there are relationships between spirit and idea, perhaps Berkeley means that terms such as 'being' are predicated of spirit and idea analogously.[5] The interpretation, however, has too many difficulties.

There are key differences between pure equivocity and analogy, and Berkeley represents spirits and ideas in terms of the former. Analogy requires some commonality between the analogates. The healthy urine and the healthy animal have in common the health itself which resides in the animal. Yet Berkeley's account of spirit and idea conforms to the definition of pure equivocation. Cardinal Cajetan (1468–1534), an influential systematizer of Aquinas' notions of analogy explains, 'By an *equivocal* name diverse things are so signified that, as such, they are united only by the external word.'[6] And again:

> As regards *equivocals*, those natures – that of the dogfish and that of the ordinary dog – are entirely different in essence. For this reason whatever *dog* predicates of a dogfish it in no way predicates of an ordinary dog, and vice versa. Therefore, it is only with respect to the name that an equivocal term is said to be, and really is, more common or greater than the equivocates.[7]

This is what Berkeley alleges: '*Thing* or *being* is the most general name of all, it comprehends under it two kinds entirely distinct, and heterogeneous, and which have nothing common but the name ...' (PHK I 89). And: '*Spirits* and *ideas* are things so wholly different, that when we say, *they exist*, *they are known*, or the like, these words must not be thought to signify any thing common to both natures' (PHK I 142).

Berkeley is clear that we can learn nothing about the nature of spirits from the nature of ideas. This doctrine is essential to his claim that we cannot have an idea of spirit. Yet this suggests that spirit and ideas are equivocal, not, analogous, since one is supposed to be able to gather knowledge about one analogate from the other. That is how one secures knowledge of God from finite beings.

And Berkeley does explicitly endorse a doctrine of analogy in *Alciphron*. He suggests that some (King and Browne) have misunderstood analogy,[8] sides with Cajetan's account of it, and alleges that wisdom is predicated analogically of God and man (ALC IV 17–22, 165–171). Given his endorsement of analogy between God and finite spirit, and his insistence that spirits and ideas have 'nothing common but the name' it would seem that the latter is not Berkeley's way of expressing an analogy between spirits and ideas. Instead, it is Berkeley's way of denying it.

One response is to suppose that as Berkeley grew more mature as a philosopher, he became more sympathetic to the subtlety of analogy.[9] Berkeley's views may have evolved on this question. However, in his early letter to Percival, Berkeley indicates that he is already well acquainted with analogy and that he rejects the Irish version of it. Moreover, in his *Essay* (1709) Berkeley aims to show that while tangible figure, extension, and motion share common names with visible figure, extension, and motion, they are nonetheless 'entirely different' (§ 137). Not only do they not belong to the same species, we merely '... imagine a likeness or an analogy between the immediate objects of sight and touch' (§ 145). If this is an earlier, rudimentary view of a young Berkeley, one wonders why Berkeley appended the *New Theory of Vision* to the initial editions of *Alciphron*. Indeed, it is hard to avoid the fact that Berkeley's negative answer to the Molyneux question has a bearing on his attitude toward the central trope of Irish analogy as promulgated by Browne, King, and Synge.

Young Berkeley even recognizes that general terms can have multiple significations. He writes in the Introduction to the *Principles*, '... in truth, there is no such thing as one precise and definite signification annexed to any general name, they all signifying indifferently a great number of particular ideas' (PHK Intro 18). The point is even sharper in the *Manuscript Introduction* (99), where he writes, 'Whereas there is in Truth a Diversity of significations in every general name' ('an homonymy or' is lined out and 'Diversity' and 'general' are inserted).

Contrast this with Hobbes' account of the distinction between univocity and equivocity (which leaves no room for analogy):

> *Univocall* [names] are those which in the same train of Discourse signifie alwayes the same thing; but *Equivocall* [names are] those which meane sometimes one thing, and sometimes another. Thus, the Name *Triangle* is

> said to be *Univocall,* because it is alwayes taken in the same sense; and *Parabola* to be *Equivocall,* for the signification it has sometimes of Allegory or Similitude, and sometimes of a certaine Geometrical figure. Also every *Metaphor* is by profession *Equivocall.*[10]

Almost as a response, Berkeley writes, '... there is no one settled idea which limits the signification of the word *triangle.* 'Tis one thing for to keep a name constantly to the same definition, and another to make it stand every where for the same idea ...' (PHK Intro 18). For Berkeley, there is something of analogy concealed within general terms. General terms apply analogically to a range of ideas.[11]

Moreover, Berkeley's account of our knowledge of God is virtually the same in the *Dialogues* and in *Alciphron.* While in the former, Berkeley does not explore the Scholastic notion of analogy, he affirms in both works that we acquire some conception of God by leaving out the imperfections of our finite spirit. And although Berkeley's immaterialism is not explicit in *Alciphron,* his extreme dualism is. Euphranor writes of soul and body as '... things so very different and heterogeneous' (ALC VI. 11 241) which hardly seems like a change from Berkeley's position in the *Principles.*

Even in the *Principles*, Berkeley discusses the notion of a scale of reality. He contrasts imagined and sensible ideas saying, 'These latter are said to have more *reality* in them than the former: by which is meant that they are more affecting, orderly, and distinct, and that they are not fictions of the mind perceiving them' (PHK I 36). This sense of 'reality' hardly applies to spirits. Instead of a placing both spirit and idea on the same scale of being, it seems Berkeley thinks there are two different scales.

Berkeley and Cajetan[12]

Cajetan distinguishes the analogy of attribution (of which the preceding health example was an instance) from the analogy of proportionality (which he views as the proper form of analogy). For Cajetan, the analogy of attribution involves only extrinsic denomination. While the food is denominated 'healthy' in virtue of the fact that it causes the perfection 'health' to exist within the animal, there is no corresponding perfection which exists within it. This kind of attribution cannot be used to ground the analogy of being (at least not by itself). Accidents are not only called 'being' in virtue of their relationship to substances, they really exist. This is something that cannot be accommodated by the analogy of attribution alone.[13]

Instead, Cajetan appeals to the analogy of proportionality which involves the similitude between proportions or any other relations. He further distinguishes between two types of this analogy, metaphoric and proper. In the former, the analogous term has 'one formal meaning' and the analogon exists in only one of the analogates in its 'proper sense' while it is predicated of the other only by way of metaphor. We say that fortune smiles as a man smiles. In such a case, there is a priority where the term is predicated primarily (and 'properly') of one and extended to another only metaphorically.[14] Such extended and metaphoric predication signifies nothing more than that the thing so predicated bears a likeness to the primary analogate. It is a similarity, however, which cannot be understood without understanding the meaning of the term's proper sense. Because of this terms which are so analogous are like terms which are analogous by analogy of attribution. Both involve extrinsic denomination.[15]

In the case of analogy of proportionality in its proper sense, the common term is predicated of both analogates without metaphor. For example, 'principle' is applied to both the heart (with respect to the animal) and the foundation (with respect to the house).[16] Likewise God and finite creature are called 'being' where there is a similitude between the relation of each to their respective 'to be-s.' In such cases, one analogate does not have to be defined by appeal to the other.

Cajetan says that this kind of analogy is midway between univocity and the analogy of attribution.[17] Yet while Cajetan recognizes proper proportionality as a midway, he does not deny that terms such as 'being' and 'goodness' apply to God in their proper and literal sense.[18,19] What makes such terms non-univocal is the fact that there is a 'double concept.' There is an imperfect common concept which is one through analogy (insofar as each of the diverse analogates imperfectly resembles the others with respect to the analogon). Yet there are as many perfect concepts as there are analogates (all of which represent themselves perfectly).[20]

What 'similarity' there is between spirits and ideas, however, is at best metaphoric. Berkeley's concern about metaphoric language applied to mental operations emerges as early as PC 176 and 176a, and it lies in Philonous' defense of using 'exists in the mind' to mean 'is perceived by the mind.' In response to Hylas' concern that he is guilty of some abuse of language, Philonous claims it is not uncommon for mental operations to be described by terms borrowed from sensible things. He says, '... the terms *comprehend*, *reflect*, *discourse*, &c. which being applied to the mind, must not be taken in their gross original sense' (3D III 250).

In *Alciphron* Berkeley discusses the translation of words used to refer to mental operations which have been borrowed from applications to sensible objects. Alciphron alleges that 'to inspire' is borrowed from the Latin, which in a strict sense means only 'to breathe or blow in.' Yet Euphranor allows for a 'secondary, figurative, and translated sense' according to which 'inspire' can denote 'an action of God, in an extraordinary manner, influencing, exciting, and enlightening the mind of a prophet or an apostle.' Euphranor points out to Alciphron that 'to discourse' taken from the Latin means 'to run about.' Yet Alciphron allows 'discourse' to mean (in a translated sense), 'an invisible action of the mind, reasoning or inferring one thing from another' (ALC VI 9 237–8). Indeed, Berkeley believes that sensible things are used to illustrate spiritual ones (ALC VII 13 306–7).

It may therefore seem that for Berkeley, spirits and ideas are not pure equivocals but metaphorically analogous. If so, Berkeley's position would still be much closer to such pure equivocity than the proper analogy which obtains between God and spirits. Hobbes, for example, views metaphor as a straightforward case of equivocation. And metaphor, while attributing a similarity, does not itself serve to augment knowledge so much as facilitate understanding through illustration, allusion, and allegory. Here, Berkeley's position about spirits and ideas would be like his view that 'higher' and 'lower' are attributed to visible ideas only by 'metaphor and analogy' (TVV 46).[21] Indeed, Berkeley's view about spirits and ideas would mirror King's view about God and human beings.

Yet I think that Berkeley's account also involves even stronger equivocity. For while the use of sensible things to illustrate spiritual ones involves allegory and metaphor, in the case of 'inspiration' and 'discourse' one doesn't need to understand the original Latin meanings in order to understand the common applications. However, in the case of Lockean 'support' of accidents, there is a suggested likeness to spatial support involved in the term which gives it what little meaning it has in its departure from common usage. Since understanding the terms 'discourse' and 'inspiration' does not require an understanding of the original meanings, this is not a case of the analogy of proportionality (metaphoric sense), while the metaphysical deployment of 'support' is. In the former case, we have (at best) a dead metaphor where the actions are named after sensible things, just as a star may be named after a dog.

In any event, this reading of Berkeley may lead one to think that Berkeley's account of mind is merely metaphorical in nature.[22] Such a conclusion runs in the face of Berkeley's clear hostility to metaphor in *De Motu* where he declares, '. . . a philosopher should abstain from metaphor' (§ 3, *Works* IV 31).[23] The danger of confounding spirits and ideas through metaphor, illustration, and transferred terms is serious, for Berkeley. It is the greatest error with respect to the soul:

> But nothing seems more to have contributed towards engaging men in controversies and mistakes, with regard to the nature and operations of the mind, than the being used to speak of those things in terms borrowed from sensible ideas. (PHK I 144)

One of Berkeley's reasons for insisting upon the 'entire distinctness' of spirit and idea is to have philosophers de-literalize what might have been helpful metaphors in understanding spirits and to avoid being tricked by borrowed language. One imagines, that it is such errors which lead some to 'hold the soul of man to be only a thin vital flame, or system of animal spirits' (PHK I 141).

Another reason for insisting upon this distinctness is to reveal a deeply dualistic ontology concealed by these metaphors. It is not a substance dualism; it is a *thing* dualism. Berkeley cannot suppose that 'thing' and 'exists' apply to spirits only metaphorically or that they are borrowed terms such as 'discourse' or 'inspiration.' That would be to suggest that figurative or metaphoric application is only one of extrinsic denomination (an unacceptable conclusion given that spirits really exist).

Recall Aquinas' distinction between the two senses of 'being.' In one sense anything can be called a being in case an affirmative proposition can be formed of it; while in another sense only 'something positive in reality' counts as a being (where being is divided by the ten categories). In the first sense spirits and ideas are equally 'beings' as are 'volitions,' 'operations,' and 'passions,' and anything else of which we can affirm a proposition. In terms of 'something positive in reality' only spirits and ideas count. He writes, '... for anyone to pretend to a notion of entity or existence *abstracted* from *spirit* and *idea*, from perceiving and being perceived, is, I suspect, a downright repugnancy and trifling with words' (PHK I 81). He does not merely mean to reject some univocal notion of entity or existence. Rather Cajetan himself had allowed for one imperfect, analogical concept of 'being.' This is likewise rejected by Berkeley since spirit and idea are so different that one cannot possibly resemble the other, even imperfectly.

Consequently there are two important respects in which Berkeley's dualism is more radical than Descartes'. Descartes allows that thinking and extended substance share a 'common concept of substance' – namely, 'things that need only the concurrence of God in order to exist.' He claims that the term 'substance' applies to mind and body univocally.[24] According to Berkeley, spirit and idea have nothing common but the name 'thing.' Second, unlike Cartesian Dualism, Berkeleian Dualism occurs at the most general level of ontology (being itself). Descartes presupposes the traditional substance-mode ontology which allows for a relatively unified concept of being. According to Berkeley however, the difference between spirit and idea is as extreme as the difference that King supposes between God and man.

Yet despite the radicalism of Berkeleian dualism, it is compatible with the substantiality thesis. The thesis that spirits and ideas are equivocates by no means undermines the view that the former are substances which support the latter. The claim that two things are 'really distinct' is different from the claim that they are 'entirely distinct.' Spirit and ideas are both bound together and yet deeply contrasting.

Part II: Berkeley, Browne, and Divine Analogy[25]

Browne and Berkeley agree that we use our selves to conceive the various attributes of God; we conceive the Divine Attributes mediately. For Browne the imperfection in us is so deeply part of our mental operations that they can only provide an analogical conception of the attributes as sounds and smells might be used to provide an indirect conception of light.[26]

The reason for this imperfection is that our spirit and body are so interblended that all mental operations are the effect of the joint operation of the two. As Browne later remarks in the *Procedure* (97), the reason why words ('apprehends,' 'separates') are borrowed from bodily actions in order to describe our mental operations is because mind and body are so intermixed that we are under a necessity to describe 'the modus' of our various operations in this way. Whenever we attempt to form notions of thinking we imagine them as motions and agitations of the soul.[27] Consequently, we have no direct grasp of a pure spirit's operations, and can only understand them analogically.

In the *Procedure*, Browne distinguishes between divine metaphor and divine analogy (132–146). The latter involves a real correspondence between the divine and the human, whereas the former does not. While speaking of God as bodily involves divine metaphor, the attribution of intellect, wisdom, and passions to God (or any pure spirit) involves *analogy* (although passions in a lesser degree) (*Analogy* 43–8).[28] This means that terms such as 'wisdom' and 'love' do not apply to God (or any pure spirit) in the proper, literal sense of the word. They are used in what he calls an analogous sense, where we use the notion of what we find in our own soul as an analogue for what is in God (or any pure spirit).

For Berkeley we are able simply to omit our imperfections and augment our powers and thereby form a direct conception of God's attributes without difficulty. Philonous explains in *Three Dialogues*:

> For all the notion I have of God, is obtained by reflecting on my own soul heightening its powers, and removing its imperfections. I have therefore, though not an inactive idea, yet in my self some sort of an active thinking image of the Deity. (3D III 231–2)

In *Alciphron* Berkeley further clarifies that body, sensations, and passions all involve defect in their 'proper signification' and are consequently applied to God only in a metaphorical sense. However, knowledge and wisdom do not involve defect in their 'proper signification' and consequently 'may be attributed to God proportionably, that is, preserving a proportion to the infinite nature of God' (ALC IV 21, 170).

On the face of it, it is easy to understand Berkeley's response to Browne. While Browne sees mental operations as the joint product of spirit and body, Berkeley has rejected the notion of material substance altogether. Corporeal things (real ideas and collections thereof) are passive and inert. Insofar as they are merely effects of spirit, there is no way mental operations could be the joint product of both.

Yet there are some peculiar questions which need to be answered: (1) Given Berkeley's departure from Browne, why does he continue to say that mental operations are explained in terms borrowed from sensible things? Browne's own motivation has been abandoned. (2) Given that no mental operation involves a deep interblending of spirit and body, why does he think that passion and sensation are imperfections?

Perfections and Imperfections

One of the major issues driving the disagreement between the two men is that, according to Browne, some type of mental conception, complex notion, or idea is required in order for a term to have any significance (*Analogy* 534–5). On this point, Browne is very clear. He takes it that we are conscious of all of our mental operations (*Analogy* 410–1). If we were not, according to Browne's view, terms such as 'thought' and the like could have no meaning. Moreover, it is through this consciousness that we can form complex notions of our activities and our mind.

Browne is led to his view about analogy through his commitment to the theses that every intelligible term requires some mental conception annexed to it and that the notion of ourselves cannot be purged of imperfection. Terms which refer to our own mental operations are given content precisely through the particular notions that we have of them. Since imperfection is a part of these notions, he needs an 'analogous' use of the terms where our imperfect notions are used to understand God.

Berkeley denies that we need some idea or notion in order for words to count as significant. Consequently, it is not surprising that Browne takes Berkeley to task for this 'modern loose and illogical' use of 'idea' (*Analogy* 525) urging him to restrict it only in 'the true logical Sence, as limited to the *Direct and Immediate Perception* of external and sensible Objects only . . .' (*Analogy* 541). In denying that we have an idea (or notion) of grace, Berkeley is not merely denying that there are sensible or imaginable ideas of it. Rather, he is denying that we have any mental 'conceptions' or 'complex notions' in Browne's sense as well. His view emerges in *Alciphron.*

Alciphron complains to Euphranor of the endless controversy surrounding the Christian notion of 'grace' and challenges Euphranor to provide a clear and distinct idea marked by the term. 'Grace' in its vulgar sense (as either beauty or favour) is easily understood. However, when used to denote an active principle which influences the mind of men, it is unintelligible. While men attempt to explicate the notion by appealing to force; the latter is clear and intelligible but the former is not.

In response, Euphranor challenges Alciphron to form an idea of 'force' exclusive of its 'subject and effects.' The latter, who has just defined force as '. . . that in bodies which produceth motion and other sensible effects' (ALC VII 6 294) finds that he can form no such idea. Euphranor then exploits this concession to argue that since 'force' can be recognized as a meaningful term despite the fact that no idea of it can be formed, by parity the same should be allowed of the term 'grace' which cannot find an idea separate '. . . from God the author, from man the subject, and from virtue and piety its effects' (ALC VII 7 296).

In the *Analogy*, Browne agrees that the idea of force cannot be separated off from its subject and effects. And he says the same is true of thinking and willing. 'Yes surely; it is the same senseless Ridicule as if you bid a Man try to form a Conception of *Thinking* or *Willing*, exclusive of any *Object* of Thought or Desire, and of a Mind operating' (545). Yet, he maintains that 'in the concrete' (without separating it off from subject and effect), one must have some sort of mental conception of the thing in question in order for terms such as 'motion' and the like to be meaningful.

Berkeley's response to Browne's criticism in their private correspondence brings out the crucial difference between the two. Berkeley claims that Browne's 'fundamental error' is his 'refusing to acknowledge that undetermined words can convey true conceptions to the mind' (391). He continues, '. . . and if a power, however described by its effects, excites no notion in the mind till its intrinsic activity be understood, 'tis strictly impossible indeed we should any ways attain the least conception of our Maker' (391–2). And then, 'For if a power, only described by its effects, be perfectly unknown, till its intrinsic nature be found out, all powers either divine or humane [*sic*] are, to use your Lordship's words, involved in midnight darkness' (392). And then, 'But so confident I am of the assertion, that I readily will trust the whole debate upon this issue. Let your Lordship but explain one single power in the whole creation, independently of its effects, and by its true internal nature, and I am a convert to *analogy*' (392).[29] Berkeley is saying, *pace* Browne, that we have no conception of any 'intrinsic activity' whatsoever. We know powers only through the effects which they produce.

This is shocking claim. One would have thought consciousness of volition counted as a kind of access to 'intrinsic activity.' And discrete 'volitions' had played an important role in Berkeley's earlier thought. Berkeley wrote in his notebooks: 'The Will not distinct from Particular volitions' (PC 615). However, the flurry of entries toward the end of the notebooks indicates an important change in Berkeley's thinking.

First, he moves away from multiple volitions to the view that spirit is one, ongoing act: 'We see no variety or difference betwixt the Volitions, only between their effects. Tis One Will one Act distinguish'd by the effects. This will, this Act is the Spirit, operative, Principle, Soul etc.' (PC 788. cf. PC 854). Second, Berkeley abandons this notion of one ongoing volition as well. He writes 'I must not give the Soul or Mind the Scholastique Name pure act, but rather pure Spirit or active Being' and 'The Will & Volition are words not used by the Vulgar, the Learned are banter'd by their meaning abstract Ideas' (PC 870 and PC 867, cf. PC 849, PC 871). By the time we get to Berkeley's published views in 1710 and 1713, volitions are nowhere to be found among the things that exist: '*Thing* or *being* ... comprehends under it ... *spirits* and *ideas*' (PHK I 89). Apparently he has dropped the claim that 'Thing comprehends also volitions or actions. Now these are no ideas' (PC 644).

When Berkeley observes in the *Principles*, 'Men have imagined they could frame abstract notions of the powers and acts of the mind, and consider them prescinded, as well from the mind or spirit it self, as from their respective objects and effects' (PHK I 143), he does not simply mean that one is incapable of separating activities or powers off by themselves (as Browne would maintain). Berkeley means that there is no perception of any such acts or powers at all: One is aware only of oneself and one's effects. One's self insofar as it makes such items can be called a power (namely 'the will'), but there is no further 'intrinsic activity' as a third element of consciousness.

Berkeley is suggesting that our understanding of the Christian mystery 'grace' is on par with our understanding of the mental operations of finite spirits, some of the Divine attributes, and even force. In all cases, we understand and define the relevant terms by appealing simply to cause, subject, effects, and circumstances.[30] Thus defined, we likewise understand the conditions under which statements about them can be true. What we lack, however, is a precise idea or notion answering to the specific term that would let us know about the 'intrinsic activity' involved.[31] This is why Berkeley speaks of Browne's 'refusing to acknowledge that undetermined words can convey true conceptions to the mind.' According to Berkeley, terms such as 'grace,' 'inspiration,' 'discourse,' and so forth can be meaningful even though there is no distinct notion corresponding to the term.

Now if there is an 'intrinsic nature' of activity of which we are unaware with respect to grace, this would constitute a 'hidden mystery.' However, Berkeley claims that the reason we have no idea of any intrinsic activity concerns illicit abstraction. This is the Berkeleian kiss of death; and it suggests that there is no such thing at all.

Indeed, the discussion of the mysteries in *Alciphron* involves some concern with abstract ideas and pointless dispute (ALC VII 9 299–301). Berkeley suggests that the mysteries only become open to dispute in advanced philosophical speculation. Crito complains of the minute philosophers who confound Scholasticism with Christianity (ALC VII 19 300).

Berkeley claims that language has different functions. He says, '... the true end of speech, reason, science, faith, assent, in all its different degrees, is not merely, or principally, or always, the imparting or acquiring of ideas, but rather something of an active operative nature, tending to a conceived good' (ALC VII 14 307). To propose that there is some unknown notion of intrinsic activity (available to God, say), suggests that the function of terms such as 'grace,' 'inspiration,' and 'discourse' is to convey (general) ideas (where the function has now somehow failed). The better view is that the function of such terms has been misunderstood and consequently resulted in endless dispute. Thus Berkeley (*pace* Browne) places mysteries such as 'grace' on par with 'mysteries' such as number and force because it is his general view that any controversies concerning such terms arise from the mistaken view that there is a settle, determined, abstract idea.

One objection is that this interpretation deflates the notion of 'mystery.' There is nothing 'beyond our reason,' since one has a handy definition of grace already (which omits any specification of the intrinsic activity), and there is nothing left to know. It invites the question: Is Berkeley actually on Toland's side?

He is not. For Berkeley, the supreme good is eternal life through Jesus Christ. Berkeley is clear that there *is* a mystery in the traditional sense that we do not have the appropriate ideas to grasp the good that is in store for us in the future state. The challenge of faith is to accept God's word that it shall be infinitely great and to act accordingly.[32] Even though mysteries such as 'grace' do not themselves conceal something incomprehensible and perplexing (abstract) they have a functional role to play in guiding us toward our mysterious end. We may lack an idea how original sin is transmitted. Yet while there is no possible clear and distinct idea or notion of it, we nonetheless understand what the words mean (defined in terms of cause, subject, and effect).[33] Any hope for an additional mental conception of the intrinsic activity is misguided however, since the point of the term is not to convey such a conception, but to produce 'a salutary sense of ... unworthiness' necessary to guide us toward our great end (ALC VII.10, 301).

Another sort of mystery comes into play when we stop to consider the radicalism of Berkeley's view concerning action. It can be appreciated by considering some comments that Locke makes. Locke finds that he has ideas of only two kinds of action – namely thinking and motion.

> ... *many words, which seem to express some Action*, signify nothing of the Action, or *Modus Operandi* at all, *but* barely *the effect*, with some circumstances of the Subject wrought on, or Cause operating; *v.g.* Creation, Annihilation, contain in them no *Idea* of the Action or Manner, whereby they are produced, but barely of the Cause, and the thing done. (E. 2.22.11, 294)

In Berkeley's view, thought has become a kind of creation. We have no awareness of volition but only an awareness of the cause and the ideas produced. Yet the action, thought, or *modus operandi* is not an element of consciousness. Consequently, finite spirits are significantly 'upgraded' in Berkeley's view, possessing a capacity akin to God's. Berkeley writes, 'Why may we not conceive it possible for God to create things out of Nothing. Certainly we our selves create in some wise whenever we imagine' (PC 830).

The capacity is by no means trivial, since in the view that ideas are mere perceptions, Berkeley would not be able to make this claim. Altering oneself (altering one's properties) is no more creation *ex nihilo* than waving goodbye. What makes this a case of creation is that spirits and ideas are so different they have nothing in common but the name. Here Berkeley abandons the view that the cause must have something of the effect within it (see PC 780). Even though our imagined ideas must be based upon the ideas received through the senses (and therefore don't completely come from nothing), there is nothing in the idea that comes from spirit itself which is to found within the effect.

There is a kind of mystery here. The mystery is not that there is some intrinsic action hidden to our awareness. Indeed, should there be some hidden intrinsic activity which explains the production of ideas, it is unclear how this could remain a case of creation *ex nihilo*. Yet, the fact remains that although we find by experience that we can create and destroy ideas, this may be insufficient to lessen our bafflement.[34]

It is no doubt in part for this very reason that Berkeley thinks that we appeal to sensible things, using figurative and borrowed language as well as allegory, as a way to illustrate mysterious mental operations. Berkeley is simply omitting Browne's hopelessly impure modus altogether. We are aware of no such interblended modifications of mind that we term 'apprehension' and 'discourse.' Mental operations merely involve the 'I' and its objects. They are therefore distinguished only in terms of their various different effects and circumstances and any suitable 'translation' of action-words borrowed from sensible things reduces to a specification of cause, subject, effects, and circumstances. Consequently borrowed terms give the appearance of providing content by distinguishing discrete modes of thought. Indeed, they can help conceal the fact that no distinct modes are available to the mind at all. The error is to take these illustrations of the subtle or mysterious activity of spirits literally. In doing so, one blends the spiritual with the corporeal; one blends thought with motion. And it would appear that Browne has fallen prey to the difficulty that so concerns Berkeley. In taking the borrowed terms seriously, Browne is led to confound the mental with the corporeal and thereby posit discrete and impure modes.

Ultimately, Berkeley can respond to Browne as follows. Knowledge and wisdom are ascribed to God in the same sense that they are ascribed to us, since no notion of a *modus* is involved our conception of them. In effect, since the only understanding we have of a power involves cause and effect, there is no difficulty in ascribing it to God in the same literal sense that it is ascribed to us. In his letter to Browne, Berkeley defines knowledge in a way that follows his account of the mysteries in *Alciphron*, '. . . a faculty in whatever kind and of whatever being it be found, by which good ends, and suitable means of attaining them, are discovered, and pursued' (390).[35]

Likewise, we can understand why Berkeley refuses to allow that sensations and passions are attributed to God except metaphorically. According to Crito, passions and sensations 'taken in the proper signification, must in every degree necessarily, and from the formal nature of the thing, include imperfection' (ALC IV 21 170). Browne complains that this is far too extreme. Suitably constrained by reason, passions constitute *perfections* of our nature, which can be attributed to God analogically (*Analogy* 442–3). While there are literally no passions in God, claims Browne, '. . . yet there may be *Inconceivable Perfections* in him some way *Answerable* to what those

Passions are in us, under a due Regulation and Subjection to Reason' (*Analogy* 45).[36] In Berkeley's view, passions are not like properties or modes that exist in the soul which may somehow correspond to realities in God.[37]

The question is why Berkeley sees them as involving defect. The only possible answer is that they involve the passive perception of ideas (PHK I 29, 3D III 240–1). Berkeley claims in the *Dialogues* that to suffer anything would be an imperfection. He denies that God does so. It therefore seems the imperfection of sensation and passion concerns their passivity.

As in the case of wisdom, there is nothing over and above the subject and the object perceived. There is no third thing, an intervening passion which can constitute some kind of perfection and correspond to something in God. Consequently the only relevant feature of passion is passivity itself. Hence, passions and sensations cannot be attributed to God except metaphorically.

Reflective Knowledge of Spirits

Besides acquiring the ability to create ideas *ex nihilo*, finite spirits are simple in something like a divine sense. Like God, they lack accidents to be gained or lost. The creation of ideas does not involve any intrinsic changes within spirit itself. Neither does the passive reception of ideas. The only variable features are elements of consciousness which are entirely distinct from spirit.

Recall Browne's concern that a complex idea cannot represent God (who is supposed to be simple).[38] Berkeley can answer this problem since it turns out that finite spirits are simple in this sense as well and can therefore serve as a representation whereby we conceive God. Recall the concern raised by Collins that the mind appears capable of gaining and losing various different mental properties. According to Berkeley, the soul could never be divided in this way, since it doesn't have any distinct faculties or powers that it can lose:

> . . . the soul is without composition of parts, one pure simple undivided being. Whatever distinction of faculties or parts we may conceive in it arises only from its various acts or operations about ideas. Hence, it is repugnant that it should be known or represented in some parts and not in others, or that there should be an idea, which incompletely resembles it. (Manuscript version of PHK I 138)

If spirits had various modifications that differed in kind or if one were aware of different modes of spiritual actions, one would be inclined to speak of different faculties or powers to receive that kind of modification or to engage in that kind of action – powers which might be lost. For Berkeley, there are no such modifications. Consequently, the soul is incorruptible.

It is because there are no different mental operations to become objects of a kind of Lockean reflection that Berkeley denies that we can secure a partial knowledge of the mind in this passage. While Browne had denied the possibility of such 'an unnatural squint,' he permitted awareness of various different acts in consciousness. According to Berkeley we are aware of no such acts in that way; and so there is nothing to turn reflection upon. We cannot have a simple idea of the faculty of understanding and a simple idea of the faculty of willing since there are no such discrete actions available for inspection.

This raises the question of how we secure knowledge of what we are. It's an important question, since we are supposed to use ourselves as the model for understanding spirits more generally. We can't accept the Cartesian view that the essence of the soul is thinking. This involves an ontological commitment to a primary property (thought) which is available to consciousness. Yet in Berkeley's view we have only the sheer 'I' and its various objects. We are aware of no such *modus*. Nor, as we have seen, can we understand what we are by appeal to a Lockean reflection.

Knowledge that one exists is more robust in Berkeley's model. For 'thing' and 'exists' involve a homonymy. Recall that the central distinction between ideas and spirits is that while the former are passive and inert, the latter are active beings or agents. I take it that awareness that one exists involves more that an awareness of one's thinghood. To be aware of oneself as a thing is *ipso facto* to be aware of oneself as an *agent*. In this way, knowledge *that one is* provides some information about *what one is*. Consequently, Berkeley can answer the Hobbesian view that 'spirit' has no significance when used in ways that depart from common or metaphorical usage. He uses consciousness of one's very being to supply 'spirit' with content and to serve as a representation of God, thereby eliminating Browne's need to appeal to a revelation-dependent notion of analogy.

Now the meaning of the term 'spirit' is *explicated* as 'that which thinks, wills, and perceives' (PHK I 138). In terms of any awareness that one has prior to language, of course, we find only the 'I' itself which is the sheer awareness that one is *qua* active being.[39] However, one can engage in various different activities as a modeling behavior. To be sure, there are no particular actions themselves available for inspection. So when Berkeley claims reflection to gain knowledge of the mind of God (and other minds), he means that in addition to the 'inward feeling' we have of our own existence, we reflect discursively upon our 'various' acts by using various different words to describe 'them'. There is no prelinguistic reflection, however.

Chapter Five

Actions and Passions

In this chapter I aim to sketch an overall account of Berkeleian mental operations. In the first part, I explain how Berkeley can allow for both the activity and passivity of finite spirits, even though he allows only spirits and ideas into his ontology. I then show how Berkeley can reconcile the passivity of finite spirits with his claim that they are simple. In the second section, I expand Berkeley's account of mental operations by illuminating his views about desire, mental activities, bodily movement, and the 'influence' of body upon spirit. Because Berkeley has so little to say about the details of mental operations, this chapter is easily the most speculative of the monograph.

Part I: The Simplicity of Spirit

Activity

While some commentators worry how a spirit can be active if it is incapable of making an impact upon the sensible world, Berkeley never denominates spirit active in terms of its abilities to make such an impact.[1] He writes of spirit, '... as it produces or otherwise operates about them [ideas], it is called the *will*' (PHK I 27, my insert). Its activity is defined in terms of its mental operations upon ideas. Berkeley writes, 'It is no more than willing, and straightway this or that idea arises in my fancy: and by the same power it is obliterated, and makes way for another. This making and unmaking of ideas doth very properly denominate the mind active' (PHK I 28).

Such passages also suggest that for Berkeley, the only mental actions are (or at least reduce to) the production and destruction of ideas. To be sure, both passages leave some latitude on this point. But consider Hylas' concession that a mind is active when '... it produces, puts an end to, or changes any thing' (3D I 196). What can a mind produce, change, end but its own ideas? Berkeley leaves the will no room to do anything else. This raises two questions. How can the sheer production and destruction of ideas account for all the activities which Berkeley wishes to attribute to spirit? And how is it that spirits produce and destroy ideas? I will answer the second question now. I defer the first until the end of this chapter.

A natural reading of PHK I 28 suggests there are two things involved in imagination, the action of willing and the action of producing and destroying the idea. But what is willing? According to Locke, to will is to choose.[2] According to Collins, it is to prefer.[3] According to Malebranche, human will is a blind love for the good.[4] What is it for Berkeley? Berkeley regards love, preference, and desire as passions, and nowhere denominates spirit active by assigning the activity of choosing. I contend that, for Berkeley, volition is nothing more than producing, changing, and destroying ideas itself.

The concern is how spirits can produce ideas. And how does one become aware of one's agency? At least, an appeal to individual volitions which precede idea-effects appears to answer these questions. In the previous chapter, I suggested that the production of ideas may be a mystery for Berkeley. However, the following might also shed some light on the issue.

If one begins with passive perception and tries to add a feeling of agency to yield a suitable model, the account will seem strained. Since Berkeley views spirit as essentially active, we ought to begin with consciousness of active thought. After all, Berkeley views mental activity as a perfection and mental passivity an imperfection.

Berkeley has experience on his side. When we actively think, we are aware that we are agents. To understand the account, we should recognize that for Berkeley it is an ordinary fact that one is aware that one is active; and that this can be determined by experience. '. . . I am conscious that I am an active being, who can and do determine myself' (ALC VII 18 314). The question is this: What are we aware of when we are aware that we are thinking? Berkeley can say that we are aware of ourselves *qua* agent and we are aware of our ideas as our effects. Thus, awareness of oneself is more robust. As I suggested in the previous chapter, it involves an awareness of oneself *qua* agent.

According to Berkeley, whenever we think, we make ideas. And whenever we make ideas, we are conscious that we make ideas. He can say that the making of ideas consists in the consciousness of making ideas. Consider the production of an imagined idea in a mind (say, a unicorn). How does one produce this imaginary unicorn? By imagining it. An imagined idea comes to exist in one's mind because one is conscious of it. In such an awareness, one is aware only of oneself and one's effects; yet it is through this awareness that one makes ideas. If the existence of an imagined idea consists in being perceived by me, it should be created precisely through my perception of it.

Contrast this lean account of imagination with the position that volition is something like the act of choosing. First, it seems entirely possible that one form the volition and yet the subsequent idea fail to appear. If so, occasionalism with respect to the mind looms large.[5] This is a disaster, given Berkeley's intention to answer Malebranche's occasionalism even with respect to bodily movement (PC 548). The problem of occasionalism within the mind is solved in my interpretation, however, since an imagined idea is produced insofar as it is perceived. There can never be an unfulfilled volition.

Moreover, volitions may require a kind of ideational content to guide the action.[6] If not, it is hard to see why one particular volition should lead to the particular upshot that it does. But one can wonder whether the ideational content of the volition guiding the production of the idea resembles it. If so, there is part of an action resembling an idea, thereby undermining the view that spirits and ideas are entirely distinct.[7] Furthermore, it is no longer clear why the imagined idea is needed, since a resemblance of it has already been produced.[8] Any subsequent production is redundant. But if there is no resemblance between the volitional content and the imagined idea, it is hard to see how such content can represent the idea produced. And we have the question how the volition itself is caused. Does this lead to an infinite regress?[9] If not, why can't the account of how we produce volitions be straightaway applied to imagined ideas?

In the proposed interpretation one does not need to perceive the content of what one is going to produce before one produces it. The very production of an idea is one with the perception of it. One is not a sighted agent because one perceives one's content before one creates it, but because it is through the perception that one creates it. Whenever one acts, one is aware of what one is doing, and it is through this awareness that one acts. Consequently, Berkeley has a powerful response to Malebranche who claims 'I deny that my will produces my ideas in me, for I do not see even how they could produce them, because my will, which is unable to act or will without knowledge, presupposes my ideas and does not produce them.'[10] For Berkeley the will acts precisely through causing ideas; and it causes them by perceiving them. The will is not blind, yet it does not presuppose the having of ideas in order to act.

This accords with experience. One does not usually need to think about what one shall think before one thinks it. One simply thinks it. I bet this is why Berkeley wonders in his notebooks: 'Qu: whether the Will can be the object of Prescience or any knowledge' (PC 875). The error is to suppose that consciousness is the vehicle by which ideas are produced. The account suggests there is no third thing. To expect any such thing is to confuse an object of perception with acting itself. One cannot wait to first perceive one's intrinsic mental activity, one must act through perceiving.[11]

Passivity

Notice a problem which confronts my own thesis that Berkeleian ideas are not modes of mind, but only objects of perception. Berkeley often represents sensible ideas as sensations. He has Philonous remark:

> But how is it possible that pain, be it as little active as you please, should exist in an unperceiving substance? In short, do but consider the point, and then confess ingenuously, whether light and colours, tastes, sounds, & c. are not all equally passions or sensations in the soul. (3D I 197)

Berkeley has Philonous argue that a great many sensible things such as intense heat, intense cold, sweetness, bitterness, odours, and apparently sounds and colours as well, involve pain or its opposite, pleasure.[12] Philonous claims, '. . . the intense heat immediately perceived, is nothing distinct from a particular sort of pain' (3D III 176). And while it is not clear, how far Berkeley takes this thesis to expand, the fact remains that many sensible ideas are pains (or pleasures), and furthermore, all sensible ideas (even indifferent ones) are to be understood as like pleasures/pains (3D I 191–2). But pains and pleasures seem to be mental states. Indeed, there is a tension that arises in Philonous' identification of intense heat with a pain. One wants to deny that heat is a property of the mind, while affirming that pain is such a state.[13]

One way to address this problem is to recognize that ideas/sensations have both a cognitive and an affective side to them.[14] One can say that sensible ideas have a positive or negative valence. Hylas remarks, '. . . things regard us only as they are pleasing or displeasing: and they can please or displease, only so far forth as they are perceived' (3D III 262). Yet it also seems the two are so fundamentally blended that they are distinguishable in name only.[15] When one experiences an intense heat, one does not merely experience pain, but burning pain. In general, it seems difficult to separate the positive valence from the sweetness or the negative valence from bitter.

There's a more serious problem. Given that an intense heat has a negative valence, it appears difficult to see how God could perceive such an idea without experiencing pain.[16] Yet Berkeley explicitly denies that God suffers pain on the grounds that to suffer a pain would constitute an imperfection (3D III 240). This suggests that while God might have ideas of our sensations, these ideas are not themselves sensations. However, it is hard to see how

God can have ideas which are even qualitatively like our painful sensations without experiencing pain.[17]

The problem is central for our purposes since according to Berkeley, '... as we conceive the ideas that are in the minds of other spirits by means of our own, which we suppose to be *resemblances* of them: so we know other spirits by means of our own soul, which in that sense is the image or idea of them ...' (PHK I 140, my emphasis). Berkeley gives no indication that this claim fails to extend to what God perceives. It would be strange if it did, since we use our own soul as an active idea or image of God (3D III 231–2). How can we do this without implicating our ideas? This point comes out when Philonous explains how we conceive of our ideas existing in some other mind (God) as follows:

> ... it is very conceivable that they [sensible ideas] should exist in, and be produced by, a spirit; since this is no more than I daily experience in myself, inasmuch as I perceive numberless ideas; and by an act of my Will can form a great variety of them, and raise them up in my imagination .... (3D II 215, my insert)

The problem is how to reconcile Berkeley's views about divine analogy with the view that intense heat is painful and God does not experience pain.

The problem unravels once we turn to Berkeley's solution. In his response to Hylas' concern that God might suffer pain, Philonous elaborates his account of what 'suffering' pain involves. In the first part of his response, Philonous points to a key difference between God's perception and our own:

> We who are limited and dependent spirits are liable to impressions of sense, the effects of an external agent, which being produced against our wills, are sometimes painful and uneasy. But God, whom no external being can affect, who perceives nothing by sense as we do, whose will is absolute and independent, causing all things, and liable to be thwarted or resisted by nothing; it is evident, such a being as this can suffer nothing, nor be affected with any painful sensation, or indeed any sensation at all. (3D III 240–1)

While we receive ideas of sensation passively, God does not. This difference suggests a possible solution to the problem: God can perceive painful heat without being in pain since to be in pain is to perceive a pain passively. Since God is never passive in his perception, while he can perceive intense heat, doing so does not require that he actually suffer pain.

It is natural to suppose the reason why somebody is in pain has to do with the qualitative character of the thing (its valence). Yet my proposed solution says that while the valence of the object perceived is relevant to a person being in pain, the idea does not actually hurt the person unless she suffers it (perceives it passively). What God perceives when he perceives pain is like what we perceive. He perceives the same negative valence. Yet God is not in pain because God does not passively receive it.

This solution may seem strange. Yet, if we consider that it is possible for finite minds to produce ideas of the imagination which are like copies of sensible ideas, then the strangeness abates. According to Berkeley, the fainter ideas we produce can 'resemble' the original ideas we receive by sensation. So we can imagine ideas of a negative valence without actually being pained by them. Berkeley can say that the reason painful ideas pain us is because they have been perceived passively. Berkeley considered imagination a way for understanding Divine perception in his own philosophical notebooks. He writes:

> God May comprehend all Ideas even the Ideas wch are painfull & unpleasant without being in any degree pained thereby. Thus we our selves can imagine the pain of a burn etc without any misery or uneasiness at all. (PC 675)

My proposal is therefore a solution to the problem which Berkeley could have endorsed. Given that it is the only obvious one available, there is evidence that Berkeley actually held the view, and there is no evidence that he did not, we ought to attribute it to him.

An objection points out that imagined pain is far less strong and vivid than the sensed idea. One might say that it is not the difference with respect to activity/passivity that determines whether an idea hurts, but the strength and vivacity. Since one would expect God's idea to be rather strong and vivid, it still ought to follow that God is in pain when God perceives intense heat.

This is not so much an objection to this interpretation as it is an objection to Berkeley's solution. Perhaps it is a good objection. But I do not see how it undermines the argument in favour of attributing this position to Berkeley. In order to do that, it would have to be shown that this position is implausible. It is surely controversial. However it is hardly out of contention. This active/passive solution is as every bit compatible with the given facts as is the faintness solution. We can willfully imagine pain without suffering it. The question is why. One difference between sense-perceived and imagined ideas is force or vivacity. Another difference concerns agency. Why is it wrong to appeal to the latter?

Berkeley might respond as follows: It is true that imagined ideas are faint and weak, while sensible ideas are vivid and strong. This difference concerns the fact that while the cause (God) of sensible ideas is exceptionally powerful, the cause (me) of the imagined ideas is unimpressive. Yet it is not my lack of power that accounts for my imagined pain's failure to hurt me. Suffering pain is a weakness, not a strength. No matter how strong my imaginative powers should expand, I could never somehow hurt myself through sheer imagination. The reason for the lack of pain in imagination has nothing to do with my weakness, but my activity in perception.

A related concern with the construal of God's perception along the lines of human imagination is that while we can admit that there is some type of awareness or perception involved in imagination, the fanciful production of ideas seems a far way off from knowledge. God is supposed to understand, while imagination seems chimerical.[18] Yet we needn't construe God's perception as effectively tantamount to imagination. The point is only that we can use human imagination to appreciate why the difference between active and passive perception matters when it comes to the experience of pain. Only to the extent that imagination is free of defect can it be attributed to God in a way that is not metaphorical.

While human imaginative powers are limited by prior sensory experience, we should not want to attribute this limitation to God. This may leave us unclear about how God could actively perceive ideas which resemble our own without having sense-perceived them first.[19] Similarly, we can say that insofar as imagination involves something of the 'unreal' this only has to do with human imperfection, and we should omit it as we strive to understand divine perception. This, too, may leave us struggling. But then, our understanding of God is 'extremely inadequate' (3D III 231).

So this proposed solution can serve to explain how God's ideas can resemble our own despite the fact that God does not suffer pain. An important upshot is that the identity principle (that ideas are states of perceiving) is refuted by means of a new argument. What is experienced in the case of pain is actually distinct from the state of being in pain. In order to be in pain, it is not sufficient to perceive something painful. One must perceive the painful object passively. And since what is perceived can also be perceived actively, it follows that what is perceived is distinct from the perception of it.

This conclusion is important because it overturns the natural view that Berkeley does not distinguish between pain and the awareness that we have of it.[20] We may speak of the pain *qua* object of awareness, and the awareness one has of the object. The difference matters, because it is precisely the modality of awareness (whether it is passive or active) which determines whether one is actually in a state of pain.

Admittedly, it seems harder to see why we should call the object of awareness a pain at all. Consider an intense heat. This intense heat is not a mental episode. It is a painful, intense heat such that whenever it is passively perceived by a spirit, that spirit will be in pain. Why call the painful heat a pain?

We can allow 'pain' to be used as a relative expression. Painful heat (ever perceived by God) is only an actual pain on the condition that the heat is passively perceived by a perceiver.[21] In such a view, Berkeley could refer to objects which are passively perceived as 'sensations.' One motivation for allowing this way of speaking would be the fact that while no longer mental properties, the variable elements of consciousness are still mind-dependent entities (incapable of existing except as elements of consciousness) and are still caused from without.

We are now enabled to distinguish between the passivity of spirits and the passivity of ideas. This is important, since if spirits and ideas share the same kind of passivity then spirits and ideas will have something in common.[22] Fortunately, the passivity of spirits consists in perceiving ideas passively (perceiving ideas that are caused by God). However, ideas do not possess this kind passivity since they don't perceive ideas at all. They are passive in the sense only that they are created and destroyed by spirits, incapable of perceiving or producing other ideas.

Removing this concern removes one good motivation for assuming that spirits are likewise active or volitional in sense-perception. Berkeley does seem to have endorsed such a volitional view in the notebooks (PC 821, 854). But it also seems to be a view he abandoned. Philonous denies that volition and action are involved in smelling and seeing (3D I 196). Moreover Berkeley writes to Johnson 'That the soul of man is passive as well as active, I make no doubt.'[23] One might insist that 'sense perceiving' is in some sort a 'doing.' But if so, it does not involve volition in it. It involves affective ideas; it seems better to view this as a kind of 'undergoing.'[24]

We are also enabled to dispel a reason for supposing sensible ideas and divine ideas cannot resemble each other. By identifying awareness and idea, one is tempted to say that sensible ideas are passive, while divine ideas are active. Such a view is a distortion of Berkeley's position; the active/passive distinction is the main grounds for distinguishing spirits and ideas.[25]

Admittedly, Philonous distinguishes his view from that of Malebranche: 'I do not understand how our ideas, which are things altogether passive and inert, can be the essence, of any part (or like any part) of the essence or substance of God, who is an impassive, indivisible, purely active being' (3D II 213–4). Yet this doesn't mean God does not perceive ideas which are passive and inert (instead, perceiving 'active ideas').[26] It means that nothing passive can be part of God; there is no passive state which God is in.[27]

Finally, we can provide the beginning of Berkeley's conception of the passions. Let's first note what Locke says about love:

> Thus any one reflecting upon the thought he has of the Delight, which any present, or absent thing is apt to produce in him, has the *Idea* we call *Love*. For when a Man declares in Autumn, when he is eating them, or in Spring, when there are none, that he *loves* Grapes, it is no more, but that the taste of Grapes delights him; let an alteration of Health or Constitution destroy the delight of their Taste, and he then can be said to *love* Grapes no longer. (E. 2.30.4, 230)

For Berkeley, a grape is going to be nothing more than a congeries of ideas and so it is not going to be a cause in the way that Locke supposes. Instead, it will have as one of its constituents a delightful taste. The passion of love will be excited in a spirit just in case the taste of the grape delights that spirit (just in case that spirit perceives the delightful taste passively). Using the distinction drawn above, to the extent that the passion of love is nothing more than the feeling of delight itself, we can say that the feeling of love is an object of consciousness (it is the taste itself passively perceived). Yet we can also say that loving (being delighted by the taste) is the spirit's passive perception of the taste.[28]

The Simplicity of Spirit

Spirits are simple, active beings (PHK I 27). Yet given that they are passive, why are they generally characterized as active? And given that they can be characterized as both, why are they characterized as simple?[29] Moreover, how can the difference between activity and passivity be determined? In the one case a finite spirit is the cause of the idea it perceives, while in the second case a finite spirit perceives an idea which is caused by God. How can this difference be known to a spirit given that only spirits and ideas are elements of conscious awareness? The additional awareness of volitions in the first case might solve this last problem. Yet it is something that my interpretation rejects.

The first step is to recognize that will and perception can be blended together in imagination as a form of active perception. Imagining a unicorn involves both will and perception since it is through the perception that one brings the idea into existence. The second step is to recognize that just as perceiving and willing are blended together in imagination, so too, sensation and passion are blended together in passive perception: Experiencing a delightful taste and being delighted by the taste are one and the same.

There is an important analogy in the two cases. In the case of active perception, one is not aware of some third volitional element. The sheer consciousness of one's effects and oneself *qua* agent constitutes the production of the effects. Similarly, the phenomenology of pain and pleasure is not a distinct element of consciousness. One perceives one's objects and oneself, just as one similarly perceives in the case of active perception. The phenomenology of experiencing pain and pleasure is tantamount to passive perception itself. To experience pain and pleasure is all one with passive perception.

The third step is this: The 'I' of self-awareness unifies active and passive perception. In the case of the active production of ideas, there are no intervening vehicles of production to constitute discrete modes existence. Likewise, passive perception itself is not some intrinsic state of spirit. Therefore, there are not two conflicting modalities of existence, there is only one simple 'I.'

Now even though spirits are not active in sense-perception, it would appear that they must always be active in order to exist. How can one be aware of oneself as both an agent and a patient at the same time given the 'I' is simple? While to suffer is all one with receiving an idea from without, this may not be the same as consciousness that one suffers. Such a consciousness requires an awareness of *oneself*, and to be aware of oneself is to be aware of oneself *qua* agent. This is fortunate, since consciousness that one is passive also requires consciousness that such ideas are independent of one's own will which, in turn, requires an awareness of oneself *qua* willing agent. We can say that to be aware of oneself as a patient is to be aware of oneself as an agent (as usual) while undergoing the phenomenology of being in pain or pleasure. It is to be aware of oneself as a suffering agent.

This is possible because the difference between activity and passivity does not concern a difference in subject or object, but the fact that in passive perception ideas are produced from without in an agent that produces its own ideas. Despite the fact that one continues thinking actively, the phenomenology of pain and pleasure does not undermine one's awareness of oneself as an agent. It makes one aware of oneself as an agent that has perceived ideas that are not one's own.[30]

Part II: Actions, Passions and the Body

Desire

While positive and negative values are blended with a great variety of sensory contents yielding a variety of delights and discomforts, this appears inadequate as a thoroughgoing account of the passions. Consider desire. Although the passive perception of a painful object may constitute a desire that the pain cease, and the passive perception of a pleasant object may carry within it a desire that the pleasure continue, it is not clear how one can desire an absent good. Imagining a pleasant idea cannot constitute a passion since it would be actively produced by the thinker (rather than passively perceived).

One solution is to appeal to a kind of 'internal sensation' (as Locke uses the expression)[31] that arises when the object is not present. One feels hunger without food, and thirst without water. Such internal sensations of uneasiness can constitute desire for the objects whose presence alleviates (or occasions the cessation of) the uneasiness. This is a good start to the account. Berkeley can allow an account of the body governed by Divine Law such that eating food alleviates hunger which is a part of the sensible body. The admission of internal sensations of this type may be good candidates for what Berkeley calls 'ideas of reflexion' (PHK I 13 and 25). However, Berkeley also rejects this as a complete account of desire in his 1708 sermon. In doing so, he rejects Locke's account of desire.

According to Locke, desire is not determined by the greatest apparent good. Men may be unmoved by many apparent goods, since the goods do not 'make a part of their present happiness.' However, one has the ability to suspend one's desires and intellectually consider the various options. Only by choosing what one considers to be the greatest good, does it become a part of one's happiness and raise the desire for it. This may take repeated contemplation so we gain 'some relish' of the good whereby its absence can then yield some uneasiness (E. 2.21.56, 270; E. 2.21.69, 280).[32]

Berkeley, however, allows for what he calls 'rational desires' which are proportional to the greatness of the good and the likelihood of its being attained. He distinguishes these desires from the brutish appetites (presumably of the type of desires that Locke has in mind). In such a view, to recognize the value of a good and its likelihood of obtaining is *ipso facto* to desire it in proportion to its value and likelihood. This is to say: The greatest (rationally) apparent good determines desire insofar as the comprehension that it is the greatest good constitutes the desire.

Berkeley can claim that a person understands a word only if upon hearing it, he is disposed to behave in the appropriate ways. He can hold that somebody who professes to understand that some object is good, but is not disposed to act in a way which demonstrates a valuing of the object is either lying or confused about what the word 'good' means. This makes sense since whenever a person passively perceives an idea with a positive-valence she will thereby value it in the very passive perception of it. In this way, 'good' is not something that one may somehow contemplate cognitively, abstracted from the affect which stirs the will.

In order to understand the basis for this view, we should note that, for Berkeley, passions may be excited by words. He writes, '. . . in hearing or reading a discourse, that the passions of fear, love, hatred, admiration, and disdain, and the like arise, immediately in his mind upon the perception of certain words, without any ideas coming between' (PHK I Intro 20). It may be that such words had originally occasioned ideas 'fit to produce those emotions' (PHK I Intro 20). Yet, once language has grown familiar, no such ideas need be suggested. This raises a couple of perplexing questions, the answers of which illuminate Berkeley's account of desire (and passion more generally).

First, in the case in which ideas are suggested by words, we want to know how passions can be excited. The idea that will be suggested by the words is one that is produced by the imagination upon hearing the relevant word. Yet, passion requires passive perception. So how could a suggested idea (an imagined idea) excite a passion? Second, if we consider the case in which no ideas are suggested, we want to know how merely hearing the right word can involve the excitation of a passion. When one perceives a beautiful colour, the valence is blended with the content. How can that valence be transferred to the mere word 'beauty'? For answers, we turn to Berkeley's notion of mediate perception.

Mediate perception involves an initial passive sensory perception by which other ideas can be suggested to the imagination. The question is how one idea suggests another idea. Berkeley cannot mean one idea causes another. Nor can he mean that one idea occasions another idea which is caused by God. The second idea is supposed to be suggested to the imagination; consequently it should be the imagination which produces it. Yet neither can Berkeley mean that the imagination just happens to cause the right idea on the occasion of the word. How does it know which idea to produce? What remains of the view that one idea *suggests* another?

Passions involved in immediate sensory perception somehow influence the will (either by a kind of attraction or repulsion). Upon the experience of intense pain, one will be inclined to think about the pain, and perhaps even cry out. The pain does not determine one's will. One can try to avoid thinking about the pain, refrain from crying out and so forth. Yet pains and pleasure attract and repulse the will in the way in which one might say that final causes attract. Ideas aren't causes for Berkeley. The attractive and repulsive power does not derive merely from the ideas themselves, but from the fact that they are passively perceived (caused by God). Yet, neither does Berkeley seem averse to the notion of 'final causation.'[33] He writes:

> ... considering the whole creation is the workmanship of a *wise* and *good* agent, it should seem to become philosophers, to employ their thoughts (contrary to what some hold) about the final causes of things: and I must confess, I see no reason, why pointing out the various ends . . . should not be thought one good way of accounting for them . . . . (PHK I 107)

Perhaps a word suggests an idea to the imagination just as passive perception of pain and pleasure attracts and repels. Suppose that repeated experience has disposed me to associate two ideas. Then upon seeing one idea I may be disposed by habit to produce the other in my imagination. The idea which is immediately perceived can be said to suggest the other (attract me to produce the other). The question now concerns this disposition or habit. What is it?

One possibility is that after repeated experience of the conjunction of two ideas, whenever I experience the one idea, an internal sensation constituting an uneasiness to behave in a certain way is occasioned. If so, the account of suggestion can reduce to the account of brute uneasiness (in the case of hunger). The difference is that in the case of hunger, the uneasiness is natural. In the case of suggestion, the uneasiness is acquired through habit.[34]

By building uneasiness into the very comprehension of the word, it then becomes a matter of whether a person believes that something is good. If she does, then she will act in a certain way. Consequently, being told that something is good and believing that it is so, is sufficient to incite (and indeed constitutes) a desire for that which is good.[35] Likewise, Berkeley asks, 'Or is not the being threatened with a danger sufficient to excite a dread, though we think not of any particular evil likely to befall us . . . ?' (PHK Intro 20). If a person has successfully mastered words such as 'dreadful' and 'dangerous' then to be threatened with a danger or some dreadful event and to understand and believe the threat is all one with being filled with dread. The account, although grounded upon uneasiness, departs from Locke in an important way. For Locke, recognizing something as good is insufficient to determine the will, it needs to become part of one's happiness. For Berkeley, recognizing something as good constitutes a desire since uneasiness is built into the comprehension of the word.

Mental Activities

The account of mental activity can be expanded to accommodate many forms of mental action. The kind of dividing and compounding of ideas

Berkeley allows reduces to nothing more than the imaginative production of ideas (PHK I Intro 10). To divide a sensible idea (say of a man), is simply to imaginatively produce an idea of a hand. Likewise to compound the idea of a man's head and horse's body is simply to imaginatively produce such an idea. And if the imagination can create the idea of a geometrical shape that it has never seen before, it can produce ideas of different shades of blue ordered accordingly. So there is no reason to believe that comparison cannot be accommodated by imagination as well.

Berkeley can expand his account of mental operations by allowing the use of various discursive symbols to count as mental operations. Berkeley admits that arithmetic, algebra, and geometry involve the manipulation of symbols according to rules and he more generally allows that terms are often used in discursive reasoning without any idea itself being appealed to or in play (ALC VII 5 293, cf. *Works* VIII Letter 5, 25). Indeed, the rule-governed nature of language and the functional use of words as devices, is pervasive. He comments to Molyneux, '... That all Grammar & every part Logic contain little else than Rules for Discourse & Ratiocination by Words. And those who do not expressly [*sic*] set themselves to study those Arts do nevertheless learn them insensibly by Custom' [*Works* VIII Letter 6, 27].

However, Berkeley can admit no mental actions except those which involve the creation, changing, and destruction of ideas. Berkeley would not have the resources to allow for mental selective attention by which one focuses on certain aspects of a complex, mixed idea to the exclusion of others, since this would not involve the creation of a new idea. One might discursively mention certain aspects of an idea without mentioning others (as one might mention an idea's color without mentioning its shape or size) (cf. 3D I 193). But this would involve the production of a new idea – namely the idea of the word.

Unfortunately, there remain mental operations which require explanation, but are difficult to accommodate. Berkeley believes that spirits have memories. Here, one is going to have to appeal to the body. How else can one explain one's loss of memory or one's slowness of recall? More generally, it seems that the body has a bearing on our thought. When one is sleepy, it is hard to concentrate and one thinks less well. But how can Berkeley accommodate such facts? While a spirit might be able to act upon body (ideas), it is unclear how the body is supposed to assist the spirit in thinking (given that ideas are inactive). Moreover, if Berkeley were to allow for such an interaction he would be in danger of conceding ground to Browne's view that mental operations reflect the joint operation of spirit and body.

Bodily Movement

Even Berkeley's claim that finite spirits have an impact upon the world is hard to understand. If God causes all sensible ideas, how can finite spirits do anything but produce their own imagined ideas? At PHK I 147 Berkeley writes, '. . . in affecting other persons, the will of man hath no other object, than barely the motion of the limbs of his body; but that such a motion should be attended by, or excite any idea in the mind of another, depends wholly on the will of the Creator' (cf. 3D III 237). Yet even granting the impact is limited, the concern that since God is the author of all ideas of sensation (PHK I 29), it is impossible for finite spirits to have any impact upon the world at all (including their own bodies) would remain.[36]

When we turn to the second part of Philonous' reply to Hylas' concern that God should feel pain, we find an answer. Philonous claims that we have a sensible body which involves the connection between corporeal motions and sensations:

> We are chained to a body, that is to say, our perceptions are connected with corporeal motions. By the Law of our Nature we are affected upon every alteration in the nervous parts of our sensible body: which sensible body rightly considered, is nothing but a complexion of such qualities or ideas ... so that this connexion of sensations with corporeal motions, means no more than a correspondence in the order of Nature between two sets of ideas . . . . (3D III 241)

It seems that the 'corporeal motions' are precisely the ideas that we ourselves are supposed to cause. And the distinction that Philonous draws suggests that they are not sensations.[37] What are they, if not sensations?

While Berkeley draws a distinction between ideas of sensation (produced by God), and ideas of imagination (produced by us), it is not clear that this distinction is exhaustive. Ideas of sensation are also characterized by strength, vivacity, and coherence, while the latter are characterized by their weakness and lack of vivacity. Berkeley does not distinguish reality from fancy by appealing to the causal source of an idea. Rather, it is in terms of the latter characteristics. He writes, 'The ideas of sense are allowed to have more reality in them, that is, to be more strong, orderly, and coherent than the creatures of the mind . . .' (PHK I 33, cf. 36).

This leaves open the possibility that our ideas of corporeal motions can be like ideas of sensation in these 'reality-making' respects. They can count as real despite the fact that we cause them.[38] Philonous points out that these corporeal motions are attended by pleasure and pain. This is important, since while he must regard these corporeal motions as real, he is likewise denying that they can constitute pleasure and pains. We know why. They are not passively perceived; they are actively perceived. Yet they are vivid, strong, and fit within the causal order by constituting the occasions of sensible ideas, thereby affording us dominion over a small part of the real world (our bodies). They constitute a distinct class of ideas ('internal kinesthetic ideas' if you will) which we cause in exactly the same way we cause imaginary ideas. Everything else is up to God.[39]

Spiritual Limitations and the Body

Our sensible body is governed by Divine Laws, just as any sensible object. To lose the capacity to see can be accounted for by the fact that it is no longer true that corporeal motions (such as opening one's eyes) are occasioned by visible sensations. Consequently, finite spirits have a constraint placed on their perception. They can only sensibly perceive certain objects.

This means that rather than viewing the body as the instrument by which we see, the fact that we need eyes is a defect or constraint upon a finite spirit's capacity to perceive. Berkeley writes to Johnson:

> Now it seems very easy to conceive the soul to exist in a separate state (i.e. divested from those limits and laws of motion and perception with which she is embarrassed here), and to exercise herself on new ideas, without the intervention of these tangible things we call bodies. It is even very possible to apprehend how the soul may have ideas of colour without an eye, or of sounds without an ear. (*Works* II, *Berkeley to Johnson* II, 6, 282)

It is likewise clear that our imaginations are constrained by sensory experience. Somebody born without vision will be unable to produce images of visible ideas. And tacitly presupposed, is that in producing our imagined ideas we will have retained past experience. Just as a person with poor vision will be imaginatively constrained, so will one with poor memory. The range of ideas that we can produce is constrained. This can be viewed as a limitation on our spirits. It is a limitation that may vary from time to time. And it is a limitation that is occasioned by facts about the body. Upon failing to eat enough, there may be a great limitation on the speed and range of imaginative production. So, while bodies may not have a causal impact upon spirits, changes in body can nonetheless occasion the variable limitations on finite spirit.

One consequence of this view is that Berkeley is enabled to explain how we can conceptualize an infinitely powerful God in a way that does not entirely derive from the sheer expansion or augmentation of our own powers as supposed by Locke (E. 2.23.33–34, 315). The Lockean approach to infinity through repetition and augmentation yields no positive notion (E. 2.17). To the extent that for Berkeley, we understand ourselves as limited in our productive powers, and conceptualize God by removing the limitations, our own self-understanding provides a more robust model of God's power than Locke had supposed.[40]

Chapter Six

Identity and Time

By identifying the will with the production of ideas, Berkeley is enabled to reject more deterministic accounts. According to Collins, to will is all one with preferring an action and preference is determined by the greatest apparent good.[1] For Berkeley, by contrast, the will is not a preference, although it is guided by it. According to Locke, willing is determined by uneasiness. We have freedom of the will to the extent that we consider the various goods and judge which one is best. This, in turn, generates a new uneasiness which determines the will (E. 2.21.45–7, 261–63). According to Berkeley, by contrast, God himself can will, despite the fact that he lacks such uneasiness (PC 610). Since the will is nothing but the production of thought itself, it is involved in the very act of judgment which Locke thinks necessarily precedes an act of the will (ALC VII 18 314).[2]

Having extricated the will from such concerns, Berkeley makes strides ensuring that finite spirits are appropriate candidates for reward and punishment. The questions that I examine now concern the identity of agents through time and Berkeley's views concerning resurrection and immortality. I conclude with Berkeley's reconciliation of human liberty with divine prescience.

Part I: Individuation, Privacy, and Bodily Resurrection

A.A. Luce is known for his controversial interpretation according to which ideas of sense are publicly available entities, capable of existing independently of finite minds.[3,4,5] According to what I shall call 'a Lucian-style interpretation' at least some of the following claims are attributed to Berkeley: (1) Finite spirits share some sensible ideas (where numerically one and the same idea is perceived by more than one finite spirit). (2) Any sensible idea perceived by a given finite spirit is also perceived by God (where that finite spirit and God perceive numerically one and the same idea). (3) A sensible idea (perceived by a given finite spirit) is not dependent upon that spirit for its existence insofar as the idea is also perceived by God, and can be perceived by God whether that finite spirit perceives it or not.[6,7,8]

A more traditional view denies that Berkeley held any of these claims, maintaining that each spirit perceives its own ideas and that such items may not exist independently of the spirit which perceives them. In this view, Berkeley's philosophical position is at odds with common sense. He 'speaks with the vulgar and thinks with the learned' (PHK 151). In a Lucian-style interpretation, Berkeley's philosophical views are in agreement with common sense; Berkeley sides '. . . in all things with the Mob' (PC 405).

I depart from both interpretations by maintaining that for Berkeley there is no fact of the matter how to numerically individuate sensible ideas per perceiver. There may obtain a mere qualitative identity between what any two spirits perceive which may be vulgarly described as 'perceiving one and the same thing.' But at a deeper level, there is no fact of the matter how to individuate sensible ideas per perceiver, and there is likewise no fact of the matter whether a sensible idea perceived by some finite spirit can exist independently of that spirit. Both traditional and Lucian-style readings are guilty of attributing to Berkeley a deep philosophical view he does not hold.

Both views misrepresent Berkeley's relationship to common sense. While the traditional view is correct that Berkeley merely 'speaks with the vulgar,' it is incorrect in attributing to Berkeley a philosophical view which is at odds with 'the vulgar.' While the Lucian-style interpretation is wrong in attributing to Berkeley a philosophical view which agrees with 'the vulgar,' it is correct that Berkeley 'sides in all things with the Mob.' According to Berkeley, the superficial views of the vulgar express the only truth to be had since there is no deeper philosophical truth.

Such a thesis seems to be virtually paradoxical. While we can see how two people may wear the very same dress to a cocktail party in the sense that they are wearing qualitatively identical ones, it is also true that there are numerically two dresses. How can ideas be qualitatively identical without there being some fact of the matter how many there are?

In the view I attribute to Berkeley, 'idea' is nothing more than a synonym for 'object of immediate perception,' 'existence in the mind' means 'immediate perception by the mind' (where immediate perception is understood as the conscious awareness of objects), and 'my ideas' can be translated into 'what I perceive.' Thus *what I perceive* may be the same as *what God perceives* (we may perceive 'the same thing'). But in these cases, the issue is one of qualitative identity, not numerical identity. The question how we numerically count perceived things is a further, trickier question.

The thought is that there ought to be some underlying ontology which tells us one way or the other. If we viewed ideas not only as objects of consciousness but also mental properties, we would have any easy way of individuating ideas per perceiver. Alternatively, if we endorsed some ontology according to which we perceived numerically one and the same accident in a material substance, we could move beyond qualitative identity. In the view I believe Berkeley holds there is no underlying ontology which tells us one way or the other.[9] Any hope for an answer derives from a philosopher's hallucinated ontology. By contrast, when two finite perceivers imagine the same content, there is a metaphysical basis for individuating the ideas because an imagined idea is produced through its finite perceiver's perception of it. Every imagined idea is consequently bound to the perceiver that produces it. Two imagined ideas can be distinguished by appeal to distinct causes. In the case of sensation, however, there is one causal source and more than one perceiver.

One objection involves the notion of content. If what I perceive is qualitatively the same as what you perceive, do we not perceive the numerically same content? The question is whether anything especially interesting is being said beyond the sheer fact that there is an exact qualitative identity between what the two of us perceive in this case. To be sure, a failure in resemblance would necessarily yield a numeric distinctness in content. But numerical identity doesn't follow from qualitative identity. Sometimes when what I perceive and what you perceive are qualitatively similar (although not exactly so), it might be said that the content is almost the same (just as two people might say almost the same thing). With respect to genuine numerical identity there is never an 'almost.' And if nothing beyond a qualitative identity between 'what we perceive' is asserted, then to speak of a numerically identical content is a verbal decision since there is no fine-spun ontology which can decide the case.[10]

Another objection involves drawing attention to one of my central theses, that immediate perception, for Berkeley, is consciousness itself. Consider the thought 'That sunset is lovely' or the imagined idea of a pink unicorn. These seem to be the sort of objects which are private since there is an important sense in which they exist in one perceiver's mind and nowhere else. Berkeley's point, in my reading, is that sensible things such as sounds and odours are likewise objects for consciousness. How can there be no fact of the matter whether such objects are individuated per perceiver? These objects are essentially private for each perceiver, and are therefore individuated per perceiver.

The response runs as follows. What motivates our desire to say thoughts such as 'That sunset is lovely' and imagined pink unicorns are private is that we do not 'look' into each other's minds and perceive each other's thoughts. The point is one about access. This is a point Berkeley considers. Hylas complains:

> Pray are not the objects perceived by the senses of one likewise perceivable to others present? If there were an hundred more here, they would all see the garden, the trees, and flowers as I see them. But they are not in the same manner affected with the ideas I frame in my imagination. Does not this make a difference between the former sort of objects and the latter? (3D III 246–7)

In drawing a public/private distinction, Hylas does not make the point that our imagined ideas are numerically individuated per perceiver. He says only that in this case other people are not affected with my ideas. It makes one wonder what it would be for other minds to be affected by imagined ideas. I bet it goes like this.

Suppose that whenever I think various different 'verbal' thoughts to myself, such as 'What a lovely sunset,' somehow you are caused to 'hear' that thought in your own mind. Indeed, suppose that we can actually converse using our own thoughts through this telepathic exchange. Suppose that we can recognize who is thinking much in the way that we recognize people based upon their voices. Is this not what we mean by mind-reading? Is this not the kind of publicity that Hylas appears to have in mind? If so, Philonous agrees that ideas of imagination lack publicity in the sense here explained (3D I 247).

Yet there is another notion of privacy which goes well beyond this example, forbidding that two minds share and experience numerically one and the same mental state or episode. It is clear that in this example there is no such denial of privacy involved. This is to be expected in my interpretation since for Berkeley ideas are not mental states or episodes. An episode is a relation between subject and object which is individuated per relata. The demand that I have this type of access to somebody else's mental life is nothing short of the demand that somebody else's awareness of the object be identical to my own; that I enter into numerically one and the same relation of passive perception as somebody else. This is impossible unless I absurdly am somebody else. But the difference discussed by Hylas and Philonous concerns objects of sensation and imagination, not episodes of them.

The question we need to ask is whether in this hypothetical case of mind-reading the thought perceived is to be individuated per perceiver. There is no good reason in principle why it should be and no good reason why it shouldn't. Every concern about privacy and publicity has already been covered. In terms of content what had been private has now been made public, while in terms of mental episode, there remains a deep privacy. I don't see how one can argue for the numerical individuation of ideas per perceiver by appealing to concerns about privacy since all concerns about privacy have been accommodated. To be sure, the vulgar can take qualitative identity as sufficient grounds for numerical identity.[11] But this is a verbal affair.

My proposed interpretation agrees very closely with what Berkeley suggests. In the *Third Dialogue*, Hylas queries Philonous, (A) 'Is it not your opinion that by our senses we perceive only the ideas existing in our minds?' (3D III 247). Philonous agrees to this claim. Then Hylas alleges that (B) 'the same idea which is in my mind, cannot be in yours, or in any other mind.' And then Hylas worries that (C) it will 'follow from your principles that no two can see the same thing? And is this not highly absurd?' (3D III 247).

It is far from obvious that Philonous accepts (B). Indeed, I take it that for Philonous, ideas just are the things themselves, so there is no distinction between (B) and (C).[12] In support of the claim that Philonous does not accept (B), consider the following:

> It is evident that the things I perceive are my own ideas, and that no idea can exist unless it be in a mind. Nor is it less plain that these ideas or things by me perceived, either themselves or their archetypes, exist independently of my mind, since I know myself not to be their author, it being out of my power to determine at pleasure, what particular ideas I shall be affected with upon opening my eyes or ears. They must therefore exist in some other mind, whose will it is they should be exhibited to me. (3D III 214)

Philonous links the expressions 'my own ideas,' 'these ideas,' and 'things by me perceived'; and the context in this passage suggests that they are interchangeable. Philonous takes the following two possibilities seriously: My ideas exist independently of my mind and the archetypes of my ideas exist independently of my mind. Yet the fact that he takes the first possibility seriously shows that for Philonous, it is allowable to say 'my own ideas' exist independently of my mind.

Philonous suggests that the question whether to individuate ideas per perceiver is merely a verbal affair. 'But who sees not that all the dispute is about a word? to wit, whether what is perceived by different persons, may yet have the term *same* applied to it?' (248) Of course, if 'the term *same* be taken in the vulgar acceptation, it is certain . . . that different persons may perceive the same thing; or the same thing or idea exist in different mind.' (247). But there are philosophers who 'pretend to an abstracted notion of identity' and are in disagreement about the correct account of 'philosophical identity' (247). Any attempt to arbitrate a merely verbal dispute by appealing to a 'simple, abstracted idea of identity' (248) fails since, according to Philonous, '. . . I know not what you mean by *your abstracted idea of identity*' (248). Surely allegations of pretending to a simple, abstract idea of philosophical identity is Berkeley's kiss of death. The point is that any attempt to bring some fine-spun ontology to bear on the question of individuation is nothing short of an illicit abstraction.

Philonous also recognizes, in his own view, there can be archetypes. He does this because, while his account allows different perceivers to 'perceive the same thing,' it seems we truly have lost the external world that the materialist could believe in. Despite the fact that two finite perceivers sometimes perceive the same thing, there is no guarantee that what they perceive will exist even when they do not perceive it. In order to secure this sort of mind-independence of what we perceive, we need to appeal to what God perceives. However, this appeal to divine archetypes does not undermine the preceding claim that there is *no fact of the matter how to numerically individuate what I perceive and what* God perceives. For a divine archetype (or idea) is simply the content of God's perception. The two moves that Philonous makes are thus compatible and necessary.[13,14]

This means that Berkeley's spirit–idea ontology departs from substance–mode ontology in an important way. In traditional substance–mode ontology, substances not only 'support' modes, they individuate them through inherence.[15] In Berkeley's view, while spirits support ideas, they do not individuate them through this support.

We can easily distinguish between the relation of support that is supposed to obtain between supporter and supported, and the capacity of substance to individuate such items. Consider the following analogy. Suppose four pillars used to support a platform and contrast this with one pillar used to support the platform. In both cases there is genuine support. In the former case all four pillars support one and the same platform. Thus we can have support despite the fact that it is shared support.

Yet, while it is true that Berkeleian substances lose their capacity to individuate items through supporting them, there is another way in which substances may be said to gain a kind of superiority over the items to which they lend support. Spirits have a self-identity which ideas lack. Ideas become things for which numerical identity between perceivers is ontologically inapplicable. Far from undermining the substantiality of spirit, Berkeley only affirms it in an idiosyncratic way.

Insofar as there is no fact of the matter how to individuate sensible ideas per perceiver, there is likewise no fact of the matter how to individuate them over time. The only way the idea I perceive now could return to me later, numerically one and the same, would be for God and I to perceive numerically one and the same idea. Yet there is no fact of the matter whether this is the case. Likewise, the only way in which the sensible idea I perceive now could be numerically distinct from the qualitatively identical idea that I perceive later would require that such ideas cease to exist when I cease to perceive them. However, there is no fact of the matter whether such sensible ideas are dependent or independent of me, and consequently no fact of the matter whether they are numerically distinct through perceptual interruption. Contrast this with the case of imagined ideas. I may imagine the same unicorn over the course of a week (every day at midnight for one minute). Here, I can distinguish between multiple productions of ideas which come into existence and then cease. They cease to exist since their existing at all consists in being perceived by me.

This interpretation squares nicely with the text. For in attempting to answer worries about bodily resurrection, Berkeley writes:[16]

> But do not the most plausible of them depend on the supposition, that a body is denominated the *same*, with regard not to the form or that which is perceived by sense, but the material substance which remains the same under several forms? Take away this *material substance*, about the identity where all the dispute is, and mean by *body* what every plain ordinary person means by that word, to wit . . . only a combination of sensible qualities, or ideas: and then their most unanswerable objections come to nothing. (PHK I 95)

Any view which requires that qualitatively identical sensible ideas be numerically individuated by perceptual interruption has no good explanation of how the fact that bodies are collections of sensible ideas is supposed to solve the problem of resurrection. If the ideas do not continue to exist intermittently, how can the collection of such ideas continue to exist intermittently? And if the collection can't exist intermittently, how is resurrection going to be possible? The only 'solution' such an interpretation proposes is the destruction of identity over time so that any account of resurrection would be one which appealed to the same verbal fiction used to smooth over the consequences of such a view.

By contrast, a view that qualitatively identical ideas which are perceptually intermittent can be numerically identical does explain resurrection.[17] Yet, it also seems to fail as an explanation of Berkeley's elucidation of bodily resurrection by appealing to other examples in nature.[18]

> All the parts of this corporeal world are in a perpetual flux and revolution, decaying and renewing, perishing and rising up again. The various successions and returns of light and darkness, winter and summer, spring and autumn, the renovation of plants and fruits of the earth, all are in some sort so many instances of this truth (*Works* VII Sermon 8, 107).

In the view that perceptually intermittent ideas can be numerically identical over time, Berkeley's appeal hardly makes any sense since the plants that die should count as numerically distinct from the ones which grow later. How does this example help us understand the doctrine that the dead shall be resurrected?

Berkeley can view these examples as analogous to bodily resurrection in case he simply rejects the numerical individuation of qualitatively identical ideas by affirming that in cases of qualitative identity there is no further fact concerning numerical identity. In this way, Berkeley is enabled to address Stillingfleet's insistence that the numerically same body be resurrected on Judgment Day by discarding such identity from the natural world; he has rejected the underlying individuating matter, and retained only 'the form or that which is perceived by sense.'

Berkeley also considers resurrection involving a 'change in form' (like Paul's transformation of seeds into plants); 'Thus the silkworm lies without sense or motion, is dead and actually buried in a tomb of her own spinning. But after some daies ... she revives and takes on a new form ...'[19] On the face of it this does not seem to be a genuine case of resurrection, while it does seem to be a change in 'form' since there is no underlying matter to secure numerically identity. Yet this constitutes a genuine resurrection which is similar to the way our bodies shall be spiritualized at resurrection.[20] Without underlying matter to raise problems about individuation, we should expect that bodily resurrections can be accounted much in the same way that the resurrection of silkworm can be so accounted (by appealing to the laws of nature). Any wrangling about numerical identity is a dispute about nothing.

Part II: Spiritual Simplicity, Time, and Identity

Berkeley affirms that time is succession of ideas relative to each individual finite subject and that no time can elapse for a spirit 'in between' going to sleep and waking up in the morning. Berkeley writes 'Time therefore being nothing, abstracted from the succession of ideas in our minds, it follows that the duration of any finite spirit must be estimated by the number of ideas or actions succeeding each other in that same spirit or mind' (PHK I 98). Berkeley means to deny that there is any objective time. That this is his intention emerges in his reply to Johnson where he affirms that time is constituted by a succession of ideas, and that there is no change, variation, or succession in God (the only possible anchor for securing objective time).[21]

Although there are many disturbing consequences which appear to follow from this view,[22] one is that according to Berkeley, it appears that no time can have passed before one was born. Consequently, no events can have occurred prior to one's birth, since there is no objective time within which they could have occurred. Perhaps one might acknowledge that events prior to one's birth were observed by other spirits. Yet this is to allocate events to other time-lines, and it is hard to see how this is relevant. If this is relevant, why is the fact that other finite spirits perceive while one is sleeping not relevant? Worse, it seems hard to fathom other spirits perceiving events prior to one's first conscious thought (or simultaneous with one's sleeping). What could 'simultaneity' mean given that there is no common time-line?

Berkeley needs to allow for the fact that many events occurred prior to his own birth (such as the Mosaic Creation of the World). And he plainly does. Philonous says:

> When I deny sensible things an existence out of the mind, I do not mean my mind in particular, but all minds. Now it is plain they have an existence exterior to my mind, since I find them by experience to be independent of it. There is therefore some other mind wherein they exist, during the intervals between the times of my perceiving them: as likewise they did before my birth, and would do after my supposed annihilation. (3D III 230–1)

But if Berkeley allows that objects exist before he was born, why should he not allow for objects to exist while he is sleeping? Yet if he allows this, then there is a time when he is sleeping, and he has given up his solution to problem of intermittent existence.[23]

Berkeley's problem is serious. The sheer vulgar use of time-words in which you bid 'your servant meet you at such a *time*, in such a *place*, and he shall never stay to deliberate on the meaning of those words . . .' (PHK I 97) cannot solve this problem. How can the perceived rising and setting of the sun serve as a 'public' (conventional) way of measuring time that serves pragmatic purposes, if it is true that at the metaphysical level, each finite spirit occupies a different time-line? How is intersubjectivity possible given that there is no *simultaneity*?[24]

It is too easy to construe Berkeleian times as individual ideas which are like frames in a moving picture.[25] In this view, times would move more quickly should the rate of temporal succession increase. Yet this view cannot be correct since it presupposes time itself in the calculation of the rate of succession (the number of ideas that succeed each other per minute or second).[26] To the extent that Berkeley's view is a radicalization of the position offered by Locke, we must understand it in a different way (E. 2.14.4–5, 182–3). For Locke, the duration of one's existence or anything else is measured by the succession of ideas: The greater the succession (i.e. the greater the number of changes in ideas), the greater the duration. If time is nothing but the succession of ideas then it ought to be measured against the backdrop of a thing's existence.

Berkeley's view that the rate of temporal succession may vary requires a fixed thing or event against which the rate is itself is to be measured. Such things exist in the mind of God. While God may not himself experience change-requiring succession, he may order ideas in a particular way such that finite spirits will perceive them in a given sequence.[27] Indeed, Berkeley himself speaks of 'the Course of Nature' by which he means 'the motions, changes, and decays, and dissolutions which we hourly see befall natural bodies . . .' (PHK I 141). Thus a history of the natural world may exist in the mind of God as an ordered set of ideas with respect to their perceptibility to finite spirits. Due to this ordering, finite spirits may exist 'simultaneously' insofar as they perceive the same event or object that is part of the Course of Nature. Likewise, they can exist 'before' or 'after' each other as they perceive different events located within the Course of Nature (contrast, for example, the finite spirit who perceives the Flood, with the finite spirit who perceives the coronation of Queen Elizabeth II).

We now have a way to say that the speed of time varies per finite perceiver. Suppose two finite perceivers are observing the same tree which is about to be chopped down. One perceiver can experience a greater succession of ideas (caused by his thinking many successive thoughts), while another perceiver may have very few thoughts. Time moves faster for the first perceiver and consequently more time elapses and the duration is therefore longer. Because the latter observes very little change, by contrast, the duration of the event is very short.

An objection to this position is that in allowing for this divine sequencing, I have represented Berkeley as re-introducing an objective time-line which all finite spirits can occupy. How does this square with Berkeley's subjectivizing of time? For Berkeley, temporal duration is a function of the subjective succession of ideas. An objective ordering of ideas is not the same as there being an objective duration of each of those ideas. Any ordering of events which appeals to time units will fail. While the ordering can tell us that the Fall occurred before the Flood, it cannot tell us how long the Flood lasted or how long the Fall took. The Scriptures teach us that it rained for forty days and forty nights. Howsoever true this may be, the measurements themselves appeal to events which occur in the Course of Nature. But how long does it take for the Earth to spin on its axis? The actual temporal duration of the time in between the Sun's rising and setting is not to be determined by appeal to further events within the Course of Nature. The duration is to be determined by the succession of ideas within a finite mind. For one person those forty days and forty nights might have been exceptionally long, for another person they might have passed rather quickly.

Because of this, a man (following Johnson's example, call him John)[28] can say that events actually occurred while he was sleeping. He can admit that he slept for an entire day during which many things took place. He would be admitting that there are certain ordered ideas in the mind of God that other people perceived while he was unconscious. One might say that there were certain events in the Course of Nature which he did not witness or attend (i.e. at which he did not exist). In this way it would look as though John had an intermittent existence (or at least that his spirit was intermittent, while his body continued on).

Fortunately, while these events may have had some duration for others, they had no duration for John. In other words, since the events that John missed had no duration for him, his failure to perceive them constituted no gap in his existence. Johnson, who is watching John sleep, can say the very same thing.[29] He can say that John does not exist during a sequence of events which occur in between two states of wakefulness. By this he can mean that there are certain events which his friend does not perceive. Johnson can also recognize that the duration of the events is ultimately relative to the perceiver. So while the events have some duration for him, they have no duration for John who has slept through them. In other words, while it is true that John does not exist while he (or rather his body) is sleeping, the period of his sleeping has no duration for John, and consequently his non-existence during that period is of no consequence (to him).

This is why Berkeley writes: 'Certainly the mind always & constantly thinks & we know this too In Sleep & trances *the mind exists not* there is no time no succession of ideas' (PC 651, my emphasis). Some commentators have represented this comment as a mistake.[30] On the contrary, it brings out the true paradoxical nature of Berkeley's claim that the resurrection follows the next moment after death.[31] One may have a gappy existence insofar as there are a great many events one does not witness (i.e. at which one does not exist), which are nonetheless attended by many others during the period between death and resurrection. Since these events are of no duration for one, no time passes at all between one's death and resurrection, and resurrection follows immediately upon one's death.

The account points to the radically different ways in which spirits and ideas are related to the course of nature and time. The sensible ideas are part of the Course of Nature. They are elements in an objectively ordered history of natural bodies which come to be and which pass away. But while these ideas constitute the Course of Nature, a spirit witnesses various different sections of the Course without itself being part of it. It is to some extent because spirits are not constituents of the Course of Nature but perceivers of it, that they are shown to be naturally immortal. Their relationship to the history of the world is fundamentally different from sensible ideas.

What drives this important difference between spirits and ideas is Berkeley's rejection of mode ontology. The variable elements of consciousness are no longer modes of mind or acts of thinking; they are things in their own right. So there is a sense in which spirit does not undergo change. There are no intrinsic changes in spirit. Spirits are now 'apart' from the changes in a way that they had not been before.

This is important in addressing concerns that naturally arise with Berkeley's account. Insofar as the 'I' is nothing other than what is revealed in self-consciousness, one might worry that since the consciousness that accompanies all thoughts is as variable as the thought itself, the 'I' will be a numerically distinct representation with each passing thought.

These problems do not arise on Berkeley's account since the substance–mode account of thought has been rejected. Numerically one 'I' is 'present' at various different events insofar as it perceives certain ideas which constitute the Course of Nature. The only changes are changes in ideas, not spirit itself which undergoes no intrinsic changes such as supposed in the preceding concerns. Indeed, the entire issue of establishing whether spirit S1 at time t1 is the same is spirit S2 at t2, is to formulate things inappropriately in Berkeley's account. Berkeley is not saying that S1 and S2 are the same just in case S2 is responsible for the actions for which S1 is responsible. One proceeds with numerically one agent, which may then exist at various different events insofar as it witnesses them. Agents do not continue to exist in or through time. Rather, they perceive various moments of time. They have eternal life in case the succession of ideas is infinite, mortal life in case the succession is finite. They are not numerically identical over time, so much as numerically identical prior to time as the required center of temporal elapse. Because of this they are not fleeting or perishable in the way that ideas are. Johnson's concern that *esse* is *percipere* undermines the natural immortality of the soul is turned on its head.

An important upshot is that Berkeley can be viewed as offering an elegant way to elucidate what had been abandoned by Locke, Clarke, Collins, Browne, and King – an understanding of the eternal now as a permanent instant. Johnson tells Berkeley that he cannot understand the eternal now except in terms of Clarke's claim that God knows everything at once. At any point in time, God knows everything that has been, is, and will be as if it were present to him.

For Berkeley this becomes the very explanation for what it means to say that God is outside time: 'By the *τὸ νῦν* I suppose to be implied that all things, past and to come, are actually present to the mind of God, and that there is in Him no change, variation, or succession. A succession of ideas I take to *constitute* Time . . . .'[32] If it is possible to conceive of God perceiving all ideas (past, present, and future) without change or succession (as Clarke allows) then, in Berkeley's view we have successfully conceived of God's atemporality.

Insofar as no time passes for God (there is no succession) and he comprehends everything in the ordered Course of Nature, we can likewise conceptualize how God is at every point in time whole. God perceives all of the ideas which constitute the Course of Nature at once, just as finite perceivers perceive some of these ideas successively. As finite perceivers exist at certain events, God exists at all of the events which occur in the Course of Nature (he perceives them). Berkeley thereby allows us to understand God's eternity (like his infinite power) in a way that goes beyond mere augmentation (in this case, infinite succession).

Moreover, Berkeley is in a good position to accommodate Stillingfleet's mystery how the eternity of God is reconcilable with his many successive actions. While we can conceive of God's eternity in terms of his successionless perception of the entire course of nature, we must accordingly conceive of all actions as occurring in time (3D III 254). This is not radical, since Aquinas allowed that certain names (importing relations to creatures) were applied to God temporally (names such as 'Creator').[33] Thus, God's divine activity *outside of time* is, for Berkeley, a genuine mystery. Philonous remarks, 'God is a being of transcendent and unlimited perfections: his nature, therefore, is incomprehensible to finite spirits' (3D III 254).[34] This makes sense. To understand God's agency as it is in itself (rather than as it relates to us) would be to understand God's very existence. This is something Berkeley would not countenance.

Yet while we may be under an obligation to conceive of God's actions as performed in time, it does not follow from this that we must conceive of God as undergoing any genuine succession. For we do not undergo any real succession. The only changes we perceive are in the objects we perceive. We can be said to undergo a change insofar as 'something new befalls us' (3D III 254). But this is only a relational change, and it is an imperfection only insofar as it entails that we are in time.

This brings us to Berkeley's reconciliation of divine prescience with human liberty. The problem is not one easily solved by *any* philosopher. Yet one of the difficulties which appeared to make this problem especially vexing was the inability to conceive the *τὸ νῦν*. Unless God atemporally perceives all things at once, it seems hard to conceive how he could know human action in advance without undermining human liberty. Clarke, distinguishing certainty and necessity, thought that it sufficed that God know everything that is to happen before it does happen (just as human beings can sometimes know what somebody is going to do before they do it).[35] In this way, he hoped to make sense of the *τὸ νῦν* without any appeal to the *punctum stans*. Yet short of positing God's knowledge of causal preconditions, it is a little mysterious how God should secure certain knowledge of contingent events in the future.[36] Once God exists outside of time and can perceive all at once, however, it is easier to conceive how God could know a contingent action without knowing a causal precondition. So in showing how this can be conceptualized, Berkeley achieves something of importance.

Chapter Seven

The Spirit and the Heap

While Berkeley's rejection of material substance involves a complete rejection of substance–mode ontology, this does not lead to a rejection of spiritual substance. Berkeley adopts a new account of substance which exhibits important features of substance. In many ways it is disanalogous from the traditional model. Ideas do not have a proprietary but a perceptual dependence, spirit–idea ontology is a robust dualism, spirits don't individuate ideas, spirits undergo no intrinsic changes. Consequently, one is hard pressed to see how Berkeley in any way remains a part of the older substance–mode tradition. Yet spirits are nonetheless basic supports and causes of ideas as well as the abiding persistents through variation. They possess key distinguishing features of substance. The concern that Berkeley's account of spirit is incoherent has been answered. In destroying the older model of substance, Berkeley has created a new one.

The concern has been answered without appeal to Berkeley's alleged 1734 introduction of 'notion' or the two exchanges between Philonous and Hylas. Since one is conscious of one's existence, one has empirical grounds for endorsing the existence of spirit. Moreover, one has the 'mental content' requisite for providing the term 'spirit' with significance. Other words (denoting mental operations) can be given content in terms of cause, subject, effect, and circumstance. It is one's awareness of oneself as an active thing which provides the anchor for the preceding, allowing mental operations to be viewed as relations between oneself and one's ideas.

In what follows I briefly examine these 1734 revisions. Then, I turn to Hume's views about the mind. In the traditional story, Hume (unlike Berkeley) realized that spiritual substance must go the way of material substance. Given that Berkeley's account has been vindicated from this incoherence, it is worth re-examining Hume's views.

Part I: The 1734 Revisions

Notions

It is probably his interaction with Browne which prompted Berkeley to add the allegedly more technical 'notion' into both the 1734 editions of the *Principles* and *Dialogues*.[1] Berkeley acquiesces in his letter to Browne, 'I am wedded to no party, and bigoted to no expressions, and to begin by an instance of compliance, I'll give up the hateful word idea, to be used as your Lordship shall think fit' (386). Moreover, it is likely that Baxter's remarks in his 1733 *Enquiry into the Nature of the Human Soul* also played some role in this change. Baxter draws attention to Berkeley's denial we have an idea or notion of spirit. He claims that if this is so, then '. . . it seems impossible that such a thing [spirit] could ever have entered into the thoughts of men' (259, my insert).

In the 1734 revisions, Berkeley alters any passage where he denies that there is notion of spirit (PHK I 138, 139); he adds passages alleging that while he lacks an idea of spirit (and its operations), he nonetheless possesses some notion of them (PHK I 27, 89, 140, 142); and he adds two new exchanges between Philonous and Hylas in which the word 'notion' recurs.

The word 'notion' is used by Berkeley in three interrelated ways.[2] First, Berkeley uses 'notion' as virtually equivalent to 'definition' (1st ed. PHK I 9, 3rd ed. 3D III 233). Here there is a distinction between idea (or any mental conception) and a 'notion.' Consider Berkeley's contrast between the definition of a triangle as 'a plane figure comprehended by three right lines' and the various ideas to which the term 'triangle' applies (while the definition is fixed, there is no one determinate signification) (PHK Intro 18). The former concerns the explication of words through words. Given Berkeley's views about 'grace,' 'discourse,' and 'force' it is clear not all definable words have ideas/mental conceptions affixed to them.

Second, one can 'have a notion of something' just in case one has 'some knowledge' of it (1st ed. 3D III 231–2, 2nd ed. PHK I 142). For example, one can have knowledge of something 'insofar as one understands the meaning of the words.' For Berkeley this is often the justification for claiming that we have 'some notion' of spirit and its operations in the 2nd edition of the *Principles* and his justification for saying that we have an idea of spirit (in a large sense) in the first. This way of possessing 'some knowledge' (some notion) suggests that one can explicate the meaning of the word by providing a definition (a notion) of it. Yet it also seems that 'having a notion' (as defined as 'some knowledge') may include knowledge of ideas. One has 'some notion' of a triangle insofar as the general (not abstract) idea of a triangle is an object of perception.

Finally, 'notion' is used as a virtual synonym for 'idea' (in the narrow sense) (1st ed. PHK I 25, 138, 139). In such uses a notion is an object of understanding (a variable element of consciousness), and so a pre-linguistic mental conception which provides content to terms. If I am correct that Berkeley uses 'notion' in something like Browne's sense at PHK 143, then despite the heralded alterations, even this third use of 'notion' remains in play in the 1734 editions as a kind of residue.

Far from introducing a technical term, at any rate, Berkeley is restricting the application of a term that continues to be used in a relatively loose way.[3] Indeed, there is no distinctive use which is particular to active things (to spirits distinctively and exclusively). The closest Berkeley comes to such as suggestion is the following: '. . . all relations including an act of the mind, we cannot so properly be said to have an idea, but rather a notion of the relations or habitudes between things' (PHK I 142).[4] But this is supposed to be a reason for denying that we have an idea of relations. As the rest of the section suggests we have 'some notion' ('some knowledge') of relations insofar as we understand the meaning of the words. This does not rule out the fact that one can have 'some notion' of a triangle, too, by way of idea.

Yet in restricting the use of 'notion' Berkeley is able to answer both Browne's and Baxter's concerns. Baxter was worried that either Berkeley was denying that spirit was an object of the understanding or departing from Locke and Descartes in his usage of 'idea' by restricting it to sensible and imagined ideas. Browne had the theological worry (shared by Stillingfleet) that the modern use of the word 'idea' was too broad (extending beyond sensible ideas). And in saying that we have a notion (but not an idea) of spirit and its operations he answers Baxter's worry that spirit is not an object of understanding. In doing so, Berkeley comes down on the side of the theologians, by restricting the usage of 'idea.' He says, 'But if in the modern way the word *idea* is extended to spirits, and relations and acts; this is after all an affair or verbal concern' (PHK I 142).

There is no modification in Berkeley's view, however, since he continues to maintain that spirits (and their operations) are not objects of understanding. Neither is he claiming we have any mental conceptions besides imagined and sensible ideas which provide mental terms such as 'discourse' with content. Instead, there can be a 'notion' of the word 'discourse' despite the fact that there is no internal mental conception of it at all (*pace* Browne). If this is right, Berkeley's introduction of the word 'notion' is hardly the deployment of a technical device or a doctrine designed to salvage his account so much as a quick cover-up.

Hylas's Two Objections[5]

According to the first concern raised by Hylas, material substance is rejected because there is no idea or 'notion of it' ('some knowledge'), and therefore spiritual substance ought to be rejected as well because there is no idea of it either (3D III 232). Philonous responds as follows.

First, he claims that he does not reject material substance merely because he has no notion of it, but because the notion of it is inconsistent. He rephrases the inconsistency as the impossibility that there be a notion. The confusing use of the term 'notion' reflects Berkeley's ambivalence about its meaning. Berkeley is pointing out that he rejects material substance because in the very 'notion or definition' there is included an inconsistency. Berkeley is faithful to his argument. At section 9 of the *Principles* he writes, 'Hence, it is plain, that the very notion of what is called *matter* or *corporeal substance*, involves a contradiction in it.' And early in the *Dialogues*, Philonous uses similar concerns against Hylas.

The point is that because the definition of 'material substance' includes a contradiction in terms, so there can be no 'notion' of it ('knowledge'). But Philonous claims there is no such contradiction in the definition of spirit since '... it is no repugnancy to say, that a perceiving thing should be the subject of ideas ...' (3D III 233). He says that many things may exist even though we lack ideas or 'notions' ('some knowledge') of them, however their definitions must be consistent.

Philonous adds that while we may believe in the existence of something without perceiving it, we must have grounds to make an inference (either by necessary consequence or a probable deduction). We have no reason for concluding the existence of matter, while we do have a reason to infer the existence of other finite spirits. We infer other finite spirits, since the signs and effects which we perceive (of a human body) give probable evidence of an intelligent finite being as cause of the bodily motions we perceive. But since ideas are not viewed as accidents, there is no necessity in concluding a substratum. And since material substance cannot be a cause, there is no reason to conclude it from the sensible ideas as effects. Philonous ends by noting that he has a notion of spirit. He points out that while we lack an idea of spirit and do not know it by means of an idea, nonetheless we 'know it by reflection.' Berkeley's point is that we have 'some knowledge' of what a spirit is by discursively thinking about ourselves (explicating the meaning of the relevant words) and through the internal awareness that we have of our own existence as active beings.

Hylas' second concern is that according to Philonous' principles it ought to follow that he is only 'a system of floating ideas, without any substance to support them' (3D III 233). 'Words are not to be used without a meaning,' he complains '... there is no more meaning in spiritual substance than material substance ....' Philonous' first response is that one's existence is available to consciousness and there is some knowledge of what we are (a thing that thinks, perceives, wills, etc.). 'But,' says Philonous, 'I am not in like manner conscious either of the existence or essence of matter.' (234)

Philonous then provides what looks to be an argument that he is distinct from his ideas: (1) I (one and the same self) perceive both colours and sounds; (2) Colours cannot perceive sounds and sounds cannot perceive colours; therefore (3) I am one individual principle distinct from colours and sounds. The point is that a system of ideas can't perceive colours and sounds. The only possibility is that I am either a colour or a sound, which is absurd, so I must be distinct from my ideas.[6]

Philonous concludes by addressing the vacuity of the expression 'spiritual substance' by pointing out that while he knows what he means when he affirms that spirits are substances (they perceive ideas), he does not know what is meant when it is said that material substance has ideas (or archetypes) inherent in it. It is a bit odd that the issue now is the vacuity of the expression 'material substance,' when earlier the concern was that it was a contradiction in terms. The reason is that 'material substance' is only a contradiction in terms if 'inherence' is vacuous. For Locke sensible qualities may be viewed as modifications of matter. It is only by rejecting the latter way of viewing sensible things that enables Berkeley to force a contradiction.[7]

Hylas' first objection may have been inspired by Baxter's objections. Baxter mistakenly believed that Berkeley allowed that material substance was not a contradiction in terms (so this would be an important corrective). And he raised the parity of reasoning worry that as Berkeley was not entitled to conclude a material substance on the basis of the qualities perceived, so too, Berkeley could not infer the existence of any other spirits. He also worried about Berkeley's denial that there was an idea or notion of spirit.[8]

Hylas' second objection, however, seems to have originated from Berkeley himself, who had considered such objections in his own earlier notebooks.[9] For example, Berkeley writes:

> Say you the Mind is not the Perceptions. But that thing wh^{ch} perceives. I answer you are abus'd by the words that & thing these are vague empty words without a meaning. (PC 581)

This raises interesting questions. Did Berkeley at some early point *accept* the objection posed by Hylas? And if so, why did he change his mind?[10]

It is worth noting that at PC 523, Berkeley has already remarked 'It seems improper & liable to difficulties to make the Word Person stand for an Idea, or to make ourselves Ideas or thinking things ideas' after noting that for Locke knowledge is only about ideas (PC 522). He also affirms at PC 547 and 563 that we have an intuitive knowledge of our own existence distinct from that of our ideas. Does Berkeley no longer accept 'thinking thing' as intelligible? Note that at PC 672, Berkeley responds to the claim that there is no idea of 'the unknown substratum of Volitions & Ideas' by arguing that there can be no such idea unless the substratum is itself, absurdly, an idea (echoing the view endorsed at PC 523).

The proto-Humean passages (PC 577, 578, 579, 580, 581) begin 'We think we know not the Soul because we have no imaginable or sensible Idea annex'd to that sound. This the Effect of prejudice' (PC 576). This suggests that in what follows, Berkeley is speaking in the voice of his opponents. It is a voice which says that words are *only* significant if they have ideas annexed to them. To be sure the *verso* entry 576a may seem to undermine this interpretation:

> Certainly we do not know it. This will be plain if we examine what we mean by the word knowledge. Neither doth this argue any defect in our knowledge no more than our not knowing a contradiction. (PC 576a)

Yet I would venture that it needs to be understood in terms of subsequent entries such as this: 'If by Idea you mean object of the Understanding. Then certainly the Will is no Idea, or we have no idea annext to the word Will' (PC 665). Note that 576a is actually an earlier formulation of Berkeley's response to Malebranche. If so, caution is needed with respect to the view that Berkeley ever maintained a congeries account of the soul. The issue is complicated by Berkeley's developing views about self-knowledge

Part Two: Hume and the Traditional Worry

The concern that in rejecting material substance, Berkeley must reject spiritual substance is connected to the view that Berkeley rejects material substance because it cannot be perceived and/or because there is no idea of it. Turbayne remarks, 'But this concept of mind is inconsistent with the rest of Berkeley's system. He should have suffered the gravest embarrassment in retaining mental substance, although it is unperceivable, and in rejecting material substance, because it is unperceivable . . . .'[11] We need to recognize that this argument is not one that Berkeley ever made.[12] Philonous is happy to allow Hylas to infer the existence of material substratum. The problem is not that he can't perceive it but that the notion of inherence is vacuous.

The irony is that this misreading of Berkeley has obscured the importance of his claim that spirits cannot be perceived. Far from an embarrassment, this is a central thesis that reflects Berkeley's denial that ideas are states of mind and his emphasis on the distinction between consciousness of ideas and consciousness of oneself. It is fundamental to understanding his answer to the concern that we lack an idea of spirit. It is fundamental to understanding his very ontology. It is entirely missed as a consequence of this reading.

One reason for this misunderstanding is that Berkeley is often read through Hume. The inability to perceive substance and our lack of an idea of it is central to Hume's rejection of both material and spiritual substance. The interesting question is this: Given Berkeley's account of spirit has survived any parity of reasoning concerns, how is Hume supposed to have responded to it?

The question is important given that it has been established beyond doubt that Hume read Berkeley and was influenced by him in important ways. The worry that Hume didn't read Berkeley was raised by Richard Popkin. And while somewhat extreme, the worry was important in combating the crude caricature of an empiricist triumvirate according to which Hume is the successor of Berkeley and informed almost exclusively by his predecessor's thought. Since then, we have clear documentation of the fact that Hume read Berkeley prior to the completion of the *Treatise*.[13]

Of course, we also have internal evidence of the influence. In one of his three published references to Berkeley,[14] Hume recognizes him as ' a great philosopher' and praises Berkeley's views on abstraction as '... one of the greatest and most valuable discoveries that has been made of late years in the Republic of Letters ...' (T. 1.1.7.1, 17; SBN 17).[15] Additionally, both Ayers and Raynor have defended the importance of Berkeley's doctrine of *minima sensibilia* for Hume.[16] Hall and Ayers have defended Hume's use of the notion of 'outness.'[17] Ayers points to the importance of the vulgar view–philosophical view dialectic in both Berkeley and Hume.[18] And Raynor has defended Hume's appeal to Berkeley's argument that primary qualities cannot be abstracted from secondary qualities, and so must be equally mind-dependent (T. I.4.4.8, 150 and ECU 12.15, 202–3; SBNE 155).[19,20,21]

Given that Hume was influenced by Berkeley, the question of how Hume responds to Berkeley's account of spirit is an important question about the nature of the relationship between Berkeley's philosophy and Hume's. Since the old story about the triumvirate has been cleared away, we ought to reassess Hume's response to Berkeley. It has already been suggested by Raynor that Hume's own account of the mind may have been inspired by the second of the two 1734 exchanges.[22] The question I wish to ask is why

Hume adopted that account of mind. Did Hume reject Berkeley's account of spirit because he thought it was incoherent? Did Hume misunderstand Berkeley's account of the mind as somehow contrary to empiricist principles?[23] Or did Hume have something more interesting to say?

That the latter might be the case is suggested by one of his three published references to Berkeley:

> . . . most of the writings of that very ingenious author [Berkeley] form the best lessons of scepticism, which are to be found . . . Bayle not excepted. He professes, however, in his title-page (and undoubtedly with great truth) to have composed his book against the sceptics as well as against the atheists and free-thinkers. But that all his arguments, though otherwise intended, are, in reality, merely sceptical, appears from this, *that they admit of no answer and produce no conviction.* Their only effect is to cause that momentary amazement and irresolution and confusion, which is the result of scepticism. (EHU 12.15, 203, note 38, SBNE 155)

This is perverse high praise, elevating Berkeley above Bayle.[24] Note that Hume doesn't identify Berkeley's arguments as sceptical on the grounds that they lead to a kind of egoism. Hume labels Berkeley's arguments sceptical on these grounds alone: That they admit of no answer and produce no conviction.

As Raynor has argued, Hume has Berkeley's *Dialogues* in mind in this passage.[25] And when Hylas and Philonous dispute the meaning of the word 'scepticism,' it is expanded beyond doubting everything (3D I 172) to '. . . distrusting the senses . . . denying the real existence of things, or pretending to know nothing of them' (3D I 173). So it is appropriate that Hume should define it in a new way as well. Indeed, as Raynor observes,[26] Hume's remarks draw on Hylas himself who says:

> To deal frankly with you, Philonous, your arguments seem in themselves unanswerable, but they have not so great an effect on me as to produce that entire conviction, that hearty acquiescence which attends demonstration. (3D II 223)

Note, also, that Hume recognizes Berkeley's arguments as *unanswerable.* Surely this is a far cry from the view that Hume corrects Berkeley's elementary blunder. And I do think that there is some considerable earnestness in Hume's remarks that can be seen in the peculiar status that Berkeley appears to occupy in his earlier *Treatise.*

For while it seems that Berkeley exerted a considerable influence upon Hume, it also seems there is something to Popkin's query '. . . why is there so little trace of Berkeley in Hume's writings?'.[27] Berkeley is simply not a central target for Hume for all of that influence. There is a tension between Hume's esteem for Berkeley and the absence of direct engagement with Berkeley as a significant opponent.

Consider that the only vehicles of cognition Hume allows are perceptions. This starting move excludes the possibility of the consciousness to which Berkeley lays claim (non-perceptual consciousness of one's own being). This is hardly inconsequential, since Berkeley departs from his predecessors in this particular. Yet there is no argument for Hume's exclusionary move. It constitutes a presupposition of the theory.

Consider as well that for Hume, perceptions are like mental states or episodes. He does not view them as the modes or accidents of the older ontology; and this raises the interesting question just what they are for Hume. The important point is that they constitute elements of the mind. As part of his starting point, Hume has rejected Berkeley's view that minds and ideas are 'entirely distinct.'

Now note the following passage in Hume's Introduction to the *Treatise*:

> I do not think a philosopher, who wou'd apply himself so earnestly to the explaining the ultimate principles of the soul, wou'd show himself a great master in that very science of human nature, which he pretends to explain, or very knowing in what is naturally satisfactory to the mind of man. For nothing is more certain, than that despair has almost the same effect upon us with enjoyment, and that we are no sooner acquainted with the impossibility of satisfying any desire, than the desire itself vanishes. When we see, that we have arriv'd at the utmost extent of human reason, we sit down contented .... (T Introduction 9, 5, SBN xvii–xviii)

While Hume writes 'we sit down contended,' Berkeley complained 'we sit down in a forelorn scepticism' in apparent response to Locke's proposal that 'we sit down in quiet ignorance.' Is Hume's allusion accidental? It seems hard to believe, since Berkeley complained that God should give us a desire for knowledge and then place it out of reach; Hume gives a response in this passage: Once we realize that the desire can't be satisfied, the desire goes away. Recall that in the *Dialogues* the definition of scepticism is expanded to include pretending to an ignorance of things (see 3D III 228), a definition which applies to Locke's ignorance of the real nature of things – the very sort of ignorance that Hume is here espousing.

The remark has a bearing on Berkeley's views about our desire for immortality and our desire to know whether the soul is immortal. Hume's accusation is that the philosopher who attempts to discover 'ultimate principles' does not show himself very knowledgeable about human nature. This fits nicely with Hume's view that Berkeley's conclusions fail to produce conviction. Unlike Berkeley, Hume is initiating a broad inquiry into human nature; it is not one which reaches for the 'ultimate principles':

> For to me it seems evident, that the essence of the mind being equally unknown to us with that of external bodies, it must be equally impossible to form any notion of its powers and qualities otherwise than from careful and exact experiments, and the observation of those particular effects . . . 'tis still certain we cannot go beyond experience; and any hypothesis, that pretends to discover the ultimate original qualities of human nature, ought at first to be rejected as presumptuous and chimerical. (T Intro 8, 5, SBN xvii)

Hume simply assumes the essence of the mind is unknown. Berkeley thought otherwise. For Berkeley, once we have established that spirit is an active, perceiving thing nothing further can be known; knowledge of the mind is complete. Hume's starting assumption that what Berkeley called ideas are 'perceptions' enables him to turn knowledge of perceptions into knowledge of mind, and so Berkeley's attempt to find ultimate principles is rejected.

Owing to his conception of the mind, Hume can place us in much the situation that Locke had left us; we cannot obtain scientific (universal and necessary) knowledge of the mind. The ultimate principles would be those which went beyond what we experience; and we may only obtain what Locke calls experimental knowledge. One wonders, however, what is to be said about Berkeley's non-perceptual awareness of the self's existence (the 'I'), grounding his own account of the mind. For this has something like the status of an empirical datum.

Let's consider Hume's arguments. Hume explicitly initiates a broad attack on competing conceptions of mind in the section 'Of the immateriality of the soul.' Hume uses the term 'mind' and 'soul' broadly to apply to his own bundle of perceptions as well as the conception of anything which stands in contrast to his own.[28] Here, Hume takes issue with more traditional conceptions according to which mind is a substance on which perceptions ontologically depend for their existence. He argues against the 'curious reasoners' concerning the question whether perceptions inhere in material or immaterial substance; his own answer is that the very question is unintelligible since there is no relevant idea of substance.

In the section 'Of personal identity' Hume argues against a simple and continued self. By simple, Hume means that the self admits of no separation, and cannot be distinguished into parts; by abiding Hume means that the self does not undergo any variation. This is virtually the first time that Hume deploys the expression 'self' and the fact that he considers it in a section distinct from the preceding indicates his care in distinguishing it from 'substance.'[29] It seems clear that he is using it in a specifically philosophical way that was pioneered by Locke.[30]

The argument Hume deploys in both sections (and the one he applies throughout the *Treatise* rather frequently) runs as follows: First, Hume denies that there is any impression of the target item. He then appeals to his principle (T 1.4.6.2, 164, SBN 251): 'It must be some one impression that gives rise to every real idea,' concluding that there is no idea of it. And finally, while he tends not to mention this important assumption, Hume appeals to the thesis that terms require annexed ideas in order to count as intelligible. He concludes that the target item is a kind of nonsense.

The semantic principle which Hume relies on is one which Berkeley explicitly rejects. Yet this is a principle which Hume at no point bothers to defend. Moreover, when Hume initially runs this argument against the soul as supporting substance and then against the simple and continued self, he stops at the conclusion that there is no idea of the item, leaving the semantic commitment unspoken. The conclusion that Hume explicitly reaches against the soul and self could not be expected to rule out Berkeleian spirit, since Berkeley would have agreed with the conclusion in both cases.

More strikingly, while Hume seems mainly happy to deny that as a matter of fact there is any such impression he also flirts with Berkeley-style arguments to the effect that there could not be such an impression. In 'Of the immateriality of the soul' Hume argues that it is very difficult, if not impossible to conceive of an impression of soul-substance: 'For how can an impression represent a substance, otherwise than by resembling it? And how can an impression resemble a substance, since, according to this philosophy, it is not a substance, and is one of the peculiar qualities or characteristics of a substance?' (T 1.4.5.3, 153, SBN 233).[31]

According to the target view, impressions are not substances (they are different from them). Consequently they cannot resemble substances, and so cannot constitute likenesses of substance. This is a line of reasoning straight out of Berkeley's work. According to Berkeley, ideas cannot resemble spirits because the two are so unlike.[32]

Arguably, a similar flirtation with Berkeleian reasoning appears in 'Of personal identity': 'For from what impression cou'd this idea be deriv'd? This question 'tis impossible to answer without a manifest contradiction and absurdity . . . self or person is not any one impression, but that to which our several impressions and ideas are suppos'd to have a reference'

(T 1.4.6.2, 164, SBN 251). It is hard to spot the absurdity. Hume goes on in the passage to note that an impression of a simple, abiding self ought to continue constant and invariable, while there is no such constant impression. Yet this hardly seems like an absurdity since it is at least possible that an impression should continue constant and uninterrupted.

I suspect the absurdity does not concern constancy but the fact that impressions are supposed to have a reference to self in the first place. The following remarks about constancy would not contribute to the absurdity claim so much as help establish the empirical claim that there is, in fact, no impression. Instead, Hume is tacitly relying on the same sort of reasoning which he has already used. For a simple and abiding impression to represent a simple and abiding self, the self would have to be sufficiently similar to that impression to be represented by it. In the target view, a self is not an impression but that to which impressions are referred (hence it is different). Hume once again appears to appeal to a Berkeley-style argument to reach a conclusion which Berkeley would have accepted.

If Hume's main arguments against the soul as substance and the simple, abiding self are arguments which reach conclusions that Berkeley would have accepted, how does Hume address Berkeley? The closest Hume comes to addressing Berkeley in the main body of the *Treatise* is not in any of these sections, but the earlier section 'Of scepticism with regard to the senses.' Here Hume undertakes to show that the *appearance of a perception in the mind* is distinct from the *existence of a perception*. He does this to undermine the apparent contradiction that a perception exists 'without being present to the mind.' He then provides an account of what it means to say that an object (a perception) becomes present to the mind. For Hume, this amounts to the fact that the perception makes a causal impact upon the bundle. To be conscious of a perception is for the perception to make a causal impact upon the bundle. Hume's point is to show that the beliefs of the vulgar (namely that objects exist without being present to the mind) are at least coherent (although false).[33] Two remarks are in order.

First, Hume is fairly clear about the nature of Berkeleian mind-dependence. The question is not whether a perception (*qua* mode) can exist without a substance in which to inhere. The 'palpable contradiction' is that a thought should exist without 'appearing in the mind.' What Hume is interested to combat is the widely held view that there is no such thing as a thought absent from conscious awareness.

Second, his strategy in solving this problem begs the question against Berkeley. He asserts that the mind is a heap of perceptions and therefore a perception can exist without appearing in the mind insofar as it can be broken off from the causally connected heap.

Curiously, an argument nowhere to be found in the *Treatise* appears in Hume's Appendix retraction where he is supposed to be summarizing the arguments that led him to view the mind and self as a bundle of perceptions in the first place: According to the doctrine of the philosophers, when one views a table and a chimney, nothing is present but perceptions. Yet according to the doctrine of the vulgar, the table and chimney can and do exist separately (independent of the mind). The doctrine of the vulgar 'implies no contradiction.' Therefore, the view that perceptions can and do exist independent of the mind likewise implies no contradiction.

This is clearly an argument against Berkeley. It parallels Philonous' concluding remarks in the *Dialogues* that he is for reconciling the views of the vulgar and philosophical (3D III 262).[34] However, it is noteworthy that it should appear (for the first time) when Hume is rehearsing his reasons for coming to doubt his own account of the self. It is likewise noteworthy that Hume should finally, for the first time, explicitly state the semantic principle behind his main argument (T. Appendix 11, 399, SBN 633).

Had Hume supposed that Berkeley's own account was incoherent (i.e. that Berkeley's own principles led to a Humean account of the mind), it is very hard to understand why an argument of this type should appear in the Appendix at all. It would be wholly unnecessary. Yet it does appear, and it appears well before Hume remarks:

> Philosophers begin to be reconcil'd to the principle, *that we have no idea of external substance, distinct from the ideas of particular qualities*. This must pave the way for a like principle with regard to the mind, *that we have no notion of it, distinct from the particular perceptions*. (T. Appendix 19. 400, SBN 635)

These remarks are the culmination of a barrage of arguments. What this suggests is that Hume does not merely dismiss Berkeley's account as incoherent.

If Hume thought that Berkeley was by his own principles obliged to view the mind as a bundle of perceptions or ideas, it is hard to see why he would have ever called Berkeley's arguments unanswerable in the *Enquiry*. The bundle account of mind is precisely what allows the appearance of a perception (in the mind) and its existence to come apart.

If Berkeley's own views led inevitably to this Humean account, then the *esse* is *percipi* principle would have failed Berkeley even with respect to thoughts. Given that *esse* is *percipi* is the backbone of Berkeleian metaphysics, however, it becomes unfathomable that Hume should ever say that Berkeley's arguments are unanswerable.

On the contrary, Hume understands that Berkeleian mind-dependence hinges on 'appearance in the mind.' He also understands that intuitions are on Berkeley's side with respect to the connection between the existence of perceptions and appearance in the mind. He realizes that he needs to explain away this 'palpable contradiction' and it is precisely his own account of the mind which facilitates such an explanation.

Hume cannot endorse his own account of the mind without further ado. In rejecting Berkeley's perceiving agent, Hume needs to explain how it is that perceptions can comprise a kind of mental system, and how the system can perceive perceptions. It is through his own account of causation that Hume is enabled to accomplish this. It allows him to say that one perception causes another; it allows him to 'link' the perceptions together in a system. He can thereby say that a perception is perceived just in case it makes a causal impact upon the system.[35]

What these facts add up to is that Berkeley's conception of spirit is *a looming background presence* in Hume's *Treatise*. The main arguments that Hume uses against soul as substance/self as simple and abiding do not apply to Berkeley at all, but rather *use* Berkeley in ways that are antithetical to his own purposes. The importance of Berkeley's views to Hume's account of the mind/self arise only outside of the main body of the *Treatise*, precisely when Hume is worried about his own account. And Berkeley's views enjoy the status of never once being argued against, but rather rejected at the starting point from which Hume proceeds.

Even the argument that Hume provides in the Appendix begs the question. Hume begins with the assumption that Berkeley's view that the objects we perceive cannot exist without a mind is false, and then concludes from this the same must true for perceptions themselves. The only account which can accommodate this conclusion, is Hume's own conception of the mind. Hume's adoption of a bundle account of the mind is, in part, supported by his initial rejection of the Berkeleian conclusion that sensible things are mind-dependent.

My hypothesis is that Hume nowhere attempts to refute Berkeley since he does not think that Berkeley can be refuted. Instead, Hume takes the failure of Berkeley's arguments to produce conviction as sufficient to brand him a sceptic. He proceeds on the assumption that while Berkeley's arguments cannot be refuted, he is nonetheless wrong. By assuming that the vulgar opinion is not contradictory, Hume is led to reject a basic Berkeleian premise (which was shared by many philosophers), namely that thoughts cannot exist except insofar as they are immediately perceived by the mind. This necessarily paves the way for Hume's account of the mind.

Berkeley and Hume proceed from very different starting points. Hume endorses, while Berkeley rejects, the Lockean view that significant (categorematic) terms require annexed ideas. More deeply, they undertake philosophical projects which are radically opposed to each other. Berkeley is engaged in the motivational project of restoring philosophers to virtue by dissolving scepticism, establishing the existence of God, and demonstrating the immortality of the soul. Instead of motivating human conduct, Hume is engaged in the scientific project of explaining human nature in the tradition of Newton; or as Hume puts it to 'anatomize human nature in a regular manner.'[36] For Hume, unlike Berkeley, scepticism has an important role to play in inducing modesty and limiting the scope of inquiry.[37]

In this way, Berkeley occupies a peculiar place in Hume's system. While Hume holds Berkeley in the highest esteem, he takes the falsity of Berkeley's system as his own starting point. This does not prevent Hume from drawing on Berkeley in important ways. What it does mean is that when Berkeley is used, he is used in ways that are largely antithetical to his own project.

Yet the dispute does not remain a stand-off. Berkeley wants to motivate men to action by his work. So the irrefutability of his arguments is no consolation given Hume's (surely correct) assessment that they nonetheless fail to induce belief. If Berkeley wants to restore men to common sense by answering perplexity and scepticism, he has failed; Hume can say that Berkeley's account is a failure in its own terms.

It is hardly surprising that the prefaces of the *Principles* and *Dialogues* should both have been omitted in the 1734 editions. The hope that he should somehow restore philosophers to virtue had been surely eradicated by that point. My suspicion is that it is mainly for this reason that Berkeley did not take the time to re-write his lost manuscript. Given that his project had been to promote positive moral change, it would have been counter-productive to publish a second part of a *Treatise* that nobody could believe. It would appear far more prudent to follow the dictates of his philosophy through virtuous action. Berkeley himself went on to live the life of virtue – striving to improve the world as he saw it – as his project to Bermuda exemplifies. Much of his subsequent writings tended to be both engaged and practical, devoted to the betterment of humankind. The moral, however, is that far from rejecting Berkeley's account of spirit on the grounds of an inconsistency, Hume rejects it on the grounds of this practical failure.

Chapter Eight

The Elusive Subject

> For my part, when I enter most intimately into what I call *myself*, I always stumble on some particular perception or other, of heat or cold, light or shade, love or hatred, pain or pleasure. I never catch *myself* at any time without a perception, and never can observe anything but the perception.[1]

Hume's Complaint has been accorded a great degree of significance with respect to issues of self and self-consciousness. Hume is sometimes viewed as the originator of the theme that there is something elusive about 'the subject of experience.'[2] Some philosophers have heard Hume echoed in Lichtenberg's suggestion that instead of saying 'I am thinking' one ought to say, 'It is thinking.'[3,4] Others suggest Hume played a role in some of Wittgenstein's cryptic remarks about the thinking subject.[5]

Hume's Complaint has been installed at the center of the well-known narrative as a response to Descartes' *cogito*[6] and a point of departure for Kant's views.[7] One can say that Hume's Complaint, like the *Cogito*, is a 'philosophical moment.' It has secured philosophical importance, generated independent interest (extending well beyond the original intentions of the author), and come to interact with other philosophical moments. It has become a kind of touch-point in the cultural and partially mythological history of the Western Philosophical tradition.

The aim of this chapter is to provide a fresh reading of Hume's Complaint and thereby re-examine this philosophical moment. By viewing these remarks in light of Hume's response to Berkeley, I reassess the significance and nature of this famous passage and so secure a deeper understanding of the elusiveness theme and our notion of modern subjecthood.

Part I: Hume's Complaint

In 'Of personal identity' Hume lodges his Complaint after running his *main argument* against the idea of a simple and continued self. The Complaint is sometimes taken as a further objection to the claim that there is such an idea of the self.[8] While there is a tight connection between Hume's denial that there is an impression of a simple, continued self and his denial that such a self may be perceived, the Complaint itself does not strictly deny that such a self may be perceived. It consists of the following two claims: (1) Whenever one enters into oneself, one always perceives perceptions; (2) Whenever one enters into oneself, one perceives only perceptions. The conjunction of these two claims constitutes Hume's argument in favour of his own conception of the self.

After arguing against the simple and continued self, Hume raises the question, 'But farther, what must become of all our particular perceptions upon this hypothesis? . . . After what manner, therefore, do they belong to self; and how are they connected with it?' (T. I.4.6.3, 164–5, SBN 252). Hume never calls into question the existence of a self. The issue concerns what the self is and how perceptions are related to it. The question has special force, because after arguing against the idea of the simple, continued self, Hume argues that all perceptions are distinct existences and require nothing to support them. The positive argument in favour of his own conception of self, flowing from the Complaint, runs: 'When I turn my reflection on *myself*, I never can perceive this *self* without some one or more perceptions; nor can I ever perceive any thing but the perceptions. 'Tis the composition of these, therefore, which forms the self' (Appendix 11, 399, SBN 634).

One reason that Hume's Complaint has been mistaken for a further objection to the view that the self is simple and abiding, is that in his original formulation of this argument, Hume grapples with a metaphysician who rejects the claim that only perceptions may be perceived, maintaining that he perceives a simple and continued self. But Hume is not at this stage arguing against a simple and continued self. He has already done that. After 'loosening his perceptions' by arguing that they are distinct existences, he defends claims (1) and (2) in an argument designed to establish that the self is a heap of perceptions.

It is far from clear what Hume means when he speaks of 'entering most intimately into what he calls *himself*' and 'turning his reflection on himself.' One suspects he thinks about himself through memory and imagination.[9] What does seem clear to me is that in providing an argument in favour of his account of the self, Hume is thereby providing a positive argument in favour of his own account of *self-consciousness*. Given that Hume has rejected the view that whenever we think we are intimately conscious of a simple and continued self, it makes sense that Hume should then provide an account of what is actually involved in consciousness of oneself and one's relation to perceptions. Indeed, the very notion of a 'self' is deeply bound up with self-consciousness. To be aware of oneself (one's existence) is to be aware of the bundle. This is why Hume bolsters his positive argument by the claim that when perceptions are removed (as in sleep) one is *insensible* of oneself and may be said not to exist. Presumably when one is awake, one *is* sensible of oneself.

While the sort of reflection in which Hume is engaged seems philosophical in nature, the point of Hume's reflection and the arguments when doing so, is to provide an account of self-consciousness.[10] I take it that consciousness that one exists and that one is thinking, is not something that is restricted to the philosophers; it is available to all. While one is insensible of oneself in sound sleep, one is sensible of oneself while awake. And it is not only the philosophers themselves who are so sensible.[11]

One might suppose that in order to perceive a perception as a perception, one needs an additional idea in order to perceive it.[12] This, however, is untrue. According to Hume, there are three kinds of sense impressions – those of the primary qualities (figure, bulk, motion), those of secondary qualities (colours, tastes, smells), and those of pleasure and pain. According to Hume, both the vulgar and the philosophers recognize the latter as perceptions which exist only in the mind (T 1.4.2.12, 128; SBN 192). By contrast, the philosophers and the vulgar believe that the first sort of impressions are mind-independent, while only the vulgar think the second sort 'are on the same footing.' So the vulgar perceive perceptions and recognize some as such. They do so without any philosophical reflection.

If one generally perceives perceptions in this way (they 'appear to the mind' by making a causal impact), and the self is nothing more than a bundle of perceptions, then one ought to be aware of oneself in the same immediate, pre-reflective way.[13] In such a view, just as one's perceptions 'appear' without second-order mediation, one's own self would thereby 'appear' without mediation, as the sum total of all causally connected perceptual appearances. The vulgar may not be aware that certain things they took for external objects were in fact constituents of themselves. However, many of the perceptions they perceive would be recognized as perceptions (grief, pain, love). And they would know they were aware of themselves. This perception would not be perfect. As Hume writes, '. . . in common life 'tis evident these ideas of self and person are never very fix'd nor determinate' (T 1.2.4.6, 127; SBN 189–90).

One objection is that Hume does not need to claim that we perceive our existence in this immediate way. He simply needs an impression or idea of the bundle. In the Appendix Hume recognizes consciousness as 'a reflected thought or perception' and in Book II he speaks of the idea and impression of the self as a bundle.[14,15] Why does he need an awareness of oneself without intervention of further perceptions?

The fact is that Hume earlier discusses 'appearance in the mind' and the 'palpable contradiction' that a perception should exist without 'appearing in the mind.' In this same section he writes, 'The only existences, of which we are certain, are perceptions, which being immediately present to us by consciousness, command our strongest assent . . .' (T 1.2.4.47, 140; SBN 212). It is hard to believe that this is not a discussion of immediate consciousness (presence to the mind). Any account of Hume's view needs to square with this. Additionally, no appeal to a secondary perception can provide an account of one's consciousness of one's present being, since Hume's account of causation involves temporal contiguity. Any account of awareness through mediation, therefore, will only deliver awareness of one's past existence.

At any rate, notice that just before mentioning this 'reflected thought,' Hume has remarked, 'It follows, therefore, that the thought alone finds personal identity, when reflecting on the train of past perceptions, that compose a mind, the ideas of them are felt to be connected together, and naturally introduce each other' (Appendix 20, 400, SBN 635). Hume is discussing reflection upon one's past perceptions and so it may very well be that it is this backwards reaching consciousness (first appealed to by Locke) that he has in mind. Hume's point is that when we engage in this reflection upon past perceptions we do not perceive any real bound among them.[16,17]

The Humean idea of the self derives from reflection upon past events. It has nothing to tell us about our existence in the present. Yet Locke had used 'consciousness' in a broad way to include memories of past thoughts and actions as well as consciousness of one's existence and thoughts in the present. While the former involved a second-order perception (a reflected thought), the latter was simply constitutive of thought. Hume cannot account for this latter kind of awareness by appealing to 'the true idea of the mind' since this derives from memory. There should be an unmediated awareness of oneself that consists in consciousness of one's own perceptions. One ought to be sensible of oneself insofar as one is now thinking.

Now note that one of the most striking features of the Complaint is the emphasis on 'perception.' Hume does not 'catch' himself without a perception; he 'observes' nothing but the perception. The stubborn metaphysician may 'perceive' something simple and continued. Could Berkeley have been that stubborn metaphysician? Could Hume have intended his talk about the perceivability of the self to somehow include Berkeley's non-perceptual awareness? Obviously not. Berkeley would have accepted Hume's premises, while protesting that Hume could not draw his conclusion. Consequently, an effectively 'gagged' Berkeley continues to 'loom in the background.'

How does Hume address this stubborn metaphysician? If perceptions are viewed as modes or accidents then one has the two-element account of consciousness according to which one is aware of one's states and oneself. However, Hume refuses to view perceptions as modes which inhere in a substance. Like Berkeley, he views variable elements of consciousness as items in their own right. In his model, awareness of oneself and one's states simply involves the appearance of mental constituents within the bundle that one is.

Recall that Berkeley denies the 'I' can be perceived because he has adopted a different model of consciousness. Variable elements of consciousness are no longer viewed as modes, the constant element of consciousness (one's own existence) is not inferentially connected to them. Consequently, one's own existence is not perceived in perceiving the variable elements of consciousness. It is not, in this way, an object of perception. It is little wonder that contrary to the stubborn metaphysician Hume does not perceive anything distinct from his perceptions. Hume has rejected the model of consciousness that would have led him to represent his own self-awareness in that sort of way. While it may seem like an empirical point that Hume is making, it is only successful because he has rejected the older model of self-consciousness. That being said, Hume rejects this older model of consciousness as a consequence of his empiricism (driven largely by the *main argument*). Since all ideas must be traceable to impressions, there isn't going to be any idea of anything besides perceptions.

This interpretation sheds considerable light on Hume's notorious doubts in the Appendix. He presents two principles which he claims are inconsistent with each other, neither of which he can renounce: (A) Distinct perceptions are distinct existences; and (B) The mind never perceives any real connection among distinct existences. Pleading the privilege of the sceptic, Hume pronounces the difficulty beyond his own understanding.

One reason Hume's concern has been so hard to understand is that the two allegedly inconsistent principles aren't inconsistent; it has been supposed that there must be some third principle which completes an inconsistent triad. In the interpretation I offer, the principle is this: *I am conscious that I exist.*

If perceptions are distinct existences, the only way one could perceive oneself would be to perceive the bundle. Yet this is inconsistent with the principle 'The mind never perceives any real connection among distinct existences.' It is unclear how one can perceive one's *existence* when one perceives only a plurality of items. One would need to perceive some sort of connection between them.

Hume has left us with a paradox. Given that distinct perceptions are distinct existences, it follows that the perception of one's existence must be nothing more than the perception of the various perceptions. Yet given that no real bound can be perceived between distinct existences, no such perception of one's own existence is possible. In this way, he returns us to a state of perplexity that echoes that of Locke's perplexity about the soul. Hume has left us with a new paradox that calls into question our very awareness of our own existence.

The only solutions Hume allows involve the perception of one's existence. Did the perceptions inhere in a substance, one would have the older model of consciousness found in Descartes and Locke. In perceiving one's mental states *qua* modes, one would thereby perceive one's existence. Did one perceive a real bound among one's perceptions, one would thereby perceive oneself.[18] The possibility of non-perceptual awareness is excluded from the range of solutions. Once again, Berkeley occupies the peculiar status of being silenced from the outset. Rather than accepting Berkeley's position as a possible solution, Hume is prepared to accept the paradox.[19,20,21]

However, the paradox appears to be the consequence of Hume's rejection of Berkeley. For if the vulgar are correct, it must be possible for perceptions to exist without appearing to the mind. The only account which allows for this is one which fails at providing a satisfactory account of self-awareness. Yet Hume scarcely misses a beat, using this as more evidence in favour of scepticism. It is little wonder, since this problem has so little affect upon his project. It is a problem which only afflicts Hume's account of present self-awareness.

While consciousness that one exists requires something more than the perception of plurality, there is no difficulty in allowing for a mind as a loose mental system. Hume's project of accounting for the human mind is in no way stymied by this problem. Hume does not even need this awareness in order to ground his account of personal identity, since reflection upon past perceptions through memory and imagination would alone suffice. Indeed, this account of personal identity seems sufficient to generate the very idea of the self as a bundle of perceptions, and Hume's Book II account of the passions pride and shame remains unhindered.

Hume's privilege of the sceptic is an especially interesting move, if we continue to keep Berkeley in mind. It is not a privilege that Berkeley ever possessed, given his intention to destroy scepticism. We might recall Hume's remarks in the Introduction, '. . . the writer may derive a more delicate satisfaction from the free confession of his ignorance, and from his prudence in avoiding that error, into which so many have fallen, of imposing their conjectures and hypotheses on the world for the most certain principles'

(T Intro 9. 5; SBN xviii). One wonders whether Hume's paradox hadn't been anticipated from the outset. If so, far from being a serious problem with his theory, it may have constituted a final solution in addressing Berkeley's conception of spirit.

Part II: The Elusive Subject

Hume's Complaint has been connected to the theme that the self is mysteriously elusive. I say 'theme' rather than 'thesis' since it is far from clear what the elusiveness thesis amounts to. I suspect this is one reason for the mystery surrounding it. Consequently, I should qualify that my foray into this murky quagmire is limited in scope. Given the host of variations played upon this theme throughout the history of Western Philosophy – in Kant, Fichte, Schopenhauer, Sartre, Russell, Wittgenstein, Anscombe, and the like – it would be vain to promise a complete account.

Consider Colin McGinn's formulation of an example of 'philosophical perplexity':

> And there is a second source of ontic elusiveness, equally familiar from the history of thought on the subject of the subject: the systematic transcendence of the self in acts of self-awareness. If I try to focus on myself, making the referent of 'I' the object of my apprehension, then the subject of this focus inevitably transcends its object. When I think of myself that which thinks occurs as subject; thus I never become merely an object of my own apprehension. The self always, and systematically, steps out of cognitive reach. . . . *Qua* subject I can never be an intentional object to myself. Yet it is *qua* subject that I have my essence.[22]

McGinn's proposed treatment of philosophical perplexity is what he calls 'transcendental naturalism,' a view which to some degree echoes Locke's, in that it supposes that such perplexities '. . . arise in us because of definite inherent limitations on our epistemic faculties . . . .'[23] A more attractive approach is a Berkeleian view that this alleged problem is a distinctively philosophical one, built upon the mistakes and confusions of philosophers themselves.

This problem might be best treated that way because it is clearly a philosopher's problem. Despite Gilbert Ryle's suggestion that these issues arise even for children, the nature of this specific problem is difficult to explain to anybody – never mind children.[24] And I doubt that it has occurred to many people who have not been raised on modern Western philosophy. A further indication of this is that the problem is often formulated by appealing to a 'subject of experience.' Chisholm, for example, speaks of '... the thesis according to which one is never aware of a *subject* of experience.'[25] But what is a subject of experience? This is certainly a philosophical expression used only by philosophers. I have never once heard this expression uttered on the bus, or even over too many drinks in the wee hours of the morning by friends who were not themselves philosophers already introduced to the expression. What does it mean?

The Oxford English Dictionary provides two different philosophical definitions of 'subject':[26]

> **6.** *Philos.* The substance in which accidents or attributes inhere. **subject of inhesion** *or* **inherence**.
>
> **9.** *Mod. Philos.* More fully ***conscious*** or ***thinking subject***: The mind, as the 'subject' in which ideas inhere; that to which all mental representations or operations are attributed; the thinking or cognizing agent; the self or ego. (Correlative to OBJECT *n.* 6.)
>
> The tendency in modern philosophy after Descartes to make the mind's consciousness of itself the starting-point of enquiry led to the use of *subjectum* for the mind or ego considered as the subject of all knowledge, and since Kant this has become the general philosophical use of the word (with its derivatives *subjective*, etc.).

It defines 'object' as follows:

> **5.** *Philos.* A thing which is perceived, thought of, known, etc.; *spec.* a thing which is external to or distinct from the apprehending mind, subject, or self. (Opposed to SUBJECT *n.*9. Cf. OBJECTIVE *n.* 1).

There is a contrast between the subject (of accidents) and the subject (versus objects). Both probably derive from the same grammatical notion of a subject, yet when deployed within philosophical contexts, there is an important difference. Contrast the accounts by Aristotle and Russell: 'The subject [*hypokeimenon*] is that of which the other things are said, but which itself is never [said] of any other thing,'[27] and 'We will define a "subject" as any entity which is acquainted with something. ... Conversely, any entity with which something is acquainted will be called an "object." '[28]

The difference concerns a contrast in philosophical categories. For example, Quassim Cassam speaks of '... a form of dualism which has had a profound influence on much theorizing about the nature of self-consciousness, namely, a dualism of subject and object.'[29] He goes on to explain, 'The central thesis of this form of dualism is that the categories "subject" and "object" are mutually exclusive.' I take it that he means *philosophical* categories. After all, it is odd that 'subject' and 'object' should carry such weight. And I suspect one reason for the *significance* of these categories is this very dualism which tells us that the subject cannot be an object to itself.

Yet there is considerable room for overlap between these two notions of 'subject'; it is presumably for this reason that the two notions are generally collapsed in discussions concerning the mind. The mind can be a subject of mental states which represent objects. Or, as the OED suggests, the mind could be a subject in which its own objects (i.e. ideas) 'inhere.' Here it would be a little unclear whether ideas are accidents, or whether ideas 'inhere' only in the sense that they depend upon the mind for their existence. For present purposes I distinguish between what I will call the 'older subject' (in which accidents inhere) and the 'modern subject' (as opposed to objects), while recognizing that modern philosophical usage actually blurs the two.

Yet even this clarification is insufficient to help us understand what 'subject of experience' means. Consider that when one stares into a mirror, one sees oneself staring. Staring is something that is typically done by 'perceiving subjects.' Is one not aware of oneself *as* a subject? If so, the subject can be an object (to itself). Why then does McGinn complain that 'the subject' is ever beyond cognitive grasp? Something else must be meant by 'subject of experience.' The problem is that in denying that one ever has any cognitive grasp of it, one worries that there is no content to the expression at all, and hence no grounds for the problem.

There is a related perplexity about the way in which Hume's Complaint is supposed to connect to the elusiveness theme. While there is a sense in which Hume is taken to originate the thesis, there is another sense in which Hume is supposed to fall prey to it. In this second sense, the worry is that Hume was 'looking in the wrong place.' He was expecting to find 'the subject' among the 'the objects' and in so doing, he could not 'catch it' for all his stumbling. The two versions are in tension with each other. Is the Complaint an instance of insight or blindness?

The tension is connected to the fact that there are two possible theses involved. There is the thesis that one is never aware of 'the subject of experience' at all. And there is the weaker thesis that the subject of experience can never be 'an object to itself.' The latter leaves open the possibility that one can be aware of 'the subject' but not aware of it 'as an object.' There could be radically contrasting modes of awareness grounding a dualism between the categories of 'subject' and 'object.' As Cassam puts it:

> The suggestion, then, is that it is a monstrous contradiction that a subject should ever become an object for itself, because awareness of something as an object, and awareness of it *qua* subject, are mutually exclusive modes of awareness.[30]

The latter would seem a more palatable version since this awareness of the subject would at least provide the expression 'the subject of experience' with content.

Yet it is the stronger thesis which is usually attributed to Hume. Fortunately, Hume does not postulate anything which exists, continuing to escape his awareness of it. He takes the fact that we have no idea of a simple and abiding self as grounds for denying that the term 'self' so used has sense at all. This contrasts with McGinn's formulation of the elusiveness theme according to which there *is* a subject of experience which is never an object of cognition. Perhaps McGinn's thesis ought to be weakened to allow for *some* awareness of the subject, awareness that does not constitute awareness of something 'as object.'

What is supposed to be at stake is a sort of non-sensory awareness which has sometimes been called 'introspection' which is connected with the content of the expression 'subject of experience.' The notion, when used philosophically, suggests a kind of inner examination of one's mental life. Yet we need to keep in mind that even for Locke there is a distinction between reflection and consciousness. Reflection is something that one only does occasionally; consciousness is something that accompanies all thoughts. It is the latter we are interested in, when we investigate the grounds for self-knowledge with respect to propositions such as: 'I am in pain,' 'I see a tree,' 'I feel tired.' In such cases, one does not necessarily stop to investigate oneself through an inner scrutiny. The awareness accompanies the event quite immediately. Indeed, philosophers such as Shoemaker and Evans argue that this sort of awareness is not to be modeled on sensory awareness and that it does not involve a sort of inner examination.[31] While it is no trivial matter to specify how 'introspection' might be analogous to sense-perception, one way is for the cognition of one's own mental states to involve mediating ideas (as in Locke) and/or higher-order cognition which takes lower-order cognition as objects.

Taken in this way, 'introspection' provides the resources for an elusiveness worry (as a kind of infinite regress). One version of this is formulated by Ryle.[32] A higher-order reflection or report cannot take itself as an object, and so with each higher-order reflection, there is always something else to be reflected upon. It therefore appears that higher-order reflections generate new objects of possible reflection (infinitely).[33]

However, Ryle's account ought not be accepted as a satisfying account of the elusiveness theme.[34] It maintains there is always a distinction between a higher- and lower-order act where the higher can never be the very object upon which it is performed. Yet this is trivially false, as is evidenced by the case of examining oneself in the mirror. There are also performative statements which appear to be about themselves (as in 'I hereby declare that you are never to eat chocolate'). And it is unclear why consciousness of mental acts must involve higher-order acts. Descartes, Malebranche, and Locke viewed consciousness as constitutive of thought.

Yet, there are related issues worth noting. It is this capacity for higher-order awareness which grounds Locke's own investigation into human understanding: 'The Understanding, like the Eye, whilst it makes us see, and perceive all other Things, takes no notice of itself: And it requires Art and Pains to set it at a distance and make it its own Object' (E. 1.1.1, 43). Yet in rejecting the possibility of forming second-order simple ideas of mental operations, Berkeley's Provost, Browne, rejects this 'unnatural squint' as impossible. Knowledge of the mind is founded only on the immediate consciousness of one's acts (directed to sensible objects) and the 'notions' are all that one can cobble out of this consciousness with sensible ideas.

Berkeley takes this one step further by eliminating discrete mental acts altogether. Lockean reflection is impossible insofar as there is nothing available to reflect upon. One has awareness only of oneself, and one's effects and objects. One may discursively reflect upon oneself using words such as 'apprehend.' But there are no mental properties available for examination. Hume restores the mind as a potential focus of investigation. By viewing variable elements of consciousness as constituents of the mind, Hume enables genuine reflection upon the mind through an appeal to one's memory and imagination. Understood in this way, we can say that Berkeley endorses the view that the mind can never be an object of investigation, while Hume can be said to answer the view by showing how it can be.

Yet this concern is more focused on mental acts than upon 'the subject' itself. As a consequence, I think that it (along with Ryle's concern) does not illuminate the concern which is supposed to specifically involve 'the subject.' In particular, I do not think such an approach can illuminate what is meant by the expression 'subject of experience.' It is this issue which is supposed to be connected up with Hume's Complaint. Kripke explains:

> So: where Descartes would have said that I am certain that "I have a tickle", the only thing Hume is aware of is the tickle itself. The self – The Cartesian ego – is an entity which is wholly mysterious. We are

> aware of no such entity that 'has' the tickle, 'has' the headache, the visual perception, and the rest; we are aware only of the tickle, the headache, the visual perception, itself.[35]

As formulated, the point is too strong. Hume is rejecting any self *distinct* from his perceptions; he is rejecting a self that is simple and abiding. He is also interested in arguing that the self is nothing but a bundle of perceptions. He, too, is aware that 'I have a tickle.' The difference concerns how this awareness is analyzed. Given that a Humean bundle itself perceives perceptions by having perceptions as causally connected elements, why shouldn't we say that to be aware of the heap is *ipso facto* to be aware of oneself as a subject of experience? To be sure, this seems intuitively wrong. And it seems intuitively wrong because we philosophers have something else in mind when we speak of a subject of experience. Hume's analysis of consciousness does not provide us with content for our notion 'subject of experience.' What does?

We have two candidates from which to choose. In the older model, the subject is related to accidents. Consequently, this model more properly reflects the older notion of 'subject.' In Berkeley's model, the subject is contrasted with objects. Consequently, it more properly reflects the modern notion of 'subject.'

The contrast can be deepened by recognizing that in the older model, it makes sense to say that the subject is an object of consciousness. One's consciousness is wholly self-consciousness. In perceiving various different mental states, one perceives that one exists; in securing knowledge of these states, one secures knowledge of oneself. In Berkeley's model, one is only aware of items distinct from oneself. One is aware of oneself only as a thing that exists *qua* perceiver of those items distinct from oneself. Berkeleian spirit, unlike the Cartesian mind, possesses no intrinsic properties. Rather, it is a bare active existent, related to its various different objects.[36]

Another way to understand the contrast is to recognize the Berkeleian model of self-consciousness as 'de-centered' since one is only ever conscious of oneself in relation to something else. When one is aware that one perceives a tree, one is centrally aware of the tree and only in a de-centered way aware of oneself as a distinct perceiver of it. By contrast, in the older model, consciousness is centered. While in seeing the tree one does not see oneself, there is another modality of perception which accompanies the seeing: the conscious awareness that one sees the tree. This modality of self-awareness is itself *centered* insofar as the central object of consciousness is *oneself*.

As I have argued, when Hume grapples with a stubborn metaphysician who claims to perceive something simple and continued, this metaphysician is not Berkeley. The metaphysician ought to be understood as one (or all) of those who accepts the older model. Hume can be understood as rejecting the view that the mental subject of inherence is an object of conscious awareness (i.e. an object of perception). In this way, Hume is looking in the right place when he does not find that mental subject.

What Hume appears to leave out is one's awareness of oneself as distinct from one's mental items. To use his metaphor, in identifying the mind with a theater, Hume leaves out the spectator. One wants to say that one has an awareness of oneself (at least one's existence) and that this is distinct from one's awareness of anything on stage.

This sort of awareness involves the model endorsed by Berkeley. In the older model of consciousness, the theater metaphor is not especially apt; the items that pass by in the theater can hardly be construed as modes of oneself. Insofar as the *Berkeleian* model of consciousness provides content to our concern that Hume has left something out, it provides content to the modern notion of a subject of experience.

Berkeley can be identified as an important transitional figure between the older notion of subject and the modern notion of subject.[37] The point is not trivial. I am not merely drawing attention to the fact that for Berkeley, ideas are not accidents which inhere in spirit but are objects perceived by them. I am making the deeper point that our understanding of the modern notion of subject is informed by a Berkeleian model of consciousness which grounds a dualism between subject and object and consequently a weak version of the elusiveness theme. In the older model of consciousness, the subject of inherence is the object of consciousness; in the Berkeleian model, the subject of perception is not. The subject has a de-centered awareness of itself as distinct from its objects. A robust contrast between 'subject' and 'object' moves to the foreground, captured by spirit–idea dualism.[38]

Since the Berkeleian model provides content to the concern that Hume left something out, we can say that Hume left out Berkeleian spirit. We can recognize Berkeley as originating something like the elusiveness theme prior to Hume. And we can see Hume as drawing on Berkeleian insight to deny that the older subject can be perceived in consciousness. His response to Berkeleian spirit is far more complicated; the story of his response needs to be understood according to my remarks in the previous chapter.

At any rate, a new story can be told which invites Berkeley into the mythological pantheon of Descartes, Hume, and Kant. Perhaps this new story supplants the older one. Hume's response to Berkeley seems far more germane to our understanding of the elusiveness theme than any potential response to Descartes.

To be sure, it would be perverse to say that Berkeley's views about the self have had a profound impact upon our modern understanding of subjecthood and self-consciousness. While the views of Descartes, Hume, and Kant have been esteemed, Berkeley's view has been misunderstood and discarded as incoherent. How could his views have any influence?

To the extent that at least Hume was influenced by Berkeley in his own views about the self and self-consciousness, Berkeley has had a profound (albeit mangled) impact through Hume. And if I am correct that Berkeley's conception of consciousness is a looming background presence in Hume's famous Complaint, then Berkeley's influence is embedded within that very moment, whether we recognize it or not. Moreover, Berkeley has had a negative influence through his absence.

If Hume left Berkeleian spirit out of his account, we can now say that we have found the elusive subject. To the extent that we have missed Berkeley's account – to the extent that Berkeley has been rendered invisible not only by Hume's own exclusion of him, but by very the dismissal of his account as incoherent – our ability to understand Hume's Complaint has been seriously impaired. It has been shrouded in unclarity.

In particular, the importance of contrasting models of ontology/ consciousness has been obscured. This contrast would have been taken seriously, had we understood the importance of Berkeley's model of consciousness as the consequence of his rejection of the older ontology. The subtle transition from the older to the modern subject characterized by Berkeley's denial that the spirit can be perceived is lost to us in the prevailing mythology. Yet it is precisely this transition which is central to understanding a modern dualism of subject and object and the elusiveness theme. Indeed, it is precisely our failure to understand this transition and the contrast between the older and the Berkeleian model of consciousness which has left us vacillating between the view that Hume originated the thesis and the view that he fell prey to it. It is only by distinguishing them that we recognize that we must look for two Humean responses rather than one.

In re-telling this story, I do not think the importance of Berkeley overshadows the importance of other philosophers. I have provided no discussion of the important contrast between subjectivity and objectivity. This has relevance to the theme of the elusiveness thesis as is evidenced by Kant's worry that the 'I think' is a mere formal requirement of thought itself. Yet this does not undermine the importance of Berkeley in understanding our modern notion of subject, as well as its connection to the elusiveness theme and Hume's Complaint.

Nor do I wish to claim that Berkeley used 'subject' and 'object' in this more modern way thereby providing the terms with philosophical content.

He didn't. The point is that once Berkeley's philosophy of spirit is vindicated from the traditional concern, we see that there is an important shift which takes place. In rejecting the older ontology, Berkeley is led to embrace a new model of consciousness. It is this new model of consciousness which plays an important role in our philosophical understanding of 'subject of experience.'

This suggests the need for more caution in the use of the philosophical expression 'subject.' Even though there may be overlap in the two uses, there are also salient ontological shifts which influence the conceptualization of consciousness. Paying attention to this is important in understanding the connection between the modern notion of subject and the elusiveness theme. For the notion is fundamentally bound up with it, deriving content in part, from a Berkeleian model of consciousness. By taking this seriously and by recognizing the importance of Berkeley to Hume, we can begin to untangle some of the confusion which surrounds Hume's own relationship to the elusiveness theme.

Once we have identified Berkeleian spirit as the elusive subject, it seems that much of the murkiness surrounding the theme is dispelled. It becomes a trivial affair that in a certain model of consciousness, the subject and object are always distinct, defined by a de-centered consciousness. To the degree to which this Berkeleian model provides such philosophical categories with content, it becomes an impossibility that the subject should ever be an object insofar as its very content derives from its precisely not being an object. This is hardly a problem of deep concern.

Yet, while my own account of the elusiveness theme deflates its significance, we are led to recognize that the standard philosophical equation of the self with the subject of experience is a non-trivial assumption. When 'subject' is taken in a purely modern sense, the view that subject and self are the same is the view that all significant self-awareness is de-centered.[39] We can ask the question: Is the self a *mere* subject of experience?

Should it turn out that the only type of significant self-awareness is de-centered, it will follow that one can never apprehend any intrinsic properties of oneself.[40] One will only ever know oneself as a thing that exists, distinct from the objects of perception. It seems clear that such a thesis must be false. Yet it might be worth investigating why it is false: Is there a fact of the matter how to analyze consciousness that one is thinking? Is there a specific ontology which informs the structure of consciousness? If so, what is it? Are there other forms of significant self-awareness besides consciousness that one is thinking (such as proprioceptive awareness or even sensory awareness of one's own body) which might be centered?

There are deep questions about modern Western philosophy itself. Even if it is false that the self is a mere subject of experience, to what extent has this been assumed? To what extent has self-consciousness been understood as de-centered? And to what extent have kinds of self-awareness only been accepted as genuine to the extent that they are de-centered? The questions have force, once we recognize that the older model of consciousness accepted by Descartes and Locke was not de-centered. If de-centered self-awareness is privileged in philosophy, it is a bias which derives from Berkeley's peculiar philosophy of spirit.

I conclude this book by observing that it is strange and yet illuminating to learn that the distinctively modern concern about an elusive subject should, in part, derive from Berkeley's philosophy of spirit. Berkeley had been concerned with theological issues like the natural immortality of the soul, our knowledge of God, and the Christian mysteries. Such concerns emerged within the context of Anglican theology, the Irish notion of analogy, and the harnessing of the 'way of ideas' by free-thinkers such as Toland and Collins. By stripping back the self to a bare 'I am' Berkeley hoped to answer these concerns. Yet in splitting the *cogito* to produce it, the distinctively modern elusive subject was born. It survived only because it was found and then hidden by David Hume. Lingering like a ghost in Hume's *Treatise* and the mythologized Complaint, it has continued to exert a deep influence on our understanding of modern subjecthood.

Perhaps now that the Berkeley's philosophy of spirit has been vindicated from the charge of incoherence, Berkeley can have an even greater impact upon our understanding of contemporary issues concerning the philosophical concept of the subject of experience. The price, however, may be the recognition of the uncomfortably idiosyncratic history of contemporary philosophical concepts as well as the power of a mythologized history in obscuring, and thereby engendering, philosophical perplexity of its own.

Notes

Introduction

1. PHK Intro 3. Citations of *A Treatise concerning the Principles of Human Knowledge* [PHK] refer to part and section. Citations of *Three Dialogues between Hylas and Philonous* [3D] refer to dialogue number and page. Citations of *Philosophical Commentaries* [PC] refer to entry number. Citations of *Alciphron or the Minute Philosopher* [ALC] refer to dialogue number, section, and page. Citations of *An Essay Towards A New Theory of Vision* [NTV] and *The Theory of Vision Vindicated and Explained* [TVV] refer to section. All references to Berkeley unless specified are from A.A. Luce and T.E. Jessop (ed.), *The Works of George Berkeley, Bishop of Cloyne*, 9 volumes (Thomas Nelson and Sons: London and Edinburgh, 1948–57). Citations of other writings of Berkeley refer to *Works* volume and page. Citations of Berkeley's manuscript introduction to the *Principles* are from Bertil Belfrage's *George Berkeley's Manuscript Introduction: An editio diplomatica transcribed and edited with introduction and commentary by Bertil Belfrage* (Doxa: Oxford. 1987).
2. See Samuel Guttenplan (ed.), *A Companion to the Philosophy of Mind* (Blackwell: Oxford. 1995), 551–3 and Kim Atkins (ed.), *Self and Subjectivity* (Blackwell: Oxford. 2005), 33–5.
3. Kenneth P. Winkler, *Berkeley: An Interpretation* (Oxford University Press: Oxford. 1989), 105.
4. See Colin M. Turbayne, 'Berkeley's Two Concepts of Mind,' *Philosophy and Phenomenological Research* 20:1 (1959), 85–92 and 'Berkeley's Two Concepts of Mind Part II,' *Philosophy and Phenomenology Research* 22:3 (1962), 383–86. See also A. J. Ayer, *Language, Truth, and Logic* (Dover: London. 1946), 126 and 141.
5. See G.L. Warnock, *Berkeley* (Penguin: London. 1953), 197.
6. See Turbayne (1959). While Turbayne does not claim the view is Humean, Robert Muehlmann does. He maintains this account is concealed by a published appeal to spiritual substance which serves none of its traditional functions. See Muehlmann, *Berkeley's Ontology* (Hackett: Indianapolis. 1992) 170–204 and his 'The Substance of Berkeley's Philosophy,' in Muehlmann (ed.), *Berkeley's Metaphysics: Structural, Interpretive, and Critical Essays* (Pennsylvania State University Press: University Park. 1995), 89–105. For a critique of this view see Marc Hight and Walter Ott, 'The New Berkeley,' *Canadian Journal of Philosophy* 34 (2004), 1–24.

7. For an account of these different positions see Phillip D. Cummins, 'Berkeley on minds and agency,' in Kenneth Winkler (ed.), *The Cambridge Companion to Berkeley* (Cambridge University Press: Cambridge. 2005), 210–11.
8. S.A. Grave, 'The Mind and its Ideas: Some Problems in the Interpretation of Berkeley,' *Australian Journal of Philosophy* 42 (1964), 199–210; reprinted in C.B. Martin and D.M. Armstrong (eds), *Locke and Berkeley: A Collection of Critical Essays* (Doubleday: New York. 1968), 296–313; George Pitcher, *Berkeley* (Routledge & Kegan Paul: London. 1977), 189–203; Kenneth Winkler (1989), 290–300, Muehlmann (1992), 226–34. Geneviève Brykman, *Berkeley et le Voile des Mots* (Vrin: Paris. 1993), 274–82.
9. For a nice statement of the conflict, see Phillip D. Cummins, 'Berkeley's Unstable Ontology,' *The Modern Schoolman* 67 (1989), 15–32; esp. 30–1.
10. For some of Berman's pioneering work in this area, see *Berkeley and Irish Philosophy* (Thoemmes Continuum. 2005) and *George Berkeley: Idealism and the Man* (Clarendon: Oxford. 1994).
11. Toland's infamous book was burned by the hangman in Dublin, and censured by the Irish Parliament. See Berman's 'Enlightenment and Counter-Enlightenment in Irish Philosophy,' reprinted in Berman (2005).
12. Toland, *Christianity not Mysterious* (London. 1696), 128; Browne, *A Letter in Answer to Christianity not Mysterious* (Dublin. 1697), 49. Reprinted together by Routledge/Thoemmes Press 1995.
13. See Berman's 'Enlightenment and Counter-Enlightenment in Irish Philosophy.'
14. For an account of the development of Berkeley's views about spirit, see Charles McCracken's 'Berkeley's Notion of Spirit,' *History of European Ideas* 7 (1989), 56–88. See also Bertil Belfrage, 'George Berkeley's Four Concepts of the Soul (1707–1709),' in *Reexamining Berkeley's Philosophy*, Stephen H. Daniel (ed.) (University of Toronto Press. Toronto. Forthcoming). Belfrage argues Berkeley's different conceptions of the soul reflect different overall philosophical stances.
15. Belfrage's 'Editor's Commentary' in his edition of Berkeley's manuscript introduction (1987).
16. Jean-Paul Pittion, David Berman, and A. A. Luce, 'A New Letter by Berkeley to Browne on Divine Analogy,' *Mind* 78 (1969), 375–92. Both the date and the authorship of this letter are disputable. However, Pittion, Berman, and Luce provide strong grounds for believing that this letter was written by Berkeley. My own use of the letter will provide further evidence in favour of Berkeley's authorship.
17. Benjamin Rand (ed.), *Berkeley and Percival: The Correspondence of George Berkeley and Sir John Percival* (Cambridge University Press: Cambridge. 1914), 73.
18. *The Procedure, Extent, and Limits of Human Understanding* (London. 1728), reprinted by Garland, 1976, 150–2, 353–63, 444. See *Letter* (129–131).
19. *The Correspondence of Jonathan Swift*, ed. Harold Williams (Clarendon: Oxford. 1963–5), III, 66–7.
20. *Works* IV 235–38
21. *Works* VII 9–15.

22. Bertil Belfrage, 'The clash on semantics in Berkeley's *Notebook* A,' *Hermathena* 139 (1985) 117–26; David Berman, 'Berkeley's Semantic revolution: 19 November 1707–January 1708,' *History of European Ideas* 7:6 (1986), 603–7 and Berman (1994), 11–17.
23. At PHK I 140 of the *Works* II, the *apparatus criticus* indicates that in an early draft of sections 85–135 (British Museum Add. MS 39304, 35–105) 'or rather a notion' can be found in the text crossed out. This would constitute textual evidence that Berkeley entertained the terminological restriction from early on. Belfrage has recently drawn attention to the fact that the 'rather a' is nowhere to be found in what he calls the *Principles Manuscript*. His paper 'The Biased Presentation of George Berkeley's *Works*' was presented at the Berkeley Conference in Tartu, Estonia (September 2005).

Chapter One

1. For discussion of Berkeley's proof of the natural immortality of the soul see Harry M. Bracken, 'Berkeley on the Immortality of the Soul,' *The Modern Schoolman* 37 (1960), 77–94 and 197–212 and Berman (1994), 58–70. As a consequence of his views about time, thinks Berman, Berkeley can show that the soul is absolutely immortal. While I agree that Berkeley's view about time is important to his view about natural immortality, I do not think that absolute immortality follows from it.
2. All references to Locke's replies to Stillingfleet are from *The Works of John Locke* (London. 1823), Volume 4.
3. Bracken (1960) emphasizes the importance of this dispute in understanding Berkeley's demonstration of the natural immortality of the soul. Bracken cites the following notebooks entries as evidence that Berkeley was familiar with the dispute: PC 517 and PC 700. He also cites PC 720 as evidence of Berkeley's departure from Toland. See Luce's *editio diplomatica* of *Philosophical Commentaries* (Thomas Nelson and Sons: Edinburgh. 1944), 720 note. Further evidence of his concern with Toland's (and possibly Collins') views may be found at PC 350 and 350a.
4. Dodwell, *An Epistolary Discourse Proving from the Scriptures and the First Fathers that the Soul is a Principle Naturally Mortal* ... abbr. (London. 1706).
5. Clarke, *A Letter to Mr. Dodwell* (London. 1707).
6. Norris, *A Philosophical Discourse concerning the Natural Immortality of the Soul* (London.1708).
7. All references to the Clarke–Collins correspondence are from *The Works of Samuel Clarke* (London. 1738), four volumes, vol. III. Reprinted by Garland (1978).
8. Collins, *An Essay concerning the Use of Reason in Propositions* (London. 1707). Reprinted by Garland (1984).
9. Introduced by David Berman and edited by Andrew Carpenter. The Cadenus Press (Dublin, 1976).
10. Citations of *An Essay concerning Human Understanding* [E] refer to book, part, section, and page from (ed.) Peter H. Nidditch (Clarendon: Oxford University Press, 1975).

11. *Christianity not Mysterious*, 74–87.
12. Boethius, trans. V.E. Watts, *The Consolation of Philosophy* (The Folio Society. 1998) Book 5, Sec. 6, 169.
13. This contrasts with the view he defends in his dispute with Clarke, *An Answer to Mr. Clarke's Third Defence* (1708), 864. Clarke was quick to point this out to him in *A Fourth Defence of an Argument* (1708), 893.
14. Locke E. 2.17.16, 219; Clarke, *A Demonstration of the Being and Attributes of God*, sec. V. See also Sermon IV: *Of the Eternity of God* (*Works* I 2).
15. *Leviathan* (London. 1651), Part 3, Ch. 34.
16. Locke, *A Letter to the Right Reverend Edward, Lord Bishop of Worcester* . . . (1697) 34–6, *Mr. Locke's Reply to the Bishop of Worcester's Answer to his Second Letter* (1699) 483–92.
17. See Berman (2005), 96.
18. Browne worries how a property can be essential to one being and only accidental to another. If to remove an originally essential property makes a thing cease to be what it is, the addition of it to another ought to make it become something else. Since thought is supposed to be taken as essential to spirit, to add the property of thought to matter is to effectively make it a spirit. See *Procedure* (150–2, 444).
19. Stillingfleet, *The Bishop of Worcester's Answer to Mr. Locke's Second Letter* (London. 1698), 27–9.
20. *Mr. Locke's . . . Answer to his Second Letter*, 476.
21. Ibid., 477.
22. *Letter to Dodwell*, 740–1.
23. *Procedure*, 234–47.
24. *An Argument concerning the Human Souls seperate Subsistance* (London. 1699), 6–7. For a discussion of Layton see John W. Yolton, *Thinking Matter: Materialism in Eighteenth-Century Britain* (University of Minnesota Press: Minneapolis. 1983), 36–9.
25. Berman (1994), 66–70, draws interesting connections between Coward's *Farther Thoughts concerning Human Soul* (London, 1903) and Berkeley's theory of time.
26. Stillingfleet (1698), 44.
27. *Mr. Locke's . . . Answer to his Second Letter* (303–4, 331–2).
28. *A Third Defence of an Argument* (1708), 851–53.
29. *An Answer to Mr. Clarke's Third Defence* (1708), 875–9.
30. *A Third Defence*, 851–3.
31. Rand (1914), 69.
32. Ibid., 68.
33. Sermon VII, 'On Eternal Life' (*Works* VII 108). See ALC VI 11, 241.
34. For other discussions of this natural desire see Berman (1994), 58 and Stephen R.L. Clark, 'Berkeley on Religion,' in Kenneth P. Winkler (ed.), *The Cambridge Companion to Berkeley* (Cambridge University Press: Cambridge. 2005), 398–99.
35. Sermon IX, 'Anniversary Sermon before the Society for the Propagation of the Gospel,' (*Works* VII 114–5).
36. Ibid., 115.
37. Guardian Essay no. 89, 'Immortality' (*Works* VII 222).

38. *Works* VII 115. I take it that this is consistent with Berkeley's claim in the notebooks that sensual pleasure is the *Summum Bonum* (PC 769) 'once rightly understood.'
39. Sermon IV, 'On the Mission of Christ' (*Works* VII 48).
40. ALC III. See also Guardian Essay no. 55, 'The Sanctions of Religion' (*Works* VII 200–1).
41. *An Essay towards preventing the Ruin of Great Britain* (*Works* VI 69).
42. Sermon I, 'On Immortality' (*Works* VII 11).
43. Ibid., 13.
44. Guardian Essay no. 27, 'The Future State' (*Works* VII 183–4).
45. Ibid., 184.
46. 'On Immortality', 13.
47. Ibid., 14–15.
48. 'On Eternal Life' (*Works* VII 108); cf. ALC VI 11. 241.
49. 'Immortality' (*Works* VII 223).
50. Ibid., 223.
51. 'The Future State,' 183.
52. *Passive Obedience* (1712) sec. 5–6 (*Works* VI 19–20), Sermon IX (*Works* VII 114–5).
53. 'Immortality' (*Works* VII 222–3).
54. 'On Immortality,' 9.
55. E. 1.1.4, p. 45; PHK I Intro 1.
56. Rand (1914), 73.
57. *A Letter to the Learned Mr. Henry Dodwell* (1707), 752.
58. *Reflections on Mr. Clarke's Second Defence* (1707), 815–6.
59. *A Fourth Defence of an Argument* (1708), 904.
60. *A Second Defence of an Argument* (1707), 787.
61. *A Third Defence*, 844–5.
62. *A Philosophical Discourse concerning the Natural Immortality of the Soul* (London. 1708).
63. Johnson to Berkeley III *Works* II 289. Johnson also wonders what Berkeley thinks of animal souls and how this affects his argument. One deficiency of this monograph is my failure to discuss this important issue. It is also a failure on Berkeley's part.
64. *A Reply to Mr. Clarke's Defence* (1707), 773.
65. *A Second Defence of an Argument* (1707), 793.
66. A.A. Luce, 'Another look at Berkeley's Notebooks,' *Hermathena* 110 (1970), 5–23. For a dissenting opinion see Bertil Belfrage, 'George Berkeley's "Philosophical Commentaries" A Review of Prof. A.A. Luce's Editions' in *Logik Rätt och Moral* (ed. Sören Halldén *et al.*) Lund: Studentlitteratur, 1969, 19–34.
67. It is hard to believe that Berkeley means something so abstract as 'being in general.' Instead, he has his own specific being or existence (as given in self-consciousness) in mind.
68. In *Alciphron*, Berkeley (like Clarke) denies that personal identity can obtain while memory fail. Moreover, he thinks that the memory account violates the law of the transitivity of identity, and cannot serve as an account of personal identity. Euphranor argues (*pace* Alciphron) that personal identity is itself a *mystery* on a

par with the mysteries about the Trinity (ALC VI.8, 298–99). The transitivity argument was apparently first formulated by Henry Grove. See Raymond Martin and John Barresi, *The Naturalization of the Soul: Self and Personal Identity in the Eighteenth Century* (Routledge. 2000), 72.

Chapter Two

1. Stephen Daniel argues that for Berkeley spirit is not a thing but the sheer existence of its ideas (and its very activity of willing and perceiving). See his 'Edwards, Berkeley, and Ramist Logic,' *Idealistic Studies* 31:1 (Winter 2001), 55–72; 'The Ramist Context of Berkeley's Philosophy,' *British Journal for the History of Philosophy* 9:3 (October 2001), 487–505; 'Berkeley, Súarez, and the 'Esse-Existere' Distinction,' *American Catholic Philosophical Quarterly* 74:4 (Fall 2000), 621–36; 'Berkeley's Stoic Notion of Spiritual Substance,' in Stephen H. Daniel (ed.), *New Interpretations of Berkeley's Thought* (Humanity Books. Amherst, NY. Forthcoming). For a critique of Daniel's position, see Ott and Hight (2004). For other rejections of the substance view, see Muehlmann (1992), Turbayne (1959), and A.C. Lloyd, 'The Self in Berkeley's Philosophy,' in *Essays on Berkeley: A Tercentennial Celebration* (ed. John Foster and Howard Robinson) (Clarendon: Oxford. 1985), 187–209.
2. See Michael Ayers, 'Substance, Reality, and the Great, Dead Philosophers,' *American Philosophical Quarterly* 7:1 (1970), 38–49. He identifies 'independent support' and 'causation' as the two main features which denominate Berkeleian spirit as substance in the common tradition (48). In his introduction to Ayers (ed.), *George Berkeley: Philosophical Works including the Works on Vision* (Everyman. 1975), he speaks of a 'single, shared concept of substance' (xxvi). He explains it as follows: 'Roughly, substances are the ultimate constituents of the universe upon which the phenomena depend' (xxvi). According to Hight and Ott the moderns shared the view that 'Substances persist through change and are ultimately simple by being independent of every other kind of thing' (6).
3. While distinctions can be drawn among 'mode,' 'accident,' 'property,' 'attribute,' Berkeley treats them as virtually interchangeable (and I will, too).
4. This interpretation was developed by Edwin B. Allaire, 'Berkeley's Idealism,' *Theoria* 29 (1963), 229–44. For a discussion of this account, see Muehlmann's introduction to *Berkeley's Metaphysics* where he provides further bibliographical information of the various articles in defense and in criticism of this view. See also George Pappas, *Berkeley's Thought* (Cornell University Press: Ithaca. 2000), 128–131.
5. For 'the adverbial account' see Pitcher (1977), 189–203, Margaret Atherton (1983), and William H. Beardsley, 'Berkeley on Spirit and Its Unity,' *History of Philosophy Quarterly* 18: 3 (2001) 259–77. For critical assessment, see Kenneth Winkler (1989), 290–300 and George Pappas (2000), 124–28.
6. See Phillip D. Cummins, 'Berkeley's Ideas of Sense,' *Nous* 9 (1975), 55–69. See also Cummins (1989).

7. See Grave (1968), 309, Winkler (1989), 298 note 18 and 309–12, and Fred Wilson 'On The Hausmans' "New Approach",' in Muehlmann (1995) 87.
8. It is sometimes claimed that Berkeleian ideas *inhere* in spirit, despite the fact that Berkeley never makes this claim. See Turbayne (1982), 297. For this general tendency to analogize, see Ayers (1975), xxv, xxviii and Winkler (1989), 192 and note 42.
9. Chapter 2, Ia20 in *Aristotle's Categories and De Interpretatione*, J.L. Ackrill (trans.) (Clarendon: Oxford. 1963), 4.
10. I do not mean that *all* predication involves accidents/modes. I mean only that accident/modes are predicated of their subjects. For a discussion of the distinction between predication and inherence in the medieval Aristotelian tradition and Spinoza, see John Carriero, 'On the Relationship between Mode and Substance in Spinoza's Metaphysics,' *Journal of the History of Philosophy* 33:2 (1995), 245–73.
11. Stillingfleet, *A Discourse in Vindication of the Trinity* (London. 1697), 236.
12. Citations of Descartes are from John Cottingham, Robert Stroothoff, and Dugald Murdoch (trans.), *The Philosophical Writings of Descartes*, 2 volumes [CSM] (Cambridge University Press: Cambridge. 1984), or from John Cottingham, Robert Stroothoff, Dugald Murdoch, and Anthony Kenny (trans.), *The Philosophical Writings of Descartes*, Volume III. *The Correspondence* [CSMK] (Cambridge University Press: Cambridge. 1991), and Charles Adam and Paul Tannery (eds), *Oevres de Descartes*, 12 Volumes [AT] (Paris. Leopold Cerf, 1897–1910, reprinted Vrin, 1964–76). Citations made by volume and page.
13. *On Being and Essence*, 2nd ed. (trans.) Armand Maurer (Pontifical Institute of Mediaeval Studies: Toronto. 1968) Chapter 1, sec. 2, 29–30.
14. Ibid., sec. 3, 30.
15. Ibid., sec. 5, 32–3.
16. See Charles J. McCracken, 'Berkeley on the Relation of Ideas to the Mind,' in Phillip D. Cummins and Guenter Zoeller (eds) *Minds, Ideas, and Objects: Essays on the Theory of Representation in Modern Philosophy* (Ridgeview: California. 1992), 187–200, 190.
17. Third Meditation, AT VII 40, CSM II 27–8.
18. Replies to First Set of Objections, AT VII 102–3, CSM II 74–5.
19. For an attempt to defend this position see William H. Beardsley, 'Berkeley on Spirit and Its Unity,' *History of Philosophy Quarterly* 18:3 (July 2001), 259–77, esp. 272–3.
20. Cummins (2005), 217.
21. Beardsley (2001), 270–1.
22. For example, Michael Ayers, *Locke: Epistemology and Ontology* (Routledge. 1991), two volumes, volume II, 15–128, Edwin McCann, 'Locke's Philosophy of Body,' in Vere Chappell (ed.), *The Cambridge Companion to Locke* (Cambridge University Press: Cambridge 1994), 56–88.
23. Stillingfleet, *Vindication*, 238.
24. Locke, *A Letter . . . to Worcester* (1697), 19.
25. The argument offered at PHK I 16 and then again in the *Dialogues* is aimed at Locke. In both cases, the target position involves the denial that there is any

positive idea or notion of the substratum and the affirmation that there is a relative notion of it. This is a distinctively Lockean position. See *Mr. Locke's Letter to the Right Reverend Bishop of Worcester* (21–2). For the view that Berkeley may not be attacking Locke, see Berman, 'On Missing the Wrong Target,' reprinted in Berman (2005).

26. There is some parity between PHK I 17 and PHK I 27, where Berkeley attacks the view that there is a complex idea of spiritual substance involving an idea of each of the principal powers and an idea 'of substance or being in general with the relative notion of its supporting . . . .' There is a contrast between the idea of substance (or being) in general and the relative notion of its supporting. If so, this is not a view that Locke would have endorsed since his idea of substance in general is not interchangeable with the idea of being in general, and his idea of substance in general is identical with the relative notion of a supporter (rather than that an idea to which the relative notion is added). This suggests that the target view at 27 is more robust than the Lockean view, and that, by parity, so too is the view attacked at 17. Possibly, Berkeley intends the expression to be sufficiently unclear to allow a criticism of Locke's deflated 'something in general' as well as the more robust '*ens*.' For a different interpretation, see Daniel Garber, 'Something-I-Know-Not-What: Berkeley on Locke on Substance,' in Ernest De Sosa (ed.), *Essays on The Philosophy of George Berkeley* (D. Reidel Publishing. 1987), 27–42.
27. Citations of *The Search after Truth* [SAT] are from Thomas M. Lennon and Paul J. Olscamp (trans. and eds) (Cambridge University Press: Cambridge. 1997).
28. I am grateful to Larry Nolan for helping me to see how Berkeley positions his work.
29. Winkler (1989) uses this passage to raise similar concerns about the status of mental acts in Berkeley's ontology (309–12).
30. See also PC 784 and 785.
31. Berman (2005) appeals to these passages to suggest that Berkeley's argument against substratum may be intended against Descartes.
32. Third Set of Objections and Replies, Reply to Third Objection, AT VII 177, CSM II 125.
33. Locke (1697) 7.
34. I do not take this to mean that Locke necessarily identifies the idea and the power as somehow the same thing. The point is that the simple ideas carry with them a supposition. For a related discussion (and a different account of Berkeley's response to Locke) see John Carriero, 'Berkeley, Resemblance, and Sensible Things,' *Philosophical Topics* 31: 1, 2 (2003) 21–46.
35. Locke (1697), 19, 21.
36. See Winkler (1989), 65–75.

Chapter Three

1. I follow I.C. Tipton's interpretation of Berkeleian spirit as something like a 'person' or 'self'. I depart from him in claiming that Berkeley's model of consciousness

differs in a serious way from Locke's. It is this difference which enables Berkeley to transform a self into a genuine substance. See Tipton's 'Berkeley's View of Spirit,' in Warren E. Steinkraus (ed.), *New Studies in Berkeley's Philosophy* (Holt, Rinehard, and Winston. New York. 1966), 59–71 and *Berkeley: The Philosophy of Immaterialism* (Methuen: London. 1974), 256–69.

2. Baxter, *An Enquiry into the Nature of the Human Soul* (London. 1733). Citations from the third edition (1745), volume two, 259–60.
3. *Second Meditation* (AT VII 29, CSM II 20).
4. Berkeley mentions passions and operations of the mind in section 1. It is doubtful that he means to list them as objects of the understanding given his view that spirits are not objects of the understanding. It is likewise doubtful that he refers to Lockean ideas of reflection *of* our mental operations. Instead, he is listing ideas which accompany them.
5. McCracken is one of the few commentators sensitive to Berkeley's spirit–idea 'dualism,' although he also sees it as fraught with difficulties. See 'Berkeley's Cartesian Concept of Mind: The Return through Malebranche and Locke to Descartes,' *The Monist* 71 (1988), 596–611.
6. *Principles of Philosophy* Part I, section 48, AT VIIIA 28, CSM I 208.
7. By '*cogito*' I refer to the first-personal consciousness that one is thinking (whenever one thinks).
8. Arnauld, *Des Vrayes et des Fausses Ideés* abbr. (Cologne. 1683), 46. trans. Elmar J. Kremar, *On True and False Ideas* (The Edwin Mellen Press. 1990), 25–6.
9. *The Passions of the Soul*, Part One, Section 19, AT XI 343, CSM I 335–6.
10. E.2.1.10, 115.
11. SAT Bk 1, Ch. 1, 3.
12. My interpretation of Descartes can be disputed. For a related discussion, see Tad Schmaltz, *Malebranche's Theory of the Soul: A Cartesian Interpretation* (Oxford University Press: Oxford. 1996), 18–21. See also Udo Thiel, 'Hume's Notions of Consciousness and Reflection in Context,' *British Journal for the History of Philosophy* 2:2 (1994), 75–115, esp. 91–2.
13. It would seem Malebranche does not allow for second-order reflection. But the issue is complex. See Thiel 96–7.
14. Second Set of Replies, AT VII 140, CSM II 100.
15. Sixth Set of Replies, AT VII 422, CSM II 285, and Second Meditation, AT VII 29, CSM II 20.
16. SAT 6, 2, 6, 480.
17. E. 4.9.3, 619.
18. Following Margaret Wilson's account of Descartes, I take this as a kind of *datum*. See *Descartes* (Routledge & Kegan Paul: London. 1978), 66–7. However, I wish to remain neutral on the question whether Descartes' *cogito* is an argument. In my view, one is immediately aware of both one's thought and one's existence. Insofar as thoughts are modes or properties of the mind, one is aware of the inferential relation which holds between thought and 'I.' This can be grasped in a simple perception.

19. For Malebranche, the soul is effectively thought itself; when one perceives a particular modification one *ipso facto* perceives one's soul. It is not obvious whether he would view the perception of one's existence as a distinct datum. Descartes' position is less clear. To the extent that Berkeley is correct in reading Descartes as distinguishing between the subject (this puzzling 'I') and the cogitation, it seems that Descartes accepted a two element model of consciousness.
20. I distinguish this from knowledge of the soul's *nature* which I discuss in the subsequent chapter.
21. For a formulation of the concern, see Cummins (2005), 208–9.
22. Pitcher (1977, 212–23) argues that for Berkeley, one has no direct awareness of one's own existence, it is merely self-evident (it is self-evident that one's ideas are *one's own*). The line between the two views is slight. The first edition version of PHK I 139 in which Berkeley recognizes that propositions 'I am nothing,' 'I am an idea,' 'I am a notion' as self-evidently absurd is evidence in favour of Pitcher's reading. However, given that Berkeley also speaks of 'that which I denote by the term I' as giving content to the term 'spirit' and seriously considers the view that this entity ought to viewed as an idea, it seems to me that Berkeley goes beyond mere self-evidence. See also S.C. Brown, 'Berkeley on the Unity of the Self,' *Reason and Reality*, Royal Institute of Philosophy Lectures 5, 1970–01 (Macmillan and St. Martin's Press: London. 1972).
23. For a discussion of such issues see Laurent Jaffro's 'Le *cogito* de Berkeley,' *Archives de Philosophie* 67 (2004). Jaffro argues (98) that that there is a difference between the knowledge of existence mentioned in the *Dialogues* and the claim that we comprehend our existence by inward feeling or reflexion (which he takes to include an awareness of one's activity). According to some of Berkeley's predecessors, one's very own existence is a constituent of the consciousness which accompanies all of our thinking and in this way constitutes a kind of datum. I take it that this is sufficiently robust to ground Berkeley's appeal to 'inward feeling.' For further relevant views see A.C. Lloyd, ' "The Self" in Berkeley's Philosophy,' in Foster and Robinson (1985) and Daniel Flage, *Berkeley's Doctrine of Notions: A Reconstruction based on his Theory of Meaning* (Croom Helm. 1987, Ch. 4).
24. *de Veritate*, Q 10, A 12, *ad.* 7. From Robert W. Mulligan, James V. McGlynn, and Robert W. Schmidt (trans.) *Truth*, 3 vols. (Henry Regnery Co.: Chicago. 1952–54). I owe this reference to John P. Carriero, 'The Second Meditation and the Essence of the Mind,' in Amélie Oksenberg Rorty (ed.), *Essays on Descartes'* Meditations (University of California Press. 1986), 202.
25. *Second Meditation*. AT VII 34, CSM II 22–3.
26. SAT 6. P 2. 6, 481.
27. SAT 6. 2. 6. 480.
28. E. 4. 9.3, 618.
29. SAT 3. 2. 5, 228.
30. This view is similar to what Tom Stoneham calls 'The Simplest Model of Perception (SMP).' See Stoneham's *Berkeley's World: An Examination of the Three Dialogues* (Oxford University Press: Oxford. 2002), 54–6.

31. *Summa Theologica* I Q 85 A.2.
32. *Elucidations of the Search after Truth. Elucidation Eleven*, 633. Citations of *The Elucidations of the Search after Truth* [EST] are from Thomas M. Lennon (trans. and ed.) (Cambridge University Press: Cambridge. 1997), 633.
33. Ibid., 633–4.
34. Ibid., 634.
35. Ibid., 636.
36. According to McCracken, Berkeley and Malebranche do not differ seriously with respect to their views about self-awareness. Because of this, McCracken represents Berkeley's denial that we can have an idea of spirit as the position that since ideas are mere images, there can be no idea of spirit. One of the questions left unanswered by this interpretation, is why the impossibility of attaining *a priori* knowledge about spirit should no longer disappoint us. See *Malebranche and British Philosophy* (Clarendon: Oxford. 1983), 248–50.
37. According to Daniel (2000, 633), spirits are not objects of perception, but active perception itself. One difficulty is that by identifying spirits with the *existence* of ideas, Berkeley's view that spirit and idea have nothing in common is undermined; an idea and the existence thereof have something in common (namely the idea itself).
38. For a related reading of Berkeley's *esse* is *percipi* principle, see Phillip D. Cummins, 'Berkeley's Ideas of Sense,' *Noûs* 9 (1975), 55–72. Unlike Cummins, I do not view Berkeleian ideas as states.
39. I take this to answer Muehlman's concern that the support relation (perception) needs explication (1992), 182–3. Consequently, spirits serve one important function of substances.

Chapter Four

1. Conversations with John Carriero stimulated my thoughts about Berkeley's treatment of analogy.
2. *De veritate* Q. 2, A. XI, d.7, ad. 7.
3. *Summa Theologica* I Q 13, A 5
4. Aristotle *Metaphysics* IV, 2 (1003a 34ff.); Aquinas, ibid.
5. Perhaps Berkeley's extreme claim is simply a 'nominalist style' endorsement of a scale of being. This is Ayers' view, who argues that what Berkeley does '. . . emphatically retain from Aristotelian theory is the conception of an ontological order of ranking, a scale of being.' See 'Berkeley and the Meaning of Existence,' *The History of European Ideas* 7 (1986), 567–73, 571–2. The following considerations show why this won't work.
6. *de Nominum Analogia* Chapter 4, § 32. From Edward A. Bushinski with Henry J. Koren (trans.), *The Analogy of Names and The Concept of Being* (Duquesne University: Pittsburgh. 1959).
7. Ibid., Ch.6, § 63.
8. TVV 6.

9. For a view that Berkeley's discussion of analogy in *Alciphron* marks a change from his official *Principles* view, see Brykman (1993), 382–3.
10. *Elements of Philosophy, The First Section Concerning Body*, translated into English (London: 1656), Part One, Ch. 2. § 12. My inserts.
11. The degree to which Berkeley's theory of general terms conforms to Cajetan's notion of analogy is a question that I do not have the opportunity to explore.
12. For another discussion of Cajetan's views, see Geneviève Brykman (1993), 380–2; and *Berkeley: Philosophie et Apologétique* (Vrin: Paris. 1984), 493–95.
13. Cajetan, ch. 2, §10–11; Ch. 4, § 34–5.
14. Ibid., ch. 3 § 25.
15. Ibid., ch. 7 § 75–6.
16. Ibid., ch. 3 § 26.
17. Ibid., ch. 7 § 77.
18. Ibid., ch. 10 § 110.
19. See J. O'Higgins, 'Browne and King, Collins and Berkeley: Agnosticism or Anthropomorphism?' *Journal of Theological Studies* 27 (1976), 88–112.
20. Cajetan, Ch. 4 § 36–37, *The Concept of Being* § 3–6
21. Flage (1987) argues that Berkeley is here concerned with metaphor (123–130). Note that in TVV, Berkeley equates 'metaphor' and 'analogy' while in NTV he equates 'likeness' with 'analogy' and denies that such analogy obtains between visible and tangible extension, figure, and motion. This shift in emphasis (from proper to metaphoric analogy) may reflect Berkeley's desire to expose the danger caused by those philosophers (TVV 6).
22. Turbayne (1959), Brykman (1983), 626–7.
23. For the concern that this conflicts with Berkeley's claim that sensible terms are borrowed for spiritual actions, see Winkler, 'Berkeley and the Doctrine of Signs,' in Winkler (2005), 125–65.
24. *Principles of Philosophy*, Part One §51–2, CSM I 210.
25. For accounts of the disagreement between Browne and Berkeley see W.W. S. March, 'Analogy, Aquinas, and Bishop Berkeley,' *Theology* 44 (1942), 321–9, Paul J. Olscamp, *The Moral Philosophy of George Berkeley* (Martinus Nijhoff: The Hague. 1970), Ch. 9, Arthur Winnett, *Peter Browne: Provost, Bishop, Metaphysician* (SPCK: London. 1973) Ch. 11; O'Higgins (1976), Brykman (1984) 531–47; 591–604; Brykman (1993) 375–84; 409–15.
26. In his section devoted to Berkeley, Browne points to the deficiencies of the example of the blind man, effectively conceding ground to Berkeley. *Analogy* 412–20. See note 28.
27. *Procedure*, 98.
28. *Things Divine and Supernatural Conceived by Analogy with Things Natural and Human* (London. 1733). Reprinted by Thoemmes 1990.
29. Berkeley is not a convert to *Irish* analogy. He does, however, accept something like Cajetan's version of it. Earlier, Berkeley had expressed a similar rejection. See p. 5.
30. I therefore reject interpretations of Berkeleian mystery as non-cognitivist in nature. See David Berman, 'Cognitive theology and emotive mysteries in Berke-

ley's *Alciphron*,' *Proceedings of the Royal Irish Academy* 81, C, no. 7 (1981), 219–29, reprinted in *George Berkeley: Alciphron or the minute philosopher in focus*, D. Berman (ed.) (Routledge: London. 1993), 200–13, and Berman (1994), 144–63. For a non-cognitivist interpretation of Berkeley's theory of meaning in his earlier work, see Belfrage (1985), Belfrage 'Berkeley's Emotive Theory of Meaning (1708),' *History of European Ideas* 7:6 (1986), 643–99, Belfrage, 'Development of Berkeley's early theory of meaning,' *Revue Philosophique de la France de l'Etranger* 3 (1986), 319–30, Belfrage (1987). For replies to Belfage see Robert McKim, '*The entries in Berkeley's Notebooks: a reply to Bertil Belfrage*,' *Hemathena* 139 (1985), 156–61, Kenneth Williford, 'Berkeley's Theory of Operative Language in the *Manuscript Introduction*,' *British Journal for the History of Philosophy* 11:2 (2003), 271–301. For further bibliographic information and a powerful critique of Berman's view, see Roomet Jakapi, 'Emotive Meaning and Christian Mysteries in Berkeley's *Alciphron*,' *British Journal for the History of Philosophy* 10: 3 (2002), 401–11.

31. Not all Christian mysteries may seem definable in terms of cause, subject, effect, and circumstances (such as the Trinity). It is interesting to note, however, that even here Euphranor glosses the three in terms of action-expressions: 'Creator,' 'Redeemer,' and 'Sanctifier' (ALC VII 8, 297).
32. According to Belfrage (1986), Berkeley's 1708 sermon 'On Immortality' reflects a middle-stage between an earlier Lockean theory of meaning and Berkeley's alleged emotivist theory (at this stage Berkeley still believes in an actual afterlife of which non-human beings have conceptions). Yet in *Guardian* Essay 27 (1713), Berkeley uses the analogy of the blind man to give some dim sense of what is in store for us after death. This suggests that after the *Manuscript Introduction* Berkeley continues to believe in the future state as a genuine mystery.
33. I differ from the view offered by Roomet Jakapi according to which mystery terms have a true sense known to God but not human beings. See his 'Faith, Truth, Revelation and Meaning in Berkeley's Defense of The Christian Religion (in *Alciphron*),' *The Modern Schoolman* 80 (2002), 23–34, 32.
34. Collins argues 'for God's existence' in his *Answer to Mr. Clarke's Third Defence* (1708, 883–5). He argues that to show matter is not self-existent, we need some conception of *creation ex nihilo*. Collins provides no clue how this is be done. As Berman insightfully argues, the 'argument' seems atheistic in nature. Berkeley has answered this worry by showing we have an example of such *creation ex nihilo* in our own thinking. See D. Berman, *A History of Atheism in Britain: From Hobbes to Russell* (Croom Helm. 1988), 79–82; and Berman (1994), 42–44.
35. Browne worries that because Berkeley thinks terms such as 'wise' apply to God literally, he views the attributes of finite spirit and God as of the same kind, differing only in degree (*Analogy* 404). Berkeley's answer may lie in his peculiar views about kinds. For it seems that even general kind terms such as 'triangle' involve analogy.
36. Browne worries that Berkeley renders finite spirits fundamentally imperfect or defective. But how could God create something imperfect? (*Analogy* 442). It is worth noting that King and Browne had earlier disputed this point. According to King, evil comes from the imperfection which is necessarily part of created beings.

Browne denies that creatures can be 'imperfect in their kind.' In a letter no longer extant, King had suggested that what seemed to be evil was not really evil at all. See Winnett (1974), 34–5. See PHK I 153.

37. That God is passionless is a disconcerting view. How does one understand the incarnation? It is the view which Berkeley holds.
38. See Chapter One.
39. According to Flage's interpretation of Berkley (1987, Ch.4), we have positive notions of perception and causation, and only relative notions of our selves and our mental acts. I have argued that Berkeley rejects modes, and as a consequence we are not aware of thoughts as properties which belong to us. Instead, we are aware only of ourselves and our objects. We are directly aware of our own existence and this awareness is sufficiently robust to yield knowledge of ourselves as agents.

Chapter Five

1. See C. C. W. Taylor, 'Action and Inaction in Berkeley,' in Foster and Robinson (1985), 211–25, Robert Imlay, 'Berkeley and Action,' in Muehlmann (1995), 171–81, Catherine Wilson, 'On "Berkeley and Action",' in Muehlmann (1995), 183–96.
2. E. 2.21.17, 242.
3. Collins *Essay* (1707), 48–9, *An Answer to Mr. Clarke's Third Defence* (1708), 872. See also *A Philosophical Inquiry concerning Human Liberty* (1717).
4. SAT bk 1 ch. 1, 5.
5. Pitcher argues that with respect to bodily movement, Berkeley maintains finite spirits are occasional causes. He argues that Berkeley is likewise relegated to occasionalism with respect the causation of images through image-volitions. See 'Berkeley on the Mind's Activity,' *American Philosophical Quarterly* 18:3 (1981), 221–7. For a clear statement of the problem that afflicts Berkeley's account, see Nicholas Jolley, 'Berkeley and Malebranche on Causality and Volition,' in *Central Themes in Early Modern Philosophy: Essay presented to Jonathan Bennett*, J.A. Cover and Mark Kulstad (eds), (Hackett: Indianapolis. 1990), 227–43. An interesting solution to the threat of occasionalism is offered by Kenneth Winkler (1989), Ch. 5. According to this view, Berkeley distinguishes between a cause and occasion not by appeal to a necessary connection but to the intelligibility conferred by volitions.
6. This interpretation of Berkeley's denial of 'blind agency' (PC 812, 841, 842) is offered by Winkler. See 'Unperceived objects and Berkeley's denial of blind agency,' *Hermathena* 139 (1985), 81–100. Robert Muehlmann argues that Berkeley's commitment to this doctrine is far more complicated and troubled. See 'Berkeley's Problem of Sighted Agency,' in Muehlmann (1995), 149–69.
7. See Phillip D.Cummins, 'Berkeley on minds and agency' (2005), 222. Muehlmann also argues that there is a tension between Berkeley's denial of blind agency and his radical distinction between volitions and ideas (1995, 163–4, 168–9).
8. See A.D. Woozley, 'Berkeley on Action,' *Philosophy* 60 (1985), 293–307, 302.

9. See Jonathan Bennett, *Locke, Berkeley, Hume: Central Themes* (Clarendon: Oxford. 1971), 207, John Immerwahr, 'Berkeley's Causal Thesis,' *New Scholasticism* 48 (1974), 153–70, 166. See also Muehlmann (1995, 164).
10. EST 15, 669.
11. I take this to answer Muehlman's concern that spirits are unneeded as causes (1992), 177–8.
12. Philonous represents sound as '*loud, sweet, acute,* or *grave*' (3D I 182). And later, 'Look!' Philonous exclaims, 'are not the fields covered with a delightful verdure ... How sincere a pleasure is it to behold the natural beauties of the earth' (3D II 210). In his notebooks, Berkeley suggests that *all* ideas involve pain: 'No Ideas perfectly void of all pain & uneasiness But wt are preferable to annihilation' (PC 833).
13. For a discussion of this tension see A. A. Luce, 'Sensible ideas and sensations,' *Hermathena* 105 (1967), 74–83.
14. Geneviève Brykman draws this distinction between two aspects of the idea ('thing-idea' and 'affect-idea'). The affective side of an idea is a '... relational property of these thing-ideas to ourselves.' See 'Pleasure and pain versus ideas in Berkeley,' *Hermathena* 105 (1967).
15. I worry about the adequacy of a distinction between the cognitive and affective. Following Tipton (1974), 231, Brykman suggests that in the case of intense pain, the cognitive aspect of heat (the thing-idea) is overpowered by pain and vanishes.
16. I assume that God perceives and that imagination counts as perception, although this has been denied in the literature. Since the existence of an idea consists in being perceived, it follows that divine and imagined ideas are perceived. The opposition comes from the view that neither involves passivity. If we understand 'perception' in the sense of 'consciousness,' there is no difficulty (especially since we recognize active perception). See George Thomas, 'Berkeley's God does not perceive,' *Journal of the History of Philosophy* 14 (1976), 163–8. See also George Pitcher (1977), 163–79. For disagreement see Grayling (1986), 110–11, Winkler (1989), 205, and Pappas (2000), 108–9.
17. For a general statement of the problem, see Donald Gotterbarn, 'Berkeley: God's Pain,' *Philosophical Studies* 28 (1975), 245–54. See also Steven Nadler's 'Berkeley's Ideas and the Primary/Secondary Distinction,' *Canadian Journal of Philosophy* 20:1 (1990), 47–61, esp. 57 for a powerful formulation of the problem. McCracken, 'Berkeley's Realism,' in Stephen H. Daniel (ed.), *New Interpretations of Berkeley's Thought* (Humanity Books. Amherst, NY. Forthcoming), uses this point to argue against A.C. Grayling's view that while numerically distinct, God's ideas resemble our own.
18. The concern is about counting self-produced ideas as objects of perception. We should distinguish between (i) ideas actively produced; and (ii) 'unreal' ideas. The two are brought together in the case of human imagination. However the real/unreal contrast is relative to human perception. The relevant distinction between real and unreal doesn't seem to be in play for God.
19. Gotterbarn (1975) raises this type of concern, 250.

20. See Charles J. McCracken, 'Berkeley on the Relation of Ideas to the Mind,' in Cummins and Zoeller (1992), 194.
21. This solution can accommodate other Berkeleian remarks which seem to undermine his identification of intense heat with pain. For example, Philonous speaks of '... pleasure and pain being rather annexed to the former [secondary qualities] than the latter [primary qualities]' (3D I 191).
22. For this argument see Robert McKim, 'Berkeley's Active Mind,' *Archiv für Geschichte der Philosophie* 71 (1989), 335–43, 337.
23. *Works* II, Berkeley to Johnson IV § 3, 293.
24. For the view that sense-perception is also active for Berkeley, see A.A. Luce, 'Berkeleian Action and Passion' in *Revue Internationale de Philosophie* 7 (1966), 3–18, I.C. Tipton, *Berkeley: The Philosophy of Immaterialism* (Methuen: London. 1974), 268–9, McKim (1989), Daniel (2001).
25. For a good discussion of this point, see Robert McKim, 'Berkeley on Private Ideas and Public Objects,' in Cummins and Zoeller (1992), 215–33, 228, and note 26.
26. For the kind of reading I am arguing against, see esp. McKim (1992), p. 228. See also Stephen H. Daniel, 'Berkeley's Christian Neoplatonism, Archetypes, and Divine Ideas,' *Journal of the History of Philosophy* 39:2 (2001), 239–58, esp. 246.
27. Grayling makes a similar suggestion (1986, 99). McCracken, 'Berkeley's Realism' (forthcoming) worries this will leave Berkeley's God with an eternal realm distinct from himself. Even so, this 'realm' would be dependent upon God. More importantly, the realm is no more than what God knows and thinks – hardly a weighty realm on a par with matter.
28. While Berkeley tends to speak of passions as momentary emotions, rather than dispositions to experience such emotions, Berkeley can allow talk of love that concerns the tendency of a person to enjoy grapes.
29. For a nice statement of this problem, see Charles McCracken, 'Berkeley's Notion of Spirit,' *History of European Ideas* 7 (1986), 597–602, 602.
30. This might provide the basis for a Berkeleian account of animals. He recognizes that beasts sense-perceive (3D I 188). The question is how to distinguish them from finite spirits. He can say that animals only perceive passively. Consequently, they are not aware of their passivity, since they lack any active component. The further question how to conceptualize their consciousness is not something I know how to answer.
31. E. 2.30.3, 229–30.
32. Locke adopted this view in the 2nd edition of the *Essay*.
33. For a related suggestion, see Brykman (1985), 135.
34. Locke accepts this type of account. 'Habits have powerful charms, and put so strong attractions of easiness and pleasure into what we accustom our selves ...' (E. 1.21.69, 280).
35. For an alternative account of how 'good' receives an 'emotive meaning,' see Belfrage's editor's commentary (1987), 46–7.

36. Robert McKim defends the view that, according to Berkeley, we can in fact cause some of our sensations. See his 'Berkeley on Human Agency,' *History of Philosophical Quarterly* 1:2 (1984), 181–94.
37. McKim (1984) considers the view that finite spirits are the actual causes of bodily motions and bodily motions the occasional causes of sensations, while claiming that corporeal motion cannot be separated from sensations (188). He does not consider this passage where Berkeley seems to be distinguishing ideas of corporeal motions and sensations.
38. Berkeley sometimes seems to suggest sensible ideas are the only real things and that being caused from without is essential to their reality. See 3D III 235. Yet in even this passage – 'But the ideas perceived by sense, that is, real things, are more vivid and clear, and . . . have not a like dependence on our will' – it isn't obvious Philonous is *restricting* real things to sensible things, rather than simply saying that they *are* real things. In this passage Philonous goes on to cite the unreality of dreams on the basis of their lack of vivacity, irregularity, and lack of connection with the rest of our lives. The unreality of dream ideas derives from their lack of connection to the laws of nature. This leaves open the possibility for unreal ideas that are caused from without.
39. According to Stoneham (2002), the difference between acting (in the world) and imagining is that the former but not the latter involves causing sensations in others (who are present to the action) or affecting the world in such a way that others perceive the right ideas under the right conditions. His policy is to 'ignore' PHK I 147 where Berkeley insists that we only cause our own corporeal motions as simply a mistake on Berkeley's part, since we would then only cause something that was private to ourselves (187). However, what makes an idea real is its vivacity and connectedness with other ideas. While an idea of my corporeal motion ('from the inside') may be in some way private, it is nonetheless the occasion of sensible ideas and therefore part of the causal order.
40. Winkler (2005), 158–9, worries that removing imperfections requires an abstraction not allowed on Berkeley's principles. I don't see the difficulty in recognizing that our imaginations are limited by sense-perception and memory, nor the difficulty in supposing God lacks those limitations.

Chapter Six

1. Collins *Essay* (1707), 48–9, *An Answer to Mr. Clarke's Third Defence* (1708), 872. See also *A Philosophical Inquiry concerning Human Liberty* (1717).
2. For a thorough discussion of Berkeley's arguments for liberty against the freethinkers in *Alciphron*, see Geneviève Brykman, 'On Human Liberty in Berkeley's *Alciphron* VII,' in Stephen H. Daniel (ed.), *New Interpretations of Berkeley's Thought* (Humanity Books. Amherst, NY. Forthcoming).
3. See *Berkeley & Malebranche: A Study in the Origins of Berkeley's Thought* (Clarendon: Oxford. 1934), 84. See also 'Mind-dependence in Berkeley,' *Hermathena* 57

(1941), 117–27. T.E. Jessop is known for a similar view, and there has been talk of a 'Luce–Jessop' interpretation, although the interpretations were apparently developed independently. See Luce on this point in *The Dialectic of Immaterialism: An account of the making of Berkeley's Principles* (Hodder and Stoughton: London. 1963), 9. This interpretation is frequently referred to as a 'common-sense realist' reading. I have avoided using this name for two reasons. First, as George Pappas shows, the position may involve a group of different theses. See, for example, Pappas, 'Berkeley and Common Sense Realism,' *History of Philosophy Quarterly* 8 (1991), 27–42. The only claims that I am interested in are formulated on pages 88–9. Second, the expressions 'common-sense' and 'realism' may be used by philosophers in so many different ways. An example of this is that while Luce took himself to be *defending* 'naïve realism' by arguing that material things are composed of sense data, Pappas takes common-sense realism to involve the claim that 'no macro-physical object has *sensa* (phenomenal individuals) as constituents.' Contrast Pappas (1991), 28 with Luce's 'A critique of Professor H. H. Price's refutation of the naïve realist theory of perception,' *Hermathena* 50 (1936), 60–85. Luce expressed discomfort with the term 'realism,' only endorsing it later on in his career. Contrast, for example, his *Berkeley's Immaterialism* (Thomas Nelson and Sons: London. 1945), 28 with what he says in *The Dialectic of Immaterialism* (166).

4. See David Berman, 'Berkeley's Quad: The Question of Numerical Identity,' *Idealistic Studies* 16 (1986), 41–5; Berman (1994), 50–2; Jonathan Dancy, *Berkeley: An Introduction* (Oxford: Blackwell. 1987), 41–56; Marc A. Hight, 'Defending Berkeley's Divine Ideas,' *Philosophia* 33: 1–4 (2005), 97–128; George Pappas, 'Berkeley, Perception, and Common Sense,' in Turbayne (1982), 3–21; *Berkeley's Thought* (Cornell University Press: Ithaca. 2000), 200–1; David Raynor, 'Berkeley's Ontology,' *Dialogue* 26 (1987), 611–20; John Yolton, *Perceptual Acquaintance from Descartes to Reid* (Blackwell: Oxford. 1984), 132–7; *Perception and Reality: A history from Descartes to Kant* (Cornell: Ithaca. 1996).
5. See Charles McCracken, 'What *Does* Berkeley's God see in the Quad,' *Archiv für Geschichte der Philosphie* 61 (1979), 280–92; 'Berkeley's Realism' (forthcoming); Robert McKim in Cummins and Zoeller (1992); George Pitcher (1977), 201–3; 'Berkeley on the Perception of Objects,' *Journal of the History of Philosophy* 24 (1986), 99–105, Kenneth Winkler (1989), 300–9; David Yandell, 'Berkeley on Common Sense and the Privacy of Ideas,' *Journal of History of Philosophical Quarterly* 12 (1995), 411–23.
6. For a related formulation from which this one originally derived, see McKim (1992), 220.
7. Jessop also accepts (2) and (3). See his *Works* Introduction to the *Principles*, 10–11.
8. While these claims are related, they are also distinct. One may assert (2) without holding (1), although it seems hard to see how (2) is not, in Berkeley's universe at least, necessary for (1). While (3) presupposes (2), (3) does not necessarily follow from (2). It may be the case that while God perceives whatever I perceive, he only perceives it on the condition that I perceive it, too.

9. See Leopold Stubenberg, 'Divine Ideas: The Cure-All for Berkeley's Immaterialism?' *Southern Journal of Philosophy* 28: 2 (1990), 221–49. Stubenberg argues that because different finite spirits have different perspectives, it is impossible for them to perceive ideas which are exactly alike. This objection is at its strongest in the case of vision where the spatial positioning of the perceiver matters. The concern is a bit harder to press with respect to sound, smell, touch, and taste. I wonder why two perceivers can't have exactly resembling visible ideas so long as they occupy the same vantage point at different times.
10. According to Hight (2005), God and finite perceiver share numerically identical sensible ideas (97), while it is unknown to us from our sensory standpoint whether two finite perceivers who perceive qualitatively identical sensible ideas perceive two qualitatively identical ideas or one numerically identical idea (114). It strikes me as highly un-Berkeleian to suppose a subtle metaphysical question (whether our ideas are numerically distinct) beyond our knowledge. Berkeley would be inclined to say that such discussions are fine-spun metaphysical nonsense. This is why he ridicules the 'abstract philosophical' idea of identity in the *Dialogues* discussion of sameness.
11. I read Philonous' claim that 'If the term *same* be taken in the vulgar acceptation, it is certain . . . that different persons may perceive the same thing . . .' (3D III 247) as the claim that the vulgar attribute *numerical identity* on the basis of *qualitative identity*. For discussion of this issue, see Donald Baxter, 'Berkeley, Perception, and Identity,' *Philosophy and Phenomenological Research* 51:1 (1991), 85–98, 89–90.
12. One may deny this by attributing to Berkeley a distinction between private sensible ideas and public qualities and things (such as tables and trees) construed as collections of the private ideas (held by the different perceivers). However, Berkeley argues for the independence of sensible things on the basis of their being caused against one's will suggesting that sensible ideas are independent as well (3D II 214).
13. This is a nice consequence of my view, since in the Lucian-style interpretation God and finite perceiver perceive numerically identical ideas, Philonous' appeal to archetypes must be rejected as not reflecting Berkeley's true view.
14. There are probably as many interpretations of this passage as there are interpreters. See Michael Ayers, 'Divine Ideas and Berkeley's Proof of God's Existence,' in *Essays on The Philosophy of George Berkeley*, Ernest Sosa (ed.), (D. Reidel Publishing: Dordrecht. 1987), 115–42; Baxter (1991), David Braybrooke, 'Berkeley on the Numerical Individuation of Ideas,' *The Philosophical Review* 64:4 (1955), 631–6; Daniel Flage, 'Berkeley, Individuation, and Physical Objects,' in *Individuation and Identity in Early Modern Philosophy*, Kenneth F. Barber and Jorge J.E. Gracia (eds), (State University of New York Press: Albany. 1994), 133–54; Luce (1934) 84; Pitcher (1977) 146–51; Raynor (1987) 617–8; Stoneham (2002), 266–70, Stubenberg (1990); Winkler (1989) 302–4.
15. Muehlmann (1992) is correct that Berkeleian substance does not fulfill one of the three major functions that he claims substances are supposed to fulfill (namely individuation), 174–5. Hight and Ott (2004) are too dismissive of the view that

substances had an important role to play with respect to individuation. Substances commonly played a key role in individuating the modes which inhered in them. Even Locke himself, whom Muehlmann, Hight and Ott recognize as departing from this view, assigns substance an important role in his reasoning: 'All other things being but Modes or Relations ultimately terminated in Substances, the Identity and Diversity of each particular Existence of them too will be by the same way determined' (E. 2.27.2, 329).

16. For a fascinating and comprehensive examination of Berkeley's views on bodily resurrection, see Marc A. Hight, 'Berkeley and Bodily Resurrection,' *Journal of the History of Philosophy* (forthcoming).
17. According to Hight (ibid.), while there is a fact of the matter whether qualitatively identical perceptually intermittent sensible ideas are numerically identical, this is not something that we know. The important point is that such questions are *idle* and hence do not undermine the analogies of resurrection that Berkeley gives to make bodily resurrection seem plausible. See my preceding note 10.
18. For a similar discussion of resurrection, see ALC VI.11, 241.
19. 'On Eternal Life,' *Works* VII 108.
20. I Corinthians 15:42–4.
21. *Works* II Berkeley to Johnson IV, 293.
22. For thorough and provoking discussion of the concerns see I.C. Tipton (1974), 272–92; see also Pitcher (1977), 203–11. For attempted solutions, see A.A Luce (1963) 176–81; Grayling (1986), 174–83; H. Scott Hestevold, 'Berkeley's Theory of Time,' *History of Philosophy Quarterly* 7:2 (1990), 179–92, See also E. J. Furlong, 'On Being "Embrangled" by Time,' in Turbayne (1982), 148–55.
23. Hestevold's solution requires that Berkeley retreat into Descartes' position by supposing that we think while sleeping (187).
24. Grayling tries to solve the difficulty by appealing to a pragmatic and public (although not metaphysically objective) notion of time (179).
25. See Hestevold (1990), 181.
26. See Tipton (1974), 274, Pitcher (1997), 210, Grayling (1986), 179.
27. Hestevold likewise appeals to God to secure an atemporal ordering, although to a different end.
28. *Works* II Johnson to Berkeley III 289.
29. For a powerful discussion of the problem that multiple perspectives seems to introduce for Berkeley, see Tipton (1974).
30. Pitcher (1977), 207, Grayling (1986), 181–2.
31. *Works* II Berkeley to Johnson IV 293.
32. Ibid.
33. *Summa Theologica* I Q 13. Art. 7.
34. This may suggest that we have a better comprehension of the divine intellect than the will. For perception does not require a beginning or end, while actions (in time) do.
35. *A Demonstration of the Being and Attributes of God*, sec. V and Sermon IV: *Of the Eternity of God* (*Works* I 2).
36. See Stillingfleet's *Vindication* (1697), 282.

Chapter Seven

1. See Brykman (1993), 412.
2. For a list of five apparent uses of 'notion,' see Désirée Park, *Complementary Notions* (Martinus Nijhoff: The Hague. 1972), 54–5.
3. There are many interpretations of the 'doctrine of notions.' In one interpretation, notions are concepts of spirits and their acts, or they are spirits and their acts themselves *qua* understood in the mind. See Harry M. Bracken, 'Berkeley and Mental Acts,' *Theoria* 26 (1960), 140–6, Bracken, *Berkeley* (St. Martin's Press: New York. 1974), 82–5 and 135–48, Park (1972), 15–16, and Tipton (1974), 270. In another, notions are identified with mental acts (Flage, 1987, Ch. 5). A third account understands 'notion' in terms of the instrumentalist use of terms. A.D. Woozley, 'Berkeley's Doctrine of Notions and Theory of Meaning,' *Journal of the History of Philosophy* 14 (1976), 427–34, Brykman (1982) 613–4, Brykman (1993), 413–4.
4. Imagined ideas are produced by an act of the mind, and this does not mean we know them by notions. What Berkeley has in mind is that in order to 'perceive' a relation we imaginatively compare two different ideas. There is no third thing which we perceive. Consequently we have no idea of it.
5. For another discussion of the parity dispute, see Phillip Cummins, 'Hylas' Parity Argument,' in Turbayne (1982), 283–94.
6. That Berkeley even gives an argument is interesting, since he usually says that we are aware of ourselves as distinct from ideas. Cummins takes the claim that one idea cannot perceive another as a metaphysical principle from which Berkeley concludes from the experienced empirical self to an unexperienced substantial self (291). In my interpretation, the 'empirical self' is the 'substantial self.' The 'I' is bound to its ideas in consciousness, the 'I' continues through time, numerically identical.
7. For a similar point see Garber (1987), 34–6.
8. For discussion of Baxter's criticisms see Harry M. Bracken, *The Early Reception of Berkeley's Immaterialism: 1710–1733*, revised ed. (Martinus Mijhoff: The Hague. 1965), Ch. 5; Brykman (1984), 518–31; Brykman (1993), 406–9; C.J. McCracken and I.C. Tipton, *Berkeley's Principles and Dialogues: Background Source Materials* (Cambridge University Press: Cambridge. 2000), Ch. 15.
9. For the intriguing view that Berkeley may have been influenced by Hume see Colin M. Turbayne, 'Hume's Influence on Berkeley,' *Revue Internationale de Philosophie* 39 (1985), 259–69.
10. For different accounts of these passages see McCracken (1984), 598, Beardsley (2001) 260–7. A standard view has been to reject them on the grounds many are marked with the '+' sign. A.A. Luce suggested that mark was used as an obelus to black-list discarded entries. This has been disputed by Bertil Belfrage. See Luce (1970) and Belfrage, 'A New Approach to Berkeley's *Philosophical Notebooks*,' in Sosa (1987), 217–30.

11. Turbayne (1959), 85.
12. According to this traditional view Berkeley *infers* a substantial soul. For a nice response see Atherton (1983).
13. See R.H. Popkin, 'Did Hume ever Read Berkeley?,' *Journal of Philosophy* 56 (1959) 535–545; Philip P. Wiener and Ernest C. Mossner in the same volume (533–5, 992–5) and Antony Flew and Wiener (twice) in *Journal of Philosophy* 58 (1961) 50–1, 207–9, 327–8. A letter (August 31, 1737) was discovered in which Hume encourages Michael Ramsay to read Berkeley's *Principles* in order to better understand 'the metaphysical parts of my reasoning,' reprinted in Popkin's 'So, Hume did Read Berkeley,' *Journal of Philosophy* 61 (1964), 773–78. Nonetheless, Popkin urges that Berkeley's influence was minimal. Discussion then focuses on whether Hume used the *Principles* in composing the *Treatise*. See Roland Hall, 'Hume's Actual Use of the Principles,' *Philosophy* 43 (1968) 278–80, Graham P. Conroy, 'Did Hume Really Follow Berkeley?' *Philosophy* 44 (1969) 238–80, Hall, 'Yes, Hume Did Use Berkeley,' *Philosophy* 45 (1970), 152–3. Michael Morrisroe Jr. provides evidence of a letter to Ramsay prior to the completion of the *Treatise* (September, 29 1734) in which Hume expresses his 'Pleasure to read over again today Locke's *Essays* and the Principles of Human Knowledge by Dr. Berkeley . . . .' See 'Did Hume Read Berkeley? A Conclusive Answer,' *Philological Quarterly* 52:2 (1973), 310–5, 314–15.
14. The second reference is from the first *Essay* (cited below). The third is from his 1763 essay 'Of National Characters' in which Hume references Berkeley's *Alciphron*. See Eugene Miller (ed.), *David Hume: Essays, Moral, Political, and Literary* (1985), 209.
15. Citations of *A Treatise of Human Nature* [T] refer to book, part, section, paragraph, and page. All references are from David Fate Norton and Mary J. Norton (eds), (Oxford University Press: Oxford. 2000). I include page references for L.A. Selby-Bigge (ed.) with revisions and notes by P.H. Nidditch (2nd ed.) [SBN] (Clarendon: Oxford. 1978).
16. D.R. Raynor '"*Minima Sensibilia*" in Berkeley and Hume,' *Dialogue* 19 (1980), 196–9; M. R. Ayers, 'Berkeley and Hume: A question of influence,' in R. Rorty, Schneewind, and Skinner (eds), *Philosophy in History* (Cambridge University Press: Cambridge. 1983), 303–27; D.R. Raynor, 'Hume and Berkeley's *Three Dialogues*,' in M.A. Stewart (ed.), *Studies in the Philosophy of the Scottish Enlightenment* (Oxford University Press: Oxford. 1990), 231–50.
17. Hall (1968), 280, Hall (1970), 152, Ayers (1983), 320.
18. Ayers, 316–20.
19. Citations of *An Enquiry concerning Human Understanding* [EHU] refer to section, paragraph, and page. All references are from Tom L. Beauchamp (ed.) (Oxford University Press: Oxford. 1999). I also include page references for L.A. Selby-Bigge (ed.) with revisions and notes by P.H. Nidditch (3rd ed.) [SBN] (Clarendon: Oxford. 1975).
20. Raynor (1980), 234.
21. For further discussion see McCracken and Tipton (2005), Ch. 16.
22. Raynor (1990), 236–7.

23. This view is endorsed by Raynor (1980), 236.
24. See Ayers (1983), 305.
25. Raynor (1980), 233–4.
26. Ibid., 234.
27. Popkin (1964), 778.
28. In the Abstract, Hume says '. . . that the soul as far as we can conceive it, is nothing but a system or train of different perceptions . . . all united together but without any perfect simplicity or identity (Abstract 28, 414; SBN 657).
29. Donald Ainslie aptly notes that many commentators have supposed this section to concern substance. In 'Hume's Anti-*cogito*,' unpublished ms.
30. George Pappas defends the view that Hume is arguing against both Locke and Berkeley. See *Hume Studies* 18:2 (1992), 275–80.
31. See Norton and Norton annotation to this passage.
32. This argument applies to non-Berkeleian accounts of a soul in which impressions inhere in substance as modes and properties. Hume's point is that there can be no positive idea of the substance, since impression and substance are so different.
33. According to Muehlmann, sensible qualities are mind-dependent for Berkeley only insofar as they are sensations. By attributing to Berkeley a congeries account of mind, Muehlmann then charges Berkeley with a lack of resources to secure the dependence of sensations upon the bundle (and he draws on this Humean passage to make the criticism). See Muehlmann (1992) 182 and 290. I take this to be a deficiency of his reading.
34. Raynor (1980), 243.
35. T 1.1.4.2.40, 138, SBN 207–8.
36. T Abstract 407, SBN 646.
37. T 1. Introduction 9, 5, SBN xviii.

Chapter Eight

1. T 1.4.6.3, 165, SBN 252.
2. Roderick Chisholm, 'On the Observability of the Self,' *Philosophy and Phenomenological Research* 30 (1969), 7–21 reprinted in Quassim Cassam (ed.) *Self-Knowledge* (Oxford. 1994), 94–108, 95, Sidney Shoemaker, 'Introspection and the Self,' in Peter A. French, Theodore E. Vehlin, and Howard K. Wettstein (eds), *Studies in the Philosophy of Mind* (Midwest Studies in Philosophy, 10: Minneapolis. 1986), 101–20 reprinted in Cassam (1994), 118–39, Cassam, 'Introduction,' in *Self-Knowledge*; Cassam, *Self and World* (Oxford University Press: Oxford. 1997), 1.
3. See Shoemaker (1994) 118.
4. See Chisholm (1969), 98.
5. See Saul Kripke, *Wittgenstein on Rules and Private Language* (Harvard University Press. 1982), 122; David Pears, *The False Prison*, 2 vols (Clarendon: Oxford. 1987), vol 1 158–9.
6. Kripke (1982).

7. See Cassam (1997), 1–2.
8. Stroud, *Hume* (Routledge & Kegan Paul: London. 1977), 118–9.
9. According to Ainslie (2001), reflection involves 'secondary ideas.' T 1.1.1.11, 10, SBN 6. See his 'Hume's Reflection on the Identity and Simplicity of the Mind,' *Philosophy and Phenomenological Research* 63:3 (2001), 557–78.
10. According to Ainslie this section applies only to philosophers. But the common-folk can also stop to think about themselves. Indeed, the sort of reflexion that Hume thinks is involved concerns the memory (something to which the common-folk ought to be able to appeal). Moreover, the belief that one is the same person over time is a view held by the vulgar. To be sure, the notion of 'simplicity' is more obscure. But the point is that we take ourselves to be something over and above our perceptions, continuing over time. This is the view that Hume tries to explain away in this section. For further comments see A.E. Pitson, *Hume's Philosophy of the Self* (Routledge: London and New York. 2002), 75–80.
11. For a more detailed defense of this position, see my 'Berkeley and Hume on the Self and Self-Consciousness,' in Jon Miller (ed.), *Topics in Early Modern Philosophy of Mind* (Springer Verlag. Forthcoming).
12. Ainslie (2001), 560.
13. Michael Green objects to this account of consciousness on the grounds that Hume admits that the mind of an oyster can have but one perception. Consciousness, Green, thinks, ought to accompany the perception even in this case. In my own view, Hume is interested in providing an account of consciousness where perceptions can come apart from it (in order to refute Berkeley). I take it that since the oyster's perception makes no causal impact it is effectively an 'unconscious perception'. See Green's 'The Idea of a Momentary Self and Hume's Theory of Personal Identity,' *British Journal for the History of Philosophy* 7:1 (199), 103–22.
14. T Appendix 20.400, SBN 635.
15. T 2.1.11.4, 206; SBN 317.
16. Don Garrett argues that Hume's phrase 'reflected thought or perception' is nothing but a reference to memory. 'Hume's Self-Doubts about Personal Identity,' *The Philosophical Review* 90:3 (1981), 337–58.
17. For some alternative accounts of Humean consciousness, see Thiel (1994), Gordon Park Stevenson, 'Humean Self-Consciousness Explained,' *Hume Studies* 24:1 (1998), 95–129.
18. Another radical possibility is that Hume may have been prepared to abandon the third principle that we are conscious of our own being. Perhaps this is the solution that he left for others to find. For more discussion of this possibility, see Bettcher (ibid).
19. While it is impossible to contrast this explanation with the great many solutions that have been offered, I do want to mention a few. Green's account is in some ways similar to my own. He argues that Hume fails to account for a kind of momentary self-consciousness. We differ in our account of what Hume thinks this self-consciousness should look like and on the seriousness of the failure. According to

Green, momentary self-consciousness is important to Hume's account of personal identity, according to me it is not.

20. Robert J. Fogelin suggests that Hume's concern may arise since he attempts to show (*pace* Berkeley) how a perception can exist independently of the mind. The problem is that the mental system of perceptions is too loose, and so cannot constitute a connected individual from which perceptions can be separated. Indeed, individual perceptions themselves constitute minds and hence cannot exist independently of the mind. See his *Hume's Scepticism in the Treatise of Human Nature* (Routledge & Kegan Paul: London. 1985). In my view, Hume's analysis of consciousness does not need the perceptions to connect together that tightly. Since a single perception does not make a causal impact it has been separated from consciousness. While an isolated perception might constitute a mind, it does not 'appear to mind.' In this way, it is 'unconscious.'
21. Ainslie (2001) offers a plausible account of the problem according to which the secondary perception which reflects upon the bundle cannot itself yet be 'associatively integrated into the rest of what we take to be our simple identical minds' and so Hume cannot explain our belief that such secondary perceptions are united with the rest of our minds (566). One difficulty with this account is that it deflates why the issue poses such a problem for Hume. It seems to me that a successful explanation of Hume's problem ought to explain why this problem is important.
22. Colin McGinn, *Problems in Philosophy: The Limits of Inquiry* (Blackwell: Oxford. 1993), 48.
23. Ibid., 2.
24. *The Concept of Mind* (Barnes and Noble. 1949), 186.
25. Chisholm (1994), 94.
26. 2nd ed. (Oxford University Press: Oxford. 2006)
27. *Metaphysics* Zeta 3, 29a36 in W.D. Ross (ed.), 12 vols. (Oxford, 1938–52) revised J. Barnes, 2 vols (Oxford, 1984).
28. Russell, 'On the Nature of Acquaintance,' in R.C. March (ed.), *Logic and Knowledge: Essays* (London. 1956), 127–174, 163
29. Cassam (1997), 72.
30. Ibid., 5.
31. Shoemaker, 'Introspection and the Self,' in Cassam (1994), Gareth Evans, ed. John McDowell (ed.), *The Varieties of Reference* (Oxford. 1982), 205–33, reprinted in Cassam (1994) as 'Self-Identification,' 184–209, 202–9.
32. Ryle (1949), 195–8.
33. In the Sixth set of objections, an especially strong version is offered with the assumption that higher-order knowledge is required in order to secure lower-order knowledge, thereby rendering knowledge impossible at all (CSM II 278).
34. For a related but different analysis of Ryle's account, see Husain Sarker *Descartes' Cogito: Saved from the Great Shipwreck* (Cambridge University Press: Cambridge. 2003), 226–35.

35. Kripke (1982), 122.
36. Both Chisholm (1994) and Shoemaker (1994) criticize the view of non-proprietary mental particulars (i.e. sense data). They prefer the view that we are aware of our states and thereby aware of ourselves. Consequently such criticism of Berkeley and Hume would be on the mark. It is interesting, however, that Berkeley and Hume have just argued to overcome the older proprietary model. See Chisholm, 100–6, Shoemaker, 123–5.
37. Brykman also recognizes Berkeley's importance. For her, the shift concerns Berkeley's explanation of spiritual substantiality in terms of personal identity, driven by his subjectivist views about time. See Brykman (1993), 106.
38. Shoemaker argues that even on a model of introspective self-awareness which is 'act-object', the awareness may not be viewed as 'perceptual.' His major reason for this is that this modality of information does not admit of certain identification errors. Unfortunately, a full discussion of this important issue is beyond the scope of this study.
39. One definition of 'significant' self-awareness might be self-awareness that does not involve the identification of an object of awareness as oneself (i.e. self-awareness that is identification free). For a discussion of these issues see Shoemaker's classic article 'Self-Reference and Self-Awareness,' *Journal of Philosophy* 65:19 (1986), 555–67, reprinted in Cassam (1994), 80–93, Shoemaker, 'Introspection and the Self,' and Gareth Evans, 'Self-Identification.'
40. Shoemaker (1994) raises a similar worry (123).

Bibliography

Primary Sources

Aquinas, Thomas. 1947–48. *Summa Theologica*. Translated by Fathers of the English Dominican Province. Revised ed. New York. Benziger Brothers.

——. 1952–54. *Truth*. 3 vols. Robert W. Mulligan, James V. McGlynn, and Robert W. Schmidt (trans.). Chicago. Henry Regnery Co.

——. 1968. *On Being and Essence*. 2nd ed. Armand Maurer (trans.). Toronto. Pontifical Institute of Mediaeval Studies.

Aristotle. 1963. *Aristotle's Categories and De Interpretatione*. J.L. Ackrill (trans.). Oxford. Clarendon Press.

——. 1984. *The Complete Works of Aristotle*. W.D. Ross (ed.). 12 vols. (Oxford. 1938–52) revised by J. Barnes 2 vols. Princeton. Princeton University Press.

Arnauld, Antoine. 1990. *On True and False Ideas*. Elmar J. Kremar (trans.). Lewiston. The Edwin Mellen Press.

Baxter, Andrew. 1745. *An Enquiry into the Nature of the Human Soul*. 3rd ed. London.

Berkeley, George. 1949–57. *The Works of George Berkeley, Bishop of Cloyne*. 9 vols. A.A. Luce and T.E. Jessop (eds). London and Edinburgh. Thomas Nelson and Sons.

——. 1944. *editio diplomatica* of *Philosophical Commentaries*. A.A. Luce (ed.). London and Edinburgh. Thomas Nelson and Sons.

——. 1975. *George Berkeley: Philosophical Works including the Works on Vision*. Michael Ayers (ed.). London. Everyman.

——. 1987. *George Berkeley's Manuscript Introduction: An Editio Diplomatica transcribed and edited with Introduction and Commentary by Bertil Belfrage*. Oxford. Doxa.

——. 1993. *George Berkeley: Alciphron or the Minute Philosopher in Focus*. D. Berman (ed.). London. Routledge.

Boethius. 1998. *The Consolation of Philosophy*. V.E. Watts (trans.). London. The Folio Society.

Browne, Peter. 1695. *A Letter in Answer to Christianity not Mysterious*. Dublin. Reprinted with Toland with a new Introduction by John Valdmir Price. London, 1995. Routledge/Thoemmes Press.

——. 1728. *The Procedure, Extent, and Limits of Human Understanding*. London, 1976. Reprinted. London & New York. Garland.

——. 1733. *Things Divine and Supernatural Conceived by Analogy with Things Natural and Human*. London, 1990. Reprinted. Bristol. Thoemmes.

Cajetan, Thomas de Vio. 1959. *The Analogy of Names and The Concept of Being*. 2nd ed. Edward A. Bushinski with Henry J. Koren (trans.). Pittsburgh. Duquesne University.

Clarke, Samuel. 1978. *The Works of Samuel Clarke*. 4 vols. London, 1738. Reprinted. London & New York. Garland.

Collins, Anthony. 1707. *An Essay concerning the Use of Reason in Propositions*. London, 1984. Reprinted with *A Discourse of Free-Thinking*. London & New York. Garland.

——. 1710. *A Vindication of the Divine Attributes* . . . abbrv. London.

Coward, William. 1703. *Farther Thoughts concerning Human Soul*. London.

Descartes, René. 1984. *The Philosophical Writings of Descartes*. 2 vols. John Cottingham, Robert Stroothoff, and Dugald Murdoch (trans.). Cambridge. Cambridge University Press.

——. 1991. *The Philosophical Writings of Descartes*. Volume III. *The Correspondence*. John Cottingham, Robert Stroothoff, Dugald Murdoch, and Anthony Kenny (trans.). Cambridge. Cambridge University Press.

Dodwell, Henry. 1706. *An Epistolary Discourse Proving from the Scriptures and the First Fathers that the Soul is a Principle Naturally Mortal* . . . abbr. London.

Hobbes, Thomas. 1656. *Elements of Philosophy, The First Section Concerning Body* translated into English. London. R. & W. Leyborn.

Hume, David. 1975. *An Enquiry concerning Human Understanding*. 3rd ed. L.A. Selby-Bigge (ed.) with revisions and notes by P.H. Nidditch. Oxford. Clarendon Press.

——. 1978. *A Treatise of Human Nature*. 2nd ed. L.A. Selby-Bigge (ed.) with revisions and notes by P.H. Nidditch. Oxford. Clarendon Press.

——. 1985. *David Hume: Essays, Moral, Political, and Literary*. Eugene Miller (ed.). Indianapolis. Liberty Classics.

——. 1999. *An Enquiry concerning Human Understanding*. Tom L. Beauchamp (ed.). Oxford. Oxford University Press.

——. 2000. *A Treatise of Human Nature*. David Fate Norton and Mary J. Norton (eds.). Oxford. Oxford University Press.

King, William. 1709. 'Divine Predestination Consistent With Freedom ... abbrv.'. Dublin. Reprinted as *Sermon on Predestination*, ed. Andrew Carpenter and Introduction by David Berman (Dublin: The Cadenus Press, 1976).

Layton, Henry. 1699. *An Argument concerning the Human Souls Seperate Subsistance (sic)*. London.

Locke, John. 1823. *The Works of John Locke*. 10 vols. London. Printed for Thomas Tegg.

——. 1975. *An Essay concerning Human Understanding*. Peter H. Nidditch (ed.). Oxford. Clarendon Press.

Malebranche, Nicholas. 1997. *The Search after Truth*. Thomas M. Lennon and Paul J. Olscamp (trans. and eds). Cambridge. Cambridge University Press.

——. 1997. *Elucidations of The Search after Truth*. Thomas M. Lennon (trans. and ed.) published with *The Search after Truth*.

Norris, John. 1708. *A Philosophical Discourse concerning the Natural Immortality of the Soul*. London.

Rand, Benjamin. 1914. *Berkeley and Percival: The Correspondence of George Berkeley and Sir John Percival*. Cambridge. Cambridge University Press.

Russell, Bertrand. 1956. 'On the Nature of Acquaintance,' in R.C. Marsh (ed.), *Logic and Knowledge: Essays*. London. George Allen & Unwin. 127–74.

Stillingfleet, Edward. 1691. *The Mysteries of The Christian Faith Asserted and Vindicated.* London.

——. 1697. *A Discourse in Vindication of the Doctrine of the Trinity* . . . abbrv. London.

——. 1697. *The Bishop of Worcester's Answer to Mr. Locke's Letter* . . . abbrv. London.

——. 1698. *The Bishop of Worcester's Answer to Mr. Locke's Second Letter* . . . abbrv. London.

Swift, Jonathan. 1963–5. *The Correspondence of Jonathan Swift.* Harold Williams (ed.). Clarendon Press. Oxford.

Synge, Edward. 1698. *An Appendix to A Gentleman's Religion*, pp. 208–37. Reprinted in David Berman and Patricia Riordan (eds). *The Irish Enlightenment and Counter-Enlightenment.* Bristol. 2002.Thoemmes.

Toland, John. 1696. *Christianity not Mysterious.* London. Reprinted with Browne (1697). London. 1995. Routledge/Thoemmes Press.

Secondary Sources

Ainslie, Donald. 2001. 'Hume's Reflection on the Identity and Simplicity of the Mind,' *Philosophy and Phenomenological Research* 63:3, 557–78.

——. 'Hume's Anti-*cogito*' unpublished ms.

Allaire, Edwin B. 1963. 'Berkeley's Idealism,' *Theoria* 29, 229–44.

Atherton, Margaret. 1983. 'The Coherence of Berkeley's Theory of Mind,' *Philosophy and Phenomenological Research* 43, 389–99.

Atkins, Kim (ed.). 2005. *Self and Subjectivity*. Oxford. Blackwell Publishing.

Ayer, A. J. 1946. *Language, Truth, and Logic*. London. Dover.

Ayers, Michael R. 1970. 'Substance, Reality, and the Great, Dead Philosophers,' *American Philosophical Quarterly* 7:1, 38–49.

——. 1983. 'Berkeley and Hume: A question of influence,' in R. Rorty, Schneewind, and Skinner (eds). *Philosophy in History: Essays on the Historiography of Philosophy*. Cambridge. Cambridge University Press. 303–27.

——. 1986. 'Berkeley and the Meaning of Existence,' *The History of European Ideas* 7, 567–73.

——. 1987. 'Divine Ideas and Berkeley's Proof of God's Existence,' in Sosa (1987), 115–42.

——. 1991. *Locke: Epistemology and Ontology*. 2 vols. London. Routledge.

Baxter, Donald. 1991. 'Berkeley, Perception, and Identity,' *Philosophy and Phenomenological Research* 51:1, 85–98.

Beardsley, William H. 2001. 'Berkeley on Spirit and Its Unity,' *History of Philosophy Quarterly* 18:3, 259–77.

Belfrage, Bertil. 1985. 'The clash on semantics in Berkeley's *Notebook* A,' *Hermathena* 139, 117–26.

——. 1986a. 'Berkeley's Emotive Theory of Meaning (1708),' *History of European Ideas.* 7:6, 643–99.

——. 1986b.'Development of Berkeley's early theory of meaning,' *Revue Philosophique de la France de l'Etranger* 3, 319–30.

——. 1987. 'A New Approach to Berkeley's *Philosophical Notebooks*,' in Sosa (1987), 217–30.

——. forthcoming. 'George Berkeley's Four Concepts of the Soul (1707–1709),' in Stephen H. Daniel (ed.). *Reexamining Berkeley's Philosophy*. Toronto. University of Toronto Press.

Bennett, Jonathan. 1971. *Locke, Berkeley, Hume: Central Themes*. Oxford. Clarendon Press.

Berman, David. 1981. 'Cognitive theology and emotive mysteries in Berkeley's *Alciphron*,' *Proceedings of the Royal Irish Academy* 81, C, no. 7, 219–29, reprinted in Berman (ed.) *Alciphron* (1993), 200–13.

——. 1986a. 'Berkeley's Quad: The Question of Numerical Identity,' *Idealistic Studies* 16, 41–45.

——. 1986b. 'Berkeley's Semantic revolution: 19 November 1707–January 1708,' *History of European Ideas* 7:6, 603–7.

——. 1988. *A History of Atheism in Britain: From Hobbes to Russell*. London and New York: Croom Helm.

——. 1994. *George Berkeley: Idealism and the Man*. Oxford. Clarendon Press.

——. 2005. *Berkeley and Irish Philosophy*. London. Continuum.

——. 2005. 'Enlightenment and Counter-Enlightenment in Irish Philosophy,' reprinted in Berman (2005).

——. 2005. 'On Missing the Wrong Target,' reprinted in Berman (2005).

Bettcher, Talia Mae. forthcoming. 'Berkeley and Hume on the Self and Self-Consciousness,' in Jon Miller (ed.). *Topics in Early Modern Philosophy of Mind*. Springer Verlag.

Bracken, Harry M. 1960a. 'Berkeley on the Immortality of the Soul,' *The Modern Schoolman* 37, 77–94 and 197–212.

——. 1960b. 'Berkeley and Mental Acts,' *Theoria* 26, 140–46.

——. 1965. *The Early Reception of Berkeley's Immaterialism: 1710–1733*. revised ed. The Hague. Martinus Nijhoff.

——. 1974. *Berkeley*. New York. St. Martin's Press.

Braybrooke, David. 1955. 'Berkeley on the Numerical Individuation of Ideas,' *The Philosophical Review* 64:4, 631–36.

Brown, S.C. 1972. 'Berkeley on the Unity of the Self,' *Reason and Reality*. Royal Institute of Philosophy Lectures 5, 1970–71. London. MacMillan and St. Martin's Press.

Brykman, Geneviève. 1984. *Berkeley: Philosophie et Apologétique*. Paris.Vrin.

——. 1985. 'Pleasure and pain versus ideas in Berkeley,' *Hermathena* 139, 127–37.

——. 1993. *Berkeley et le Voile des Mots*. Paris. Vrin.

——. forthcoming. 'On Human Liberty in Berkeley's *Alciphron* VII,' in Stephen H. Daniel (ed.). New *Interpretations of Berkeley's Thought*.

Carriero, John. 1986. 'The Second Meditation and the Essence of the Mind,' in Amélie Oksenberg Rorty (ed.). *Essays on Descartes' Meditations*. University of California Press.

——. 1995. 'On the Relationship between Mode and Substance in Spinoza's Metaphysics,' *Journal of the History of Philosophy* 33:2, 245–73.

——. 2003. 'Berkeley, Resemblance, and Sensible Things,' *Philosophical Topics* 31: 1 & 2, 21–46

Cassam, Quassim (ed.). 1994. *Self-Knowledge*. Oxford. Oxford University Press.

——. 1997. *Self and World*. Oxford. Oxford University Press.

Chappell, Vere (ed.). 1994. *The Cambridge Companion to Locke*. Cambridge. Cambridge University Press.

Chisholm, Roderick. 1994. 'On the Observability of the Self,' *Philosophy and Phenomenological Research* 30 (1969), 7–21 reprinted in Cassam (ed.) (1994), 94–108.

Clark, Stephen R.L. 2005. 'Berkeley on Religion,' in Winkler (2005), 369–404.

Conroy, Graham P. 1969. 'Did Hume Really Follow Berkeley?,' *Philosophy* 44, 238–80.

Cummins, Phillip D. 1975. 'Berkeley's Ideas of Sense,' *Nous* 9, 55–69.

——. 1982. 'Hylas' Parity Argument,' in Turbayne (1982), 283–94.

——. 1989. 'Berkeley's Unstable Ontology,' *The Modern Schoolman* 67, 15–32.

——. 2005. 'Berkeley on minds and agency,' in Winkler (2005), 190–229.

Cummins, Phillip D. and Guenter Zoeller (eds). 1992. *Minds, Ideas, and Objects: Essays on the Theory of Representation in Modern Philosophy*. California. Ridgeview.

Dancy, Jonathan Dancy. 1987. *Berkeley: An Introduction*. Oxford. Blackwell Publishing.

Daniel, Stephen H. 2000. 'Berkeley, Súarez, and the 'Esse-Existere' Distinction,' *American Catholic Philosophical Quarterly* 74:4, 621–36.

——. 2001a. 'Edwards, Berkeley, and Ramist Logic,' *Idealistic Studies* 31:1, 55–72.

——. 2001b. 'The Ramist Context of Berkeley's Philosophy,' *British Journal for the History of Philosophy* 9:3, 487–505.

——. 2001c. 'Berkeley's Christian Neoplatonism, Archetypes, and Divine Ideas,' *Journal of the History of Philosophy* 39:2, 239–58.

——. forthcoming. 'Berkeley's Stoic Notion of Spiritual Substance,' in Stephen H. Daniel (ed.) *New Interpretations of Berkeley's Thought*.

Evans, Gareth (1994). John McDowell (ed.). *The Varieties of Reference*. Oxford. 1982, 205–33; reprinted in Cassam (1994) as 'Self-Identification,' 184–209.

Flage, Daniel. 1987. *Berkeley's Doctrine of Notions: A Reconstruction Based on his Theory of Meaning*. London & Sydney. Croom Helm.

——. 1994. 'Berkeley, Individuation, and Physical Objects,' in Kenneth F. Barber and Jorge J.E. Gracia (eds). *Individuation and Identity in Early Modern Philosophy*. Albany. State University of New York Press, 133–54.

Flew, Antony. 1961. 'Did Hume Ever Read Berkeley?' *Journal of Philosophy* 58, 50–1.

Fogelin, Robert J. 1985. *Hume's Skepticism in the Treatise of Human Nature*. London. Routledge & Kegan Paul.

Foster, John and Robinson, Howard (eds). 1985. *Essays on Berkeley: A Tercentennial Celebration*. Oxford. Clarendon Press.

Fritz, Anita D. 1954. 'Berkeley's Self – Its Origins in Malebranche,' *Journal of the History of Ideas* 15:4, 554–72.

Furlong, E.J. 1982. 'On Being "Embrangled" by Time,' in Turbayne (1982), 148–55.

Garber, Daniel. 1987. 'Something-I-know-Not-What: Berkeley on Locke on Substance,' in Sosa (1987), 27–42.

Garrett, Don. 1981. 'Hume's Self-Doubts about Personal Identity,' *The Philosophical Review* 90:3, 337–58.

Gotterbarn, Donald. 1975. 'Berkeley: God's Pain,' *Philosophical Studies* 28, 245–54.

Grave, S.A. 1968. 'The Mind and its Ideas: Some Problems in the Interpretation of Berkeley,' *Australian Journal of Philosophy* 42 (1964), 199–210; reprinted in C.B. Martin and D.M. Armstrong (eds). *Locke and Berkeley: A Collection of Critical Essays*. New York. Doubleday, 296–313.

Grayling, A.C. 1986. *Berkeley: The Central Arguments*. La Salle. Open Court.

Green, Michael. 1999.'The Idea of a Momentary Self in Hume's Theory of Personal Identity,' *British Journal for the History of Philosophy* 7:1, 103–122.

Guttenplan, Samuel (ed.). 1995. *A Companion to the Philosophy of Mind*. Oxford. Blackwell.

Hall, Roland. 1968. 'Hume's Actual Use of the Principles,' *Philosophy* 43, 278–80.

——. 1970. 'Yes, Hume Did Use Berkeley,' *Philosophy* 45, 152–53.

Hestevold, H. Scott. 1990. 'Berkeley's Theory of Time,' *History of Philosophy Quarterly* 7:2, 179–92.

Hight, Marc A. 2005. 'Defending Berkeley's Divine Ideas,' *Philosophia* 33: 1–4, 97–128.

——. forthcoming. 'Berkeley and Bodily Resurrection,' *Journal of the History of Philosophy*.

Hight, Marc and Ott, Walter. 2004. 'The New Berkeley,' *Canadian Journal of Philosophy* 34, 1–24.

Imlay, Robert. 1995. 'Berkeley and Action,' in Muehlmann (1995), 171–181.

Immerwahr, John. 1974. 'Berkeley's Causal Thesis,' *New Scholasticism* 48, 153–70.

Jaffro, Laurent. 2004. 'Le *cogito* de Berkeley,' *Archives de Philosophie* 67, 85–111.

Jakapi, Roomet. 2002a. 'Emotive Meaning and Christian Mysteries in Berkeley's *Alciphron*,' *British Journal for the History of Philosophy* 10: 3, 401–11.

——. 2002b. 'Faith, Truth, Revelation and Meaning in Berkeley's Defense of The Christian Religion (in *Alciphron*),' *The Modern Schoolman* 80, 23–34.

Jolley, Nicholas. 1990. 'Berkeley and Malebranche on Causality and Volition,' in J.A. Cover and Mark Kulstad (eds). *Central Themes in Early Modern Philosophy: Essays presented to Jonathan Bennett*. Indianapolis. Hackett. 227–43.

Kripke, Saul. 1982. *Wittgenstein on Rules and Private Language*. Cambridge, Massachusetts. Harvard University Press.

Lloyd, A.C. 1985. 'The Self in Berkeley's Philosophy,' in Foster and Robinson (1985), 187–209.

Luce, A.A. 1934. *Berkeley & Malebranche: A Study in the Origins of Berkeley's Thought*. Oxford. Clarendon Press.

——. 1936. 'A critique of Professor H.H. Price's refutation of the naïve realist theory of perception,' *Hermathena* 50, 60–85.

——. 1941. 'Mind-dependence in Berkeley,' *Hermathena* 57, 117–27.

——. 1945. *Berkeley's Immaterialism*. London. Thomas Nelson and Sons.

——. 1963. *The Dialectic of Immaterialism: An Account of the Making of Berkeley's Principles*. London. Hodder and Stoughton.

——. 1966. 'Berkeleian Action and Passion,' in *Revue Internationale de Philosophie* 7, 3–18.

——. 1967. 'Sensible ideas and sensations,' *Hermathena* 105, 74–83.

——. 1970. 'Another look at Berkeley's Notebooks,' *Hermathena* 110, 5–23.

March, W.W.S. 1942. 'Analogy, Aquinas, and Bishop Berkeley,' *Theology* 44, 321–29.

Martin, Raymond and Barresi, John. 2000. *The Naturalization of the Soul: Self and Personal Identity in the Eighteenth Century*. London & New York. Routledge.

McCann, Edwin. 1994. 'Locke's Philosophy of Body,' in Chappell (1994), 56–88.

McCracken, Charles J. 1979. 'What *Does* Berkeley's God see in the Quad,' *Archiv für Geschichte der Philosphie* 61, 280–92.

——. 1983. *Malebranche and British Philosophy*. Oxford. Clarendon Press.

——. 1988. 'Berkeley's Cartesian Concept of Mind: The Return through Malebranche and Locke to Descartes,' *The Monist* 71, 596–611.

——. 1989. 'Berkeley's Notion of Spirit,' *History of European Ideas* 7, 56–88.

——. 1992. 'Berkeley on the Relation of Ideas to the Mind,' in Cummins and Zoeller (1992), 187–200.

——. forthcoming. 'Berkeley's Realism,' in Stephen H. Daniel (ed.) *New Interpretations of Berkeley's Thought*.

McCracken, C.J. and Tipton, I.C. 2000. *Berkeley's Principles and Dialogues: Background Source Materials*. Cambridge. Cambridge University Press.

McGinn, Colin. 1993. *Problems in Philosophy: The Limits of Inquiry*. Oxford. Blackwell Publishing.

McKim, Robert. 1984. 'Berkeley on Human Agency,' *History of Philosophical Quarterly* 1:2, 181–94.

——. 1985. 'The entries in Berkeley's *Notebooks*: a reply to Bertil Belfrage,' *Hermathena* 139, 156–61.

——. 1992a. 'Berkeley's Active Mind,' *Archiv für Geschichte der Philosophie* 71, 335–43.

——. 1992b. 'Berkeley on Private Ideas and Public Objects,' in Cummins and Zoeller (1992), 215–33.

Morrisroe Jr., Michael. 1973. 'Did Hume Read Berkeley? A Conclusive Answer,' *Philological Quarterly* 52:2, 310–15.

Mossner, Ernest C. 1959. 'Did Hume ever Read Berkeley? A Rejoinder to Professor Popkin,' *Journal of Philosophy* 56, 992–95.

Muehlmann, Robert G. 1992. *Berkeley's Ontology*. Indianapolis. Hackett.

——. (ed.). 1995. *Berkeley's Metaphysics: Structural, Interpretive, and Critical Essays*. University Park. Pennsylvania State University Press.

——. 1995a.'The Substance of Berkeley's Philosophy,' in Muehlmann (1995), 89–105.

——. 1995b. 'Berkeley's Problem of Sighted Agency,' in Muehlmann (1995), 149–69.

Nadler, Steven. 1990. 'Berkeley's Ideas and the Primary/Secondary Distinction,' *Canadian Journal of Philosophy* 20:1, 47–61.

O'Higgins, James 1976. 'Browne and King, Collins and Berkeley: Agnosticism or Anthropomorphism?' *Journal of Theological Studies* 27, 88–112.

Olscamp, Paul J. 1970. *The Moral Philosophy of George Berkeley*. The Hague. Martinus Nijhoff.

Pappas, George. 1982. 'Berkeley, Perception, and Common Sense,' in Turbayne (1982), 3–21.

——. 1991. 'Berkeley and Common Sense Realism,' *History of Philosophy Quarterly* 8, 27–42.

——. 1992. 'Perception of the Self,' *Hume Studies* 18:2, 275–80.

——. 2000. *Berkeley's Thought*. Ithaca. Cornell University Press.

Park, Désirée. 1972. *Complementary Notions*. The Hague. Martinus Nijhoff.

Pears, David. 1987. *The False Prison*. 2 vols. Oxford. Clarendon Press.

Pitcher, George. 1977. *Berkeley*. London. Routledge & Kegan Paul.

——. 1981. 'Berkeley on the Mind's Activity,' *American Philosophical Quarterly* 18:3, 221–27.

——. 1986. 'Berkeley on the Perception of Objects,' *Journal of the History of Philosophy* 24, 99–105.

Pitson, A.E. 2002. *Hume's Philosophy of the Self*. London & New York. Routledge.

Pittion, Jean-Paul, Berman, D. and Luce, A.A. 1969. 'A New Letter by Berkeley to Browne on Divine Analogy,' *Mind* 78, 375–92.

Popkin, Richard H. 1959. 'Did Hume every Read Berkeley?' *Journal of Philosophy* 56, 535–45.

——. 1964. 'So, Hume did Read Berkeley,' *Journal of Philosophy* 61, 773–78.

Raynor, David R. 1980. '"*Minima Sensibilia*" in Berkeley and Hume,' *Dialogue* 19, 196–99.

——. 1987. 'Berkeley's Ontology,' *Dialogue* 26, 611–20.

——. 1990. 'Hume and Berkeley's *Three Dialogues*,' in M.A. Stewart (ed.). *Studies in the Philosophy of the Scottish Enlightenment*. Oxford. Oxford University Press. 231–50.

Ryle, Gilbert. 1949. *The Concept of Mind*. New York. Barnes and Noble.

Sarker, Husain. 2003. *Descartes' Cogito: Saved from the Great Shipwreck*. Cambridge. Cambridge University Press.

Schmaltz, Tad. 1996. *Malebranche's Theory of the Soul: A Cartesian Interpretation*. Oxford. Oxford University Press.

Shoemaker, Sidney. 1986. 'Self-Reference and Self-Awareness,' *Journal of Philosophy* 65:19 (1986), 555–67.

——. 1994. 'Introspection and the Self,' in Peter A. French, Theodore E. Vehlin, and Howard K. Wettstein (eds). *Studies in the Philosophy of Mind*. Midwest Studies in Philosophy 10. Minneapolis, 1986. 101–20. Reprinted in Cassam (1994) 118–39.

Sosa, Ernest (ed.). 1987. *Essays on The Philosophy of George Berkeley*. Dordrecht. D. Reidel Publishing.

Steinkraus, Warren E (ed.). 1966. *New Studies in Berkeley's Philosophy*. New York. Holt, Rinehard, and Winston.

Stevenson, Gordon Park. 1998. 'Humean Self-Consciousness Explained,' *Hume Studies* 24:1, 95–129.

Stoneham, Tom. 2002. *Berkeley's World: An Examination of the Three Dialogues*. Oxford. Oxford Press.

Stroud, Barry. 1977. *Hume*. London. Routledge & Kegan Paul.

Stubenberg, Leopold. 1990. 'Divine Ideas: The Cure-All for Berkeley's Immaterialism?' *Southern Journal of Philosophy* 28: 2, 221–49.

Taylor, C.C.W. 1985. 'Action and Inaction in Berkeley,' in Foster and Robinson (1985) 211–225.

Thiel, Udo. 1994. 'Hume's Notions of Consciousness and Reflection in Context,' *British Journal for the History of Philosophy* 2:2, 75–115.

Thomas, George. 1976. 'Berkeley's God does not perceive,' *Journal of the History of Philosophy* 14, 163–68.

Tipton, I.C. 1966. 'Berkeley's View of Spirit,' in Steinkraus (1966), 59–71.

——. 1974. *Berkeley: The Philosophy of Immaterialism.* London. Methuen.

Turbayne, Colin M. 1959. 'Berkeley's Two Concepts of Mind,' *Philosophy and Phenomenological Research* 20:1, 85–92.

——. 1962. 'Berkeley's Two Concepts of Mind Part II,' *Philosophy and Phenomenology Research* 22:3, 383–86.

—— (ed.). 1982. *Berkeley: Critical and Interpretive Essays.* Minneapolis. University of Minnesota Press.

——. 1982. 'Lending a Hand to Philonous: The Berkeley, Plato, Aristotle Connection,' in Turbayne (1982).

——. 1985. 'Hume's Influence on Berkeley,' *Revue Internationale de Philosophie* 39, 259–69.

Warnock, George L. 1953. *Berkeley.* London. Penguin Books.

Weiner, Philip P. 1959. 'Did Hume ever Read Berkeley?' *Journal of Philosophy* 56, 533–35.

Williford, Kenneth. 2003. 'Berkeley's Theory of Operative Language in the *Manuscript Introduction*,' *British Journal for the History of Philosophy* 11:2, 271–301.

Wilson, Catherine. 1995. 'On "Berkeley and Action"' in Muehlmann (1995), 183–96.

Wilson, Fred. 1995. 'On The Hausmans' "New Approach"' in Muehlmann (1995), 67–88.

Wilson, Margaret. 1978. *Descartes.* London. Routledge & Kegan Paul.

Winkler, Kenneth P. 1985. 'Unperceived objects and Berkeley's denial of blind agency,' *Hermathena* 139, 81–100.

——. 1989. *Berkeley: An Interpretation.* Oxford. Oxford University Press.

—— (ed.). 2005. *The Cambridge Companion to Berkeley.* Cambridge. Cambridge University Press.

——. 2005. 'Berkeley and the Doctrine of Signs,' in Winkler (2005).

Winnett, Arthur. 1973. *Peter Browne: Provost, Bishop, Metaphysician.* London. SPCK.

Woozley, A.D. 1976. 'Berkeley's Doctrine of Notions and Theory of Meaning,' *Journal of the History of Philosophy* 14, 427–34.

——. 1985. 'Berkeley on Action,' *Philosophy* 60, 293–307.

Yandell, David. 1995. 'Berkeley on Common Sense and the Privacy of Ideas,' *Journal of History of Philosophical Quarterly* 12, 411–23.

Yolton, John W. 1983. *Thinking Matter: Materialism in Eighteenth-Century Britain.* Minneapolis. University of Minnesota Press.

——. 1984. *Perceptual Acquaintance from Descartes to Reid.* Oxford. Basil Blackwell.

——. 1996. *Perception & Reality: A History from Descartes to Kant.* Ithaca. Cornell.

Index

Lightning Source UK Ltd.
Milton Keynes UK
UKOW06n0052190717
305601UK00008B/106/P

9 780826 486431